JESUS IN HISTORY
AND MYTH

JESUS
IN HISTORY
AND MYTH

edited by R. Joseph Hoffmann
and Gerald A. Larue

Prometheus Books

700 East Amherst St. Buffalo, New York 14215

Published 1986 by Prometheus Books
700 East Amherst Street, Buffalo, New York 14215

Library of Congress Cataloging-in-Publication Data

Jesus in history and myth.

    1. Jesus Christ—History of doctrines—Early church,
ca. 30-600—Congresses. 2. Bible. N.T. Gospels—
Criticism, interpretations, etc.—Congresses.
I. Hoffmann, R. Joseph. II. Larue, Gerald A.
BT 198.J475   1986   232.9   86-5052
ISBN 0-87975-332-3

Printed in the United States of America

Contents

Part III: The Development of Christology

Part IV: Philosophical and Theological Implications

Preface

This volume comprises papers presented at the First International Symposium on "Jesus and the Gospels" held in April, 1985, at the University of Michigan, Ann Arbor, Michigan. The program was under the auspices of the Committee for the Scientific Examination of Religion and its Religion and Biblical Criticism subcommittee. Distinguished scholars from Europe and America presented papers pertaining to Jesus in myth and history.

This particular conference was, in actuality, the fourth of a series. In 1982, a symposium held at the University of Buffalo, Buffalo, New York, dealt with "Science, the Bible, and Darwin." In 1983, a conference convened in the National Press Club in Washington, D.C., addressed the theme of "Religion in American Politics." The third meeting, held at the University of Southern California, Los Angeles, California, in 1984, focused on "Armageddon and Biblical Apocalyptic." Papers from these symposia were published in issues of *Free Inquiry* magazine.

The Religion and Biblical Criticism Project came into being immediately after the 1982 meeting. The purpose of the project was not to develop new critical research, but to disseminate the results of scholarly investigation of the Bible. The best systems of critical research were to be employed, together with findings from studies in comparative religion and folklore, scientific archeology, historical and literary analyses of texts, etc. Eminent scholars were invited to participate.

The history of biblical research has been anchored in synagogue and church. Over the centuries, intelligent Bible readers raised questions about inconsistencies, contradictions, anachronisms and inaccuracies, and the linguistic confusions in some texts. Different literary forms have been identified in the Bible including history, legend, myth, folktale, fable, allegory, maxims and aphorisms, parables and novella, letters and tracts, varying types of poetry, differing kinds of prophetic oracles, and so on. Near-eastern archeology continues to uncover structures, artifacts, and texts that provide new insight into biblical life patterns and modes of thought, and that demonstrate the intimate relationship that existed between people of ancient Palestine and their near neighbors. Biblical law codes reflect older Mesopotamian regulations. Biblical psalms and Wisdom literature exhibit links with Egyptian writings. Biblical cosmological concepts parallel beliefs held by Israel's neighbors. The recovery of religious literature belonging to Canaanites, Assyrians, Babylonians, and Egyptians has demonstrated that some biblical concepts may have been borrowed from other cults, and that festivals sacred to Jews and Christians have roots that reach back into pagan religious celebrations. In other words, the Bible, rather than proving to be a product of divine revelation, is clearly a human product, limited in what it contains by its setting in time (first millennium before the common era, and the first two centuries of the common era) and space (the ancient near-eastern world).

Unfortunately, these valuable and exciting findings have not been shared with the general public. Clergy, well trained in biblical criticism in the best universities and seminaries, consistently fail to communicate to their parishioners what they have been taught. Consequently, in synagogue and church more than a generation of biblical illiterates have become easy prey for media evangelists, simply because they are unfamiliar with the methodologies and information with which to reject the claims of the fundamentalists.

What is equally disturbing is the vigorous campaign being waged by right-wing evangelicals against modern scientific inquiry and free thought. Their persistent pressure, based on their interpretation of what the Bible teaches and their insistence that biblical ethics become the law of the land, threatens the free choice of reading materials in public libraries, the teaching of evolutionary theories in public schools, the freedom citizens enjoy in their private lives, sexual behavior not endorsed by the Bible, the efforts of women to achieve equal rights under the law, etc. It was, in part, in response to these threats to free and open inquiry from the fundamentalist right wing that the Bible project had its beginnings.

Immediately following the Michigan Conference, the Committee for the Scientific Examination of Religion was formed under the auspices of the prestigious Academy of Humanism, which is composed of humanist laureates from various fields of inquiry. This new committee will not limit its inquiry to biblical research but will feel free to investigate any and all expressions of religious belief or commitment. The Bible project is now a subgroup within the committee.

This present volume contains important materials pertaining to the study of the life and teachings of Jesus. Because differing points of view are represented, the long history of scholarly debate is reflected as it pertains to the historicity of Jesus, the influence of the developing church on the New Testament interpretation of Jesus, and the theological dialogues that developed out of the New Testament. Most churchgoers are not familiar with these issues. For example, few Christians will question the Gospel birth narratives that locate Jesus' birthplace in Bethlehem. Indeed, congregations make pilgrimages to the Church of the Nativity that is built over the supposed birthplace. Modern scholars cast grave doubts on these birth stories and suggest that Jesus was born and raised in Nazareth. Even there, the numerous church structures that are supposed to be associated with Jesus' life have nothing to do with Jesus. Many sayings attributed to Jesus appear to be the product of the developing church. Writers put in Jesus' mouth what the church wanted him to say. In fact, knowledge about the historical Jesus is scant, and it is this fact that forms the basis for the first papers in this volume. Professor George Wells questions whether Jesus ever lived. Professor Morton Smith presents his arguments to prove that he did.

In the next section, the results of inquiry into the social, political, and religious environment of the first century C.E. comes under review. Professor Ellis Rivkin investigates the references to Jesus in the writings of Josephus. Professor David Noel Freedman and Professor John Allegro look at Qumran and the Dead Sea Scrolls for relationships to Jesus' life and times. Professor Tikva Frymer-Kensky examines the Jesus tradition to try to understand Jesus' relationship to the Law.

The third section deals with Christology and explores the writings of early Christians as they attempted to explain the nature of Jesus' messiahship. The final section includes papers that present differing interpretations of the implications of critical scholarship for theology and belief.

The committee plans to hold future conferences and also to publish the papers presented in subsequent volumes in this series. Through conferences and publications we plan to continue to contribute to broader appreciation of the ongoing critical examination of the claims of religions, validating where the evidence is supportive, exposing error or misinterpretation where the evidence is negative. Both conferences and publications will reflect the continuing dialogue that goes on among competent scholars.

Gerald A. Larue, Chairman
Committee for the Scientific
Examination of Religion

University of Southern California
Los Angeles

Introduction

The Life of Jesus in Research

The life of Jesus as New Testament scholarship knows it today did not become a "problem" until the eighteenth century.[1] Since that time, scarcely a decade has gone by that has not seen an attempt, either by some well-intentioned defender of the historicity of the gospels or by one of their detractors, to supply an answer to the question, "Who was Jesus of Nazareth?" Did he really exist, or was he the creation of one of the radical messianic movements of first-century Palestine—a figure not different in genesis from Adonis, Dionysus, or Horus.[2] If he did exist, as a majority of biblical scholars would still today contend,[3] what was his mission and message, his "quest"? Was it something he meant to outlast him in the form of institution and doctrine, or was it confined to his life and culture and subject to the disconfirming experience of his associates? Especially in our own day, when it seems possible to dispense with most difficulties by knowing the right code and pressing the proper keys, the "problem" of the historical Jesus is one that refuses to go away.

The contours that normally define historical personalities are enormously hard to come by when we enter into a discussion of the gospels. *That* Jesus was a man of his time, a propounder of religious opinions easily located in the Jewish theology of his day, is more and more widely accepted by scholars. But it is a conclusion that comes to us from notoriously uncooperative sources—sources that offer us a picture not of an apocalyptic preacher from the Galilean hill country, but of a man "attested by God with mighty wonders and signs," the "lord and Christ" (Acts 2:22f., 35), the eternal *logos* of God himself (John 1:1f.). Just as uncooperative are the sources for reconstructing his teaching: Did he call twelve apostles (Mark 2:13f.) or seventy disciples (Luke 10:1–16)? Did he speculate about the signs of the last days (Mark 13:4–27) or discourage such speculation as being wicked and impious (Mark 8:13)? Did he swear people to secrecy concerning his identity (Mark 8:26, 30) or announce himself openly as the messiah and son of God (John 5:31)? Did he repudiate the Mosaic law and its orthodox interpretation by the scribes of his day or uphold it, with the injunction that the piety of his followers must exceed even the orthodoxy of the Pharisees (Matt. 5:20ff.)? So numerous are the aporias of the gospels that one can only assume that it was not part of their authors' intention that they should be read side-by-side as mutually corroborating testimony of the events of Jesus' life; that indeed was the view of the fathers of the church, the architects of the Christian doctrine of plenary inspiration. But it is not possible in the twentieth century to apply patristic logic to a body of literature that declares its origins in the mythology and legend of the Hellenistic world more eloquently than many scholars have been able to do on its behalf.

Since the appearance of David Friederich Strauss's *Das Leben Jesu, kritisch bearbeitet* (*The Life of Jesus Critically Examined,* 1835) it has been a matter of scholarly custom, varying chiefly in emphasis and confessional preference, to regard the gospels as literary compositions whose components or "traditions" are mythopoetic rather than biographical.[4] For Strauss, this recognition mattered very little since he believed with the majority of the Hegelians of his day that "true" religion was based not on facts but on ideas. Consequently, it was unimportant that the gospels were not records from which a life of Jesus could be reconstructed; it mattered only that they were the "symbolical expression of some higher truth."[5] In England, the poet Matthew Arnold (himself an amateur biblical scholar) arrived at a dilute version of the same conclusion, recommending that the gospels should be viewed not as historical annals but as products of the human imagination; their "truth" consisted in the fact that they had inspired Western civilization with the purity of their ethical teaching. Arnold advocated esthetic and literary sophistication ("culture") as a way around the manifold problems of the text, then being inventoried with alarming success by the German biblical scholars. The "fundamentalist" error as he saw it was not in regarding the literal word of God too highly, but in taking too little account of the conditions under which the gospels were composed—in sanctifying text and disregarding context: "The man with no range in his reading must inevitably misunderstand the Bible.[6] . . . It is because we cannot trace God in history that we stay the craving of our minds with a fancy account of him, made up by putting scattered expressions of the Bible together and taking them literally."[7]

The conclusions of Strauss and his sympathizers caused quite a commotion in theological circles from 1836 onwards. A certain Pastor Eschenmeyer called Strauss a "modern day Iscariot" for his seeming betrayal of the gospel and the Protestant faith, and the Prussian government considered for a time suppressing *The Life of Jesus* by edict. What Strauss had brought to the fore was the question of the relationship of the Jesus of history and the Christ of the Church's faith. Previously it had been widely accepted that the gospel "functioned" essentially as a biographical account composed by people interested in preserving a record of Jesus' life and teachings for future generations. After Strauss, it became more and more difficult to assign such an intention to first-century missionaries whose primary interest, it was becoming clear, was to win converts to their cause through the propagation of a synthetic religious myth. Jesus himself, Strauss came to conclude after 1870 (*The Old Faith and the New,* 1872), was a fanatic, a Schwärmer, who had predicted the end of the world order in his own lifetime. His prophecies, all of them mistaken, had been finally belied by his unexpected death, an event that threw his followers into a panic and precipitated the "mass hallucinations" that the gospels record in the form of stories about a risen Christ. With this verdict in sight, Strauss went on to declare that biblical criticism had brought an end to the "christian" era as nineteenth-century society had known it: "We can no longer believe this absurd nonsense," he wrote of German theology. "My conviction is . . . if we would not try to twist and explain away the facts . . . if we were to speak as honest, upright men, then we must confess: We are no longer Christians."[8]

Between 1835 and 1872, an enormous amount of energy was devoted to repairing the damage assumed to have been done to the gospels by Strauss and his myth theory. Perhaps the name of Ernest Renan stands out above the rest, less because of the scholarly weight of his masterwork (which Proust called "*une espèce de belle Hélène du Christianisme*")[9] than because of its popular appeal and easy style. "The gentle Jesus, the beautiful Maries, the fair Galilean women who form the escort of the 'charming carpenter,'" declared Schweitzer, "might simply have stepped out of one of the windows of an ecclesiastical art shop on the Place St Sulpice."[10] In the *Vie de Jésu* Renan depicted Jesus as a visionary Galilean who had no thought of founding a religion—a dreamer finally brought down by the dramatic events he put into motion. Unlike Strauss, however, Renan made no attempt to gird his life of Jesus with theoretical props: "The intuition of the artist supplements the scarcity of historical material."[11] Renan had done what liberal theologians some sixty and more years beyond would become accustomed to doing: He had used the gospels as a reflecting pool for his own values. In so doing he made explicit a tendency of biblical exegesis since the time of the church fathers. But while in the previous history of the church scripture was seen as an infallible guide and support for teaching,[12] the nineteenth century (in no small measure propelled by Renan's theological impressionism) witnessed a tendency to extract from the gospels such ideas as were congenial to the beliefs of increasingly literate and "democratic" societies. Jesus of Nazareth was more and more seen as the moral man of post-Kantian idealism, the *homo religiosus,* the ethical absolute whose message was working itself out in history.

Alongside the romanticizing biographies ran the independent stream of critical investigation headed by F.C. Baur at Tübingen.[13] A Hegelian by training, Baur understood the development of Christianity as being due to a reconciliation between an original "Judaizing" form of the religion, represented in the gospels by Peter and the apostles, and a gentile form represented by Paul and the early missionaries to the Greeks. Paul, argued Baur, spent most of his life opposing the judaizing tendencies of the apostolic community; this opposition did not lead to a Pauline "victory," however, but to an ideological synthesis: Catholicism. As a biblical critic, Baur investigated not only the historical problems relating to the development of the church, but also questions relating to the dating and authorship of individual New Testament writings.[14] Based on its theological tendencies (which Baur saw as reflecting the Montanist and gnostic movements of a later period), the Gospel of John was assigned to the second century; likewise, Matthew's gospel, because it reflected the theological disposition of the judaizing party, was seen to be the earliest. Baur had not substantially altered the traditional order of the canonical four, but he had called attention to their theological differences and, indirectly, to the necessity of regarding the gospels as independent creations of scattered communities.

More extreme than F. C. Baur was his fellow Hegelian, Bruno Bauer, who was deprived of his teaching post at Bonn in 1842 for arguing that the original gospel was the work of a single author who lived during the reign of Hadrian (117–38). In his *Kritik der Paulinischen Briefe* (1850–52), Bauer confessed that his original aim—that of "restoring the person of Jesus from the inanation to which the apologists had reduced it"—had failed.[15] His work had led him, as it would lead the Dutch Radical school later, to the problem implied in the assertion that the Jesus of the gospels was a product of the human imagination. In 1850 he addressed the question directly by challenging the attribution of the four "Great Epistles"— Galatians, 1 and 2 Corinthians, and Romans—to Paul, and in his *Criticism of the Gospel History* he argued that the development and success of Christianity does not depend on postulating a historical founder. Less cogent was Bauer's critique of Christian origins, which Schweitzer observed "relinquished all pretense of following an historical method."[16]

By 1850 at the latest, the thoroughgoingly skeptical hypothesis concerning the historical existence of Jesus had been advanced as a conclusion based on internal tendencies that no theory of synoptic relationships or prior sources available to individual evangelists could weaken. Indeed it was not long after there was something approaching scholarly consensus on the "priority" of Mark's gospel,[17] and with it the belief that the earliest gospel was a virtually unadorned record of Jesus' life and teaching, that the professor of New Testament at Breslau, Wilhelm Wrede, showed that Mark's gospel was saturated with the theological beliefs of the early Christian community. Rather than a biography, the gospel was a reading back into Jesus' life the faith and hope of the early Church that Jesus was the Messiah and Son of God. Otherwise, queried Wrede, how do we account for the obviously disjunctive character of the narrative and the mass of improbabilities and inconsistencies that characterize Jesus' actions? To cite only a few examples: Why does Jesus speak (Mark 4:10-12) of parables as being designed to conceal the mystery of the kingdom of God when he immediately gives the disciples an explanation that has nothing mysterious about it? Why does he forbid his miracles to be made known, even when there is no apparent reason for the prohibition; and further, why does he wish his messiahship to remain a secret when it is already known not only to the disciples but also to the demoniacs, the blind man at Jericho, and to the multitude at Jerusalem?[18] Wrede's answer to these and a dazzling array of similar questions imported that Mark was interested less in providing factual information about Jesus than in applying a theological theory to an accumulation of materials, the implications of which were not in every case consistent with the beliefs of the community. With Wrede's *Das Messiasgeheimnis in den Evangelien* (*The Messianic Secret in the Gospels*, 1901) came the recognition that Bauer's skepticism would not be washed away. The situation was summarized at the end of the nineteenth century by Pfleiderer:

> It must be recognized that in respect of the recasting of history under theological influences, the whole of our gospels stand in principle on the same footing. The distinction between Mark, the other two synoptists, and John, is only relative—a distinction of degree corresponding to different stages of theological reflection and the development of the ecclesiastical consciousness.[19]

And if the gospels were to be understood as theological tracts rather than as biographical annals, what residuum of fact remained upon which a coherent account of Jesus' teaching and ministry could be based?

It would seem that at the turn of the century two answers to this question were possible. One, harkening back to Bruno Bauer, denied the possibility of arriving at any such residuum and so left open the question of Jesus' actual existence without emphasizing *e silentio* that he was a fiction of the early community. The Bremen pastor and scholar Albert Kalthoff suggested in 1902 that *either* Jesus of Nazareth never lived or, if he had, he had been but one of many Jewish messianic figures engaged in preaching the judgment of God on his generation. The story of Jesus that stands before us today, Kalthoff reasoned, is in reality the story of the way in which the picture of the Christ arose—a biography of the Christian community. Furthermore, he charged the theologians of his day with dishonesty in adopting a method that obliged them to assume, at the point where the history of the Church begins, "an immediate declension from a pure, original principle."[20]

What Kalthoff called into question was the liberal position of German Protestant theology that still hinged on the belief that a pure and unspoiled truth was contained beneath a mythological and dogmatic husk.[21] To say that these dogmatic developments characterized even the earliest of the gospels (so Wrede) was unsettling but not ultimately destructive: it could still be argued that the kernel—the original principle—was "contained" in the New Testament, perhaps as a kind of accumulative truth, or in discrete sections of individual gospels. Further, it was reckoned, such a principle must exist for it could not otherwise be easily explained how a community came into existence to dogmatize it! Kalthoff did not advance merely another version of the familiar Lutheran *disjunctio membrorum* between the originality of Jesus and the missionary preaching of the early Church; rather, he advanced a theory of Christian origins that could as easily do without a historical founder as with one. Christianity had arisen by spontaneous combustion when "the inflammable materials, religious and social, that had collected together in the Roman empire, came into contact with Jewish messianic expectations." In the empire, among the oppressed masses especially, a communistic movement arose to which the influence of the Jewish element in the proletariat gave a messianic-apocalyptic coloring: "The crude social ferment in the Roman Empire amalgamated itself with the religious and philosophical forces of the time to form the new Christian social movement."[22] As to how the historicizing of the Christ took place, Kalthoff held that early Christian writers had learned from the synagogue to construct personifications: Christ, Sophia, the Son of Man, and all the rest of the titles known to us from late Jewish literature suggest the frequency of this convention. The Christ was the ideal figure of the Christian community; in a religious sense, he was their founder,[23] and he achieved historical reality in their missionary stories about him, stories that grew more elaborate following the severance of the Christ cult from the synagogues of the diaspora. In Kalthoff's view there was no need to defend a Judean provenance for the gospels since such a defense could be premised only from a mistaken assumption about the social process through which the cult was called into existence. "From the socio-religious standpoint the figure of the Christ was the sublimated religious expression for the sum of the social and ethical forces that were at work in a certain period." Kalthoff followed the then-current anthropological theory that the Lord's Supper was the memorial reenactment of the hero's death and resurrection, as well as a symbolic expression of the belief that he would come again suddenly as the judge of their enemies. Thus to explain the success of the Christian movement, one needed not to look to the message of Jesus (which in any case develops out of the praxis and needs of the cult); rather, it was the message of the cult itself, their successful adaptation of the messianic belief, their futurist eschatology, and their promise of salvation to believers that explained their dynamic growth and endurance.

The second answer to the question was in some respects more intellectually satisfying, especially to those who regarded the new sciences of sociology and psychology as overrefined and careless of hard evidence. As Bauer and Kalthoff had found the imagination of the early writers or their collectivities sufficient explanation of the evolution of the Christ myth, scholars like Albert Schweitzer preferred to probe the consciousness of Jesus himself and to find there the raison d'être of the movement. Like Wrede before him, Schweitzer considered eschatology the key to understanding Jesus' view of the world: it was, in essence, a world that stood condemned, a world upon which God would soon pronounce judgment. In its historical development, Christianity had inevitably lost touch with the eschatological world view, and so had lost sight of the Jesus of history. Moreover, the gospels do not provide access to this Jesus but rather originate in the attempt to rationalize his own expectations and eschatological vision. They are, said Schweitzer, "dogmatic history,"[24] history as molded by dogmatic beliefs. Jesus' teaching centered on the arrival of the messianic parousia in the near future (cf. Mark 9:1); his actions were the actions of someone who taught others to believe that "the kingdom of God had drawn near" (Luke 21:31). As recapitulations of Jesus' teaching, written after the delay of the parousia had been factored into the Christian experience, the gospels are indeed uncooperative sources, but they are not falsifications of history. True, as Schweitzer reckoned, they have less to do with the empirical run of events than with a community's perception of their role in a suprahistorical scheme of salvation; but they are nonetheless founded on the concrete expectations of a real individual and his associates: "The whole history of Christianity down to the present day . . . the real inner history of it, is based on the delay of the *parousia,* the non-occurrence of the *parousia,* the abandonment of eschatology, the progress and completion of the deeschatologizing of religion which has been connected therewith."[25] Once this conclusion is accepted, reasoned Schweitzer, contemporary theology cannot but bear the consequences: the historical Jesus unmasked by scholarship "will be a Jesus who was Messiah and lived as such either on the ground of a literary fiction of the earliest evangelist, or on the ground of a purely eschatological messianic conception."[26] In either case, he would not be a Christ to whom preachers and theologians could appeal in order to defend their various confessional theologies; nor would he be a figure easily intelligible and accessible to the Christian believer of the twentieth century: "The historical Jesus will be to our time a stranger and an enigma."

Since Schweitzer penned his conclusion to *The Quest of the Historical Jesus,* the investigation of the problem has undergone no dramatic developments. Such a statement will seem at first sight harsh, even uninformed; but I am convinced that a reading of twentieth-century "lives" of Jesus and of the theological literature built around them (were there a Schweitzer to do the job) would bear the assertion out. Neither New Testament scholars nor theologians could successfully challenge the new psychological twist that the rediscovery of apocalyptic in Jesus' teaching had given to the problem. Indeed, it was now seen that to speak of any part of Jesus' message apart from its eschatological context—whether the beatitudes, the parables, or the Lord's Prayer—was a risky business. The disjunction between the allegorizing preachment of the Church and the preaching of the man from Nazareth was absolute; it could even be argued that the survival of a church to carry on his mission was a glaring contradiction of what he himself understood his mission to be. The Church was a reification of its own disappointment—a community of the Last Days condemned to live through history. The theologians were not naive about the implications of the quest and their reactions were as predictable, in retrospect, as they were atavistic. The theology of Karl Barth and his disciples is a case in point. Harkening back to Paul in his ground-breaking book *The Epistle to the Romans* (1918), Barth reasserted the patristic doctrine of the fallenness of human reason and conveyed the view that the quest was mistaken and impious. God had spoken once and once only through his son, Jesus Christ; looking to the historical documentation of this revelation in order to satisfy our intellectual craving was to miss the point that the gospel was, in essence, a paradox: the affirmation that God became man. "Nothing must be allowed to disturb this paradox," wrote Barth; "nothing must be retained of that illusion which permits a supposed religious or moral or intellectual experience to remove the only sure ground of salvation."[27] Barth's view, in modified form, was that of Rudolf Bultmann, the much-misunderstood proponent of "demythologizing" the gospels. Clinging to the bare datum of Jesus' historical existence, Bultmann emphasized the pervasively mythological components of the gospels as proof that their truth for the Church was not susceptible to historical demonstration. Historical investigation, while not profitless, was profitable only in the sense that it paved the way for faith as an alternative to the skepticism that the quest had brought about. The gospel message was to be redefined, its language recast in terms amenable to the situation of men and women in the modern world. For Bultmann, this was to be done in Heideggerian terms: "For the [preaching] of the church maintains that the eschatological emissary of God is a concrete figure of a particular historical past, that his eschatological activity was wrought out in a human fate, and that therefore it is an event whose eschatological character does not admit of a secular proof."[28] In other words, the quest might have discovered that Jesus' message was essentially a message about the kingdom of God, but there was no reason to consign that message to the historical dustbin: what was "religiously" or "kerygmatically" true about it was not discoverable by applying the methods of secular historical or literary criticism to the gospels.

Naturally enough, among those who still regarded the gospels as chronicles of supernatural events, Bultmann's program was considered blasphemous; its central postulate, after all, required one to give up the historicity of the narrative as a prerequisite to comprehending its historic, transcultural value. In actuality, Bultmann stood firmly on Barthian ground in emphasizing the paradoxical nature of the gospel narratives, and in his effort to restructure their message was obliged again and again to assert the *credo quia absurdum* of patristic exegesis: "It is precisely its immunity from proof which secures the Christian proclamation against the charge of being mythological."[29]

One of Bultmann's pupils, Ernst Kaesemann, formally reopened the quest after the hiatus occasioned by the Barthian theology. Kaesemann accepted the positive results of the "thoroughgoing eschatological" school of the turn of the century, arguing that since something *can* be known about the Jesus of history, New Testament scholars should concern themselves with discovering what these additional data might be. Since the appearance of Kaesemann's manifesto, a sizable number of scholars have responded to the challenge—for different reasons, with different ends in view, and with different methodologies at hand. A very eclectic list of these scholars would include the names of Nils Dahl ("Der historische Jesus als geschichtswissenschaftliches und theologisches Problem," *Kerygma und Dogma* 1 [1955]:104–32); Joachim Jeremias ("Der gegenwärtige Stand der Debatte um das Problem des historischen Jesus," *Wissenschaftliche Zeitschrift der Ernst Moritz* [1956]:165–70); Ernst Fuchs ("Die Frage nach dem historischen Jesus," *Zeitschrift für Theologie und Kirche* 53 [1956]:210–29); Gustav Aulen (*Jesus in Contemporary Research*, Philadelphia, 1976); James M. Robinson (*A New Quest of the Historical Jesus,* Nashville, 1959). This list could be extended without difficulty; to it could be added such works as C. C. Anderson's *The Historical Jesus, A Continuing Quest* (Grand Rapids, 1972) and a string of twentieth-century "lives" of Jesus—Gunther Bornkamm's *Jesus of Nazareth* (New York, 1960); H. Braun's *Jesus of Nazareth, The Man and His Time* (Philadelphia, 1979); and the eminently readable but historiographically naive study, *Jesus the Jew* (New York, 1973) by Geza Vermes. A common fault and feature of twentieth-century "lives" of Jesus is that they do not improve on the nineteenth-century models: the same romanticizing, naturalistic, and theological special interests of the authors are not far to discover— a failing that in part must be explained by the fact that the evidence has not substantially changed from the past century to this. Nonetheless, New Testament studies have been greatly encouraged by the work of Helmut Koester of Harvard (cf. *Einführung in das Neue Testament,* 1980), James M. Robinson of the Claremont School of Theology, and Werner Kelber of Rice University. Credit must also be given to the deconfessionalizing work of historians of Christian doctrine; one thinks especially of the debates at Oxford and Cambridge during the 1970s that raised anew the question of New Testament and patristic Christologies and their doctrinal "normativeness" in contemporary Christian churches (cf. *The Myth of God Incarnate,* ed. John Hick, Philadelphia, 1977). It is too soon to know whether at the end of this long and often circuitous road concrete historical results remain to be discovered. It is unarguably true that much of twentieth-century biblical scholarship, and especially studies relating to the

New Testament and Christian origins, has mistaken its independent discovery of conclusions reached in the nineteenth century for original insight. At the same time, the revival of the quest—in whatever form—cannot but be seen as a healthy sign. It means, among other things, that Christian theology is not content to accept the theological bifurcation of the Jesus of history and the Christ of faith as a sound *historical* warrant for its faith and teaching. Indeed, it is doubtful that such a separation was ever more than a slogan for the alienation of theology from the historical methods it had helped to enrich.

This brief survey brings us to the essays collected in the present volume, *Jesus in History and Myth*. In April of 1985, scholars from the leading universities in the English-speaking world gathered in Ann Arbor for a two-day symposium on Jesus and the Gospels. The purpose of the gathering was less to break new ground than to share information with a public too often misled to think that biblical scholarship is "beyond" the average person to comprehend. A great deal is going on these days in the study of Christian origins. The results are not, of course, "kept" from the public by some Machiavellian inner circle; but the way in which such results are normally disseminated—not by scholars but by the media in its three-minutes-that's-a-wrap simplicity—leads to an inevitable distortion of the facts.

Scholarship is a slow-moving business, and in an age of "information" the progress of biblical scholarship looks to the casual observer like rigor mortis. Still, progress is being made, not just in the accumulation of data—"finds," if you will—but in the interpretation of these finds. New gospels have been discovered, late and "heretical" to be sure, but gospels nevertheless; the so-called Dead Sea Scrolls from Khirbet Qumran have yielded new information about the Judaism of Jesus' day and about the religious conditions of the monastic community that produced them. Old questions are being asked in new ways: Is it possible to speak of "authentic" sayings of Jesus, and can these be garnered from the written gospels? To what extent was early Christianity an apocalyptic movement? What insights can be gained from knowing something about the social sciences, contemporary literary theory, and the dynamics of oral cultures in studying the gospels? More broadly, what theological and philosophical implications residuate from the study of Christian origins?

The essays presented here suggest a discussion in progress. They are a sampling of educated opinion; they offer no full or decisive solutions to the problems they envisage. It is through such discussion, however, that we avoid the dogmatism of the past and learn to respect uncertainty as a

mark of enlightenment. If the twentieth-century quest differs in any significant way from that of the nineteenth, it is in this: that we are rather less
convinced that we have all the pieces of the puzzle, and rather more
convinced that when we finish we will have only one of a still-to-be-
determined number of possible configurations.

R. Joseph Hoffmann   Ann Arbor, Michigan
                                                           January 1986

NOTES

1. The reader is referred to the Bibliography in Joachim Jeremias's *The Problem of
the Historical Jesus* (Philadelphia, 1964), and the Introduction to Maurice Goguel's *The
Life of Jesus,* trans. Olive Wyon (London, 1933), 37–69.
2. So the conclusion of the so-called Dutch Radical school. An overview of their
theories is supplied by G. A. van den Bergh van Eysinga, *Die hollandische radikale Kritik
des Neuen Testaments* (Jena, 1912); cf. Arthur Drews, *Die Christusmythe* (Jena, 1909).
3. For example, Rudolf Bultmann, "The idea of the historicity of Jesus does not
need to be defended" (*Jesus,* [Berlin, 1926], 16).
4. An educated and informative dissenting view is provided by Charles Talbert,
What Is a Gospel? (Philadelphia, 1977), 132–35. Talbert does not suggest however that the
gospels are "biographies" in the sense of being transcripts of Jesus' teaching by disinterested observers. He maintains, on the contrary, that such a biography was unknown
in the Hellenistic world.
5. Cf. Strauss's discussion in *The Life of Jesus Critically Examined,* trans. George
Eliot (1892; rpt., ed. Peter Hodgson [Philadelphia, 1972]), 69.
6. Matthew Arnold, *Literature and Dogma,* ed. R. H. Super (Ann Arbor, 1968), 152.
7. Arnold, *Literature and Dogma,* 152.
8. Cited in Horton Harris, *Strauss and His Theology* (Cambridge, 1973), 241.
9. M. Proust, *Revue de Paris,* 15 Novembre 1920, 171.
10. Albert Schweitzer, *The Quest of the Historical Jesus,* trans. W. Montgomery
(1906; rpt., with Introduction by James M. Robinson [New York, 1961]), 182. Citations
are from the Montgomery translation.
11. Goguel, *The Life of Jesus,* 52.
12. Cf. for example, Article 6 of the *Thirty-Nine Articles.*
13. See *Paulus, der Apostel Jesu Christi* (1845).
14. In *Kritische Untersuchungen über die kanonischen Evangelien* (1847) and later
works.
15. Cited in Schweitzer, *Quest,* 156.
16. Schweitzer, *Quest,* 157.
17. Marcan priority (the theory that Mark's gospel was written first, and that Matthew
and Luke made use of some version of that gospel together with other sources) was
asserted by a number of scholars beginning in the early nineteenth century as a solution to

the so-called synoptic problem—the question of the literary connections between the first three gospels. Cf. Lachmann, "De ordine narrationum evangeliis synopticis," in *Theologische Studien und Kritiken* 8 (1835):570–90.

18. Wilhelm Wrede, *Das Messiasgeheimnis in den Evangelien* (Goettingen, 1901); see further Schweitzer's discussion, *Quest,* 334–35.

19. Pfleiderer, *Das Urchristentum, seine Schriften und Lehren,* 2d ed. (Berlin, 1902), 1:615.

20. Kalthoff, *Das Christusproblem* (Leipzig, 1902), 87; cf. *Die Entstehung des Christentums* (Leipzig, 1904).

21. The liberal Protestant theologians were inclined to stress the moral "center" of Jesus' teaching as the irreducible essence of early Christianity; thus, especially A. v. Harnack, *Das Wesen des Christentums* (Berlin, 1900).

22. Cited in Schweitzer, *Quest,* 317.

23. In contrast to the liberal Protestant view of Jesus as a propounder of moral truth, the myth school held that "the synoptic Jesus [not to be considered historical] taught neither a new nor loftier morality . . . nor a deepened consciousness of life" (Drews, *The Christ Myth,* trans. C. D. Burns [London, 1910]), 255. In time, the originality of Jesus' ethical teaching would be challenged by historical study of its midrashic analogues.

24. Schweitzer, *Quest,* 359.

25. Schweitzer, *Quest,* 361.

26. Schweitzer, *Quest,* 398.

27. Barth, 100.

28. Bultmann, *Kerygma and Myth,* 44.

29. Bultmann, *Kerygma and Myth,* 44.

I

The Historicity of Jesus

G. A. Wells*

The Historicity of Jesus

It is customary today to dismiss with amused contempt the suggestion that Jesus never existed. The question was hotly debated at the beginning of this century,[1] and scholars who at that time denied his historicity impaired their case in three ways: they tried to explain away his biography by unduly stressing its parallels with the lives of pagan gods, thus obscuring the fact that, as Christianity is Jewish in origin, it is its Jewish background that is primarily important; they set aside as interpolations all passages they found inconvenient, particularly those in the New Testament books written earlier than the gospels that might be taken as confirming the record of the gospels; and they were sometimes badly wrong in their dating of the documents, misled here by radical Dutch theologians of the day (e.g., W. C. van Manen) who regarded all the Pauline letters, the earliest witnesses to a human Jesus, as second-century forgeries. The tone of the whole controversy was also highly polemical and lacking in the detachment necessary for fruitful inquiry. Because a defective case was argued seventy years ago, most scholars today think it certain that Jesus did exist. I shall try to show that, whatever the final upshot of the debate may be, there are good reasons for at least doubting this.

The sparse notices of Jesus from pagan or Jewish writers are too late in their dates of origin to be accepted as evidence independent of Christian tradition. Tacitus, for instance, merely repeated in the second century what Christians already believed about Christ. The references to Jesus in the Talmud also date only from the beginning of the second century.[2] There are admittedly two passages about him in the first-century Jewish historian Josephus. But no one can accept the glowing paragraph that is the longer of these two as from the hand of this orthodox Jew, and it has to be regarded as being at best a Christian reworking of a passage original-

*G. A. Wells is Professor of German at Birkbeck College, University of London.

ly hostile to Jesus. I have argued elsewhere that the whole, as it stands, is foreign to the context in which it occurs and must therefore be set aside. The other, shorter passage is often defended as authentic, but has nevertheless been—as S. G. F. Brandon has said—"the subject of long and unceasing controversy."[3] That the non-Christian evidence is unhelpful has been repeatedly conceded by Christian scholars, e.g., by Schweitzer.[4]

We turn, then, to the Christian evidence. Everyone knows that the four canonical gospels unambiguously attest that Jesus lived and died in Pontius Pilate's Palestine. Four gospels sound impressive, but this is not *multiple* testimony, as these works are not independent of each other. For instance, Matthew and Luke take a substantial portion of their material verbatim from Mark, and much of their remaining material is drawn either from another common source (not extant) or taken by Luke directly from Matthew. As for the fourth gospel, it on the one hand markedly fails to substantiate many elements of the story told by the other three, and on the other has been shown to have reworked source material that resembled theirs.[5] Furthermore, it is now widely admitted that all four are the work of unknown authors—their titles "according to Matthew," etc., resulted from what F. W. Beare has called "second-century guesses"[6]—authors not personally acquainted with Jesus who were writing between forty and eighty years after his supposed lifetime. Much in these gospels is mere legend, the mutually exclusive virgin-birth stories of Matthew and Luke being but a particularly striking example.[7] Even the Passion narratives, long considered the bedrock of gospel biography, are now admitted to have been shaped by the theological convictions of the writers.[8] For instance, since Mark and Matthew were sure that Jesus was the Messiah, they could readily imagine that the Jews, who they knew did not accept him as such, had killed him for making such claims. So they wrote a story in which the Sanhedrin try to condemn him. Jewish scholars have shown that it is an unlikely story as it breaks every rule in the book of Jewish legal procedure.[9] The trial before Pilate also poses formidable historical difficulties. All three synoptic gospels represent this Roman governor, constantly faced as he was with the threat of sedition, as asking Jesus whether he is the king of the Jews, receiving either an affirmative answer or none at all, and then immediately doing his best to have him set free. In the fourth gospel any attempt to keep Pilate's references to Jesus within the bounds of plausibility has been abandoned. He repeatedly calls Jesus "the King of the Jews," and when the people demand his crucifixion, counters with "Shall I crucify your King?" (John 19:15). The motive of this markedly anti-Jewish evangelist in constructing such a story was presumably to show that the Jews have rejected their true king and thus forfeited their status as the chosen people.[10]

These gospels were written after Palestinian Christianity had been destroyed or dispersed in the Jewish War with Rome that had culminated in the destruction of Jerusalem in A.D. 70[11] and had occasioned a serious break in continuity that made it very difficult for Christian writers of later date, including the evangelists, to have reliable knowledge of what had been going on in Palestine in the first half of the century. It is thus not surprising that the author of the gospel of Luke, who is also the author of the Acts of the Apostles, is in complete confusion over the chronology of events that we know (from independent sources) occurred there at that time.[12] Even Mark, the earliest extant gospel, was written for gentile Christians (for whom Jewish practices had to be laboriously explained, as at Mark 7:3-4) in some part of the Roman Empire probably remote from Palestine, by an author who may well have been a gentile himself.[13] Even his knowledge of the geography of Palestine is hazy,[14] and he puts into Jesus' mouth arguments of which gentile Christians might well have believed him capable, but which a Palestinian Jew is very unlikely to have delivered.[15]

Many scholars nevertheless claim to discern in Mark a number of episodes that they regard as too unedifying to be Christian inventions and that therefore guarantee a minimum of historical fact about Jesus. I have tried to show in my three books on Christian origins that what may seem unedifying to the modern commentator, or even to evangelists who revised Mark, may not have appeared so to him; and that, in the words of H. J. Cadbury, "mixed motives" guided him in his choice of material from earlier tradition and indeed were responsible for elements in this tradition itself.[16]

If we are to believe the gospel story that Jesus suffered under Pilate, we shall want to find it confirmed by earlier Christian writers. It is not as widely known as it ought to be that the earliest Christian documents we have are not the gospels, but some of the New Testament epistles. Paul, for instance, wrote before the Jewish War; he repeatedly refers to sharp disagreements he was having with a powerful Christian community at Jerusalem that was obviously flourishing, and so had not yet experienced the disruption and worse that the war would occasion. And he in no way suggests that Jesus was crucified under Pilate. He and other epistle writers earlier than the gospels did believe that Jesus had lived on earth. But the idea that he had lived *early in the first century* is not documented in these epistles, where he is regarded as a supernatural personage whom God had sent in human form into the world to redeem it, and who had died there by crucifixion in unspecified circumstances. Paul implies that Jesus had lived sufficiently obscure a life to pass unrecognized by evil spirits who, in ignorance of his true identity, caused him to be crucified.[17] This is quite incompatible with the later view of Jesus given in the gospels, where he is repeatedly recognized by evil spirits because he works prodigious miracles, to their discomfiture: casting them out, for instance, from persons in whose bodies they had lodged (e.g., Mark 1:23-24, 34). Those who doubt Jesus' historicity can argue that Paul and the other very early Christian writers are so vague in what they say about his life that they may well have believed that he had been crucified long (one or two centuries) before their time in obscure circumstances, and that they may have been wrong in believing even this much of him. Paul does, of course, allege that Jesus' ghost (the risen Jesus) had appeared recently, not in the distant past. But he does not allege that the crucifixion and resurrection were recent occurrences; and he thought that the recent appearances of Jesus' ghost signaled that the long-awaited general resurrection of the dead and the final judgment of both living and dead could not be much further delayed.

The resurrection of Jesus was the central tenet of the nascent Christian faith. Nevertheless, we should not think of this tenet as initiated by the discovery of an empty tomb in Jerusalem about A.D. 30 by persons who had been Jesus' companions in his lifetime. Paul knows nothing of a place of burial. His letters make it clear that the earliest Christians simply asserted that "Christ is risen." This declaration was made in a preaching formula that consisted essentially of two statements: "Christ died for us" and "God raised him from the dead." According to 1 Cor. 15:12, to "preach Christ" means to preach the saving events summarized in such words, which recur in the epistles in stereotype form and so obviously represent a standard affirmation of the faith. Paul describes this affirmation if not as tradition, at any rate as information he "received" from elsewhere (1 Cor. 15:3). The next stage in the developing tradition was to support this affirmation (as Paul himself does in this same context) by alleging that some had seen the risen Lord. His appearances were, at this stage, simply listed, not narrated or described in any way. Descriptions of resurrection appearances represent a yet later layer of tradition and are not found in documents earlier than the gospels. Furthermore, by the time we reach the gospels, the very nature of these appearances has changed. Paul links Jesus' rising from the dead directly with his being at the right hand of God. He seems to have taken for granted that Jesus ascended to heaven immediately, with a body of heavenly radiance, and that his postresurrection appearances were therefore made from heaven. The evangelists, however, represent him as returning to the conditions of earthly life before ascending. (Not until the postascension appearance recorded in Acts 9 is there any suggestion at this stage of the tradition that he had acquired a body of glory.) Their motive was to supply narratives that, in the face of Jewish and gentile incredulity, established in this way the physical reality of his resurrection. But major discrepancies stamp these narratives as legends. Matthew locates the appearances to the disciples exclusively in Galilee, whereas Luke confines them to Jerusalem seventy miles away. Such stories did not form the basis of the resurrection faith but resulted from it. A yet further stage in the developing tradition is reached with the apocryphal Gospel of Peter, which does not restrict itself to appearances but includes a description of the actual resurrection itself.

The silence of those letters ascribed to Paul that are now accepted as genuinely written by him—Romans, 1 and 2 Corinthians, Galatians, Philippians, 1 Thessalonians, and possibly also Colossians—about so much of what is known of Jesus from the gospels is admitted by the defense to be a problem. The extent of this silence is truly staggering. None of these letters makes any allusion to the parents of Jesus, let alone to the virgin birth. (Paul believed that Jesus had been "born of a woman" [Gal. 4:4] and this excludes the idea of a virgin mother.) They do not refer to a place of birth (e.g., by calling Jesus "of Nazareth"). They mention neither John the Baptist (even though Paul stresses the importance of baptism) nor Judas, nor Peter's denial of his master. (They do, of course, mention Peter, but do not imply that he, any more than Paul himself, had known Jesus while he had been alive.) They give no indication of the time or place of Jesus' earthly existence. They never refer to his trial before a Roman official, nor to Jerusalem as the place of his execution. In a passage typical of Paul's standpoint, Jesus is said to be "the image of the invisible God, the firstborn of all creation, for in him were all things created" (Col. 1:15). Such references do not read like allusions to a near-contemporary human being, particularly when coupled, as they are, with vagueness about where and when and how he lived on earth.

Neither could one gather from Paul's letters that Jesus had been an ethical teacher, even though they are full of ethical admonitions. On the one occasion when he does appeal to the authority of Jesus to support an ethical teaching (on divorce), it is not necessary to suppose that he believed the doctrine to have been taught by the historical (as opposed to the risen) Jesus; for in Paul's day Christian prophets gave directives in the name of the risen one, and this will have been the obvious way of supporting rulings that they were anxious to inculcate.[18] At a later stage it would naturally be supposed that Jesus must have said in his lifetime what the risen one had said through Christian prophets, and so the relevant doctrines came to be put into the mouth of the historical Jesus and recorded as such by evangelists.

Paul is also totally silent about Jesus' miracles, even though he believed in the importance of miracles as a means of winning converts. He repeatedly refers to the "power" of Christian preachers to work "signs and wonders and mighty works," which presumably include miraculous cures effected by casting out demons or unclean spirits. But he never suggests that Jesus effected such practices or worked miracles of any kind. Nor is he alone in this respect. Other very early writers (e.g., the author of the epistle to the Hebrews) also combine silence about Jesus' miracles with declarations that Christian preachers accredit themselves by "signs, wonders and powers." This was obviously a standing phrase in those early days, and it is very significant that, only when we come to a much later work, the Acts of the Apostles, do we find this phrase applied to Jesus (as "a man attested . . . by God with mighty works [literally, "with powers"] and wonders and signs" [Acts 2:22]) and not just to Christian missionaries. Paul even comes very near to actually denying that Jesus worked miracles. He cannot, he says, preach that Jesus was a miracle worker, but only that Jesus had been crucified (1 Cor. 1:23).

If Jesus did not in fact work miracles, one ought to be able to explain how, in the course of the developing tradition, they came to be attributed to him. This is not difficult. Paul's letters show him contending against rival Christian teachers who were making what in his view were excessive claims to supernatural powers. If they asked themselves what sort of life Jesus had lived, they would surely have assumed that he—from whom they derived their great powers—had worked miracles as they did and had been as conspicuous as they themselves were. They will have agreed with Paul that the preexistent Christ did come to earth as the man Jesus, but not that he displayed his true strength by living in weakness and obscurity.[19] Traditions about his conspicuous powers, originated by such men, surely fed the very un-Pauline tradition, strongly represented in the gospels, that Jesus was a man of signs and wonders. Furthermore, among the manifold and far from uniform messianic expectations of the time was the belief that power to work miracles would come with the Messiah—a belief actually alluded to at Matt. 11:2-5. The power of demons was to be crushed in the messianic age. Paul and the author of the letter to the Hebrews represent Jesus as crushing their power by submitting to a shameful death at their instigation and then revealing himself to them in his glory at his resurrection.[20] But it is intelligible that this complicated theological argument was soon dropped. It came to be supposed that Jesus, in his lifetime, had mastered demons in the same manner that the leaders of many postresurrection churches claimed to do so, namely, by miraculously casting them out of the bodies of afflicted persons. Once the miracle stories told of Jesus had entered the tradition, they remained in it because they were a good advertisement for Christianity (as is admitted at John 20:30-31). And we need not be surprised at the fact of which Prof. Morton Smith has made so much, namely, that non-Christian documents of the second century and later say that Jesus was a magician and therefore admit that he did effect cures; for in antiquity, belief in miracles was part of the way in which everyday reality was comprehended. If someone was said to work them, a religious rival would not deny this but denigrate them as magic. Second-century pagan and Jewish acquiescence in Jesus' miracles is thus no guarantee of their authenticity; for this acquiescence dates only from the time when the gospels existed and called for critical comment.

My reader may object that silence proves nothing, that any writer knows a great many things that he fails to mention. Of course, a writer's silence is significant only if it extends to matters obviously relevant to what he has chosen to discuss. Now if we believe the gospels, there is much in Jesus' teaching and behavior that would have been relevant to the disputes in which Paul was embroiled. One of the major issues confronting him was: Should gentiles be admitted to Christianity at all, and if so, should they be required to keep the Jewish law? One would never suppose, from what he says, that Jesus had views on this matter—as, according to the gospels, he had. Again, is Jesus' second coming, which will bring the world to an end, imminent? And will it be preceded by obvious catastrophes or occur without warning? On these points, 2 Thessalonians (probably not written by Paul, although it claims to be from his hand) contradicts the doctrine of the genuinely Pauline 1 Thessalonians; but neither appeals to any teaching of Jesus (such as that detailed in Mark 13). This is very hard to understand if Jesus had in fact given such teachings, and that only a decade or two before Paul wrote. Again, Paul tells his Christian readers to "bless those that persecute you," bids them "judge not," and urges them to "pay taxes." Surely in such instances he might reasonably be expected to have invoked the authority of Jesus, *had he known* that Jesus had taught the very same doctrines. It seems much more likely that certain precepts concerning forgiveness and civil obedience were originally urged independently of Jesus, and only later put into his mouth and thereby stamped with his supreme authority, than that he really gave such rulings and was not credited with having done so by Paul—nor, indeed, as I shall show, by other early Christian writers.

Before I leave Paul, I must repeat that my arguments concerning him are not based exclusively on his silence, and that to some extent his view of Jesus is incompatible with that of the gospels. But even an argument from silence will be greatly strengthened if one can show that several writers, independent of each other, are all silent on matters that could not have been indifferent to them, had they known of them. And we do in fact find that not only Paul but all extant Christian epistles that can be plausibly dated as among the earliest refer to Jesus in essentially the same manner as he does. They stress one or more of Jesus' supernatural aspects— his existence before his life on earth, his resurrection, and his second coming—but say nothing of the teachings of miracles ascribed to him in the gospels, and give no historical setting to the crucifixion, which remains the one episode in his incarnate life that they mention at all.

These early post-Pauline epistles constitute a considerable body of literature: 2 Thessalonians, Ephesians, Hebrews, 1 Peter, and possibly also the letter of James and 1, 2, and 3 John, although these four may be of slightly later date. Can these writers, independent of each other as they mainly are, all be supposed to have believed that Jesus lived the kind of life portrayed in the gospels and yet have been silent even about the where and when of his life? The first Christian epistles to depict him in a way that shows significant resemblances to the gospels' portrait of him are some of those that are widely agreed to have been written between A.D. 90 and 110: namely, the three pastoral epistles (1 and 2 Timothy and Titus), 2 Peter, 1 Clement, and the seven letters of Ignatius of Antioch. Since these later epistles do give biographical references to Jesus, it cannot be argued that epistle writers generally were uninterested in his biography. It becomes necessary to explain why only the earlier ones (and not only Paul) give the historical Jesus such short shrift. The change in the manner of referring to him after A.D. 90 becomes intelligible if we accept that this earthly life in first-century Palestine was invented late in the first century, but it remains very puzzling if we take his existence then for historical fact.

A typical example of the earlier epistles is 1 Peter, today widely conceded to be pseudonymous, written some time between A.D. 70 and 90. The author tells his readers to love each other, to have unswerving faith, to put away malice, and so on. But he seems never to have heard of the Sermon on the Mount, and when he quotes authorities, he appeals to passages from the Old Testament, not to words of Jesus. The author knows not of Jesus' manner of life, but only of his death as exemplary behavior, and even what he says about that is based on the Old Testament (on the story of the suffering servant of Yahweh in Isaiah 53), not on historical reminiscence. As in the Pauline letters, Jesus in 1 Peter figures only as a preexistent supernatural personage—i.e., he existed before he was born on earth—who came down and died for us. In the early Christian epistles generally, any ethical inferences made apropos of his behavior are drawn from these bare facts of his coming to earth and dying—as when Paul argues that he showed exemplary humility in condescending to take human form. What he did or taught between birth and death remains, at this stage of Christian tradition, utterly unknown. Commentators, noting the marked similarities between the ethical precepts formulated—on his own authority—by the author of 1 Peter and those of the Sermon on the Mount, say that the former are "echoes of" or "recall" the latter. But it is surely possible to argue that the true view is the very opposite, namely, that after certain ethical and religious precepts had become established in early Christianity, it came to be believed that Jesus had taught them while on earth.

Liberal New Testament scholars may retort that they do not suppose that the sermon—whether in its Matthean or in its significantly different Lucan form—was ever historically delivered by Jesus, as it has long been shown to be a compilation drawn from disparate items of older Jewish teaching. This, however, does not militate against my position, but merely concedes that there is evidence, additional to the silence of earlier Christian writers (or to the incompatibility of their record with that of the gospels), that this item must be deleted from traditions about Jesus that have any claim to be accepted as authentic.

Other items of substance that must similarly be deleted include the tradition that Jesus suffered under Pilate; for the author of 1 Peter urges his Christian readers to obey Roman governors, who, he says, have been sent by the emperor to punish those who do wrong and to praise those who do right (1 Pet. 2:13-14). Can he then have accepted any tradition that Jesus—who, he expressly says, had done nothing but right—had been condemned to death by a Roman governor? Paul, writing a little earlier, and also silent concerning Pilate, had also said that the governing authorities punish only wrongdoers (Rom. 13:1-7). When, however, we turn to a *later* epistle—namely, the pastoral 1 Timothy, written by general consent after A.D. 90, by which time Christians had come to believe that Jesus had suffered under Pilate—and that expressly links him with Pilate, we do not find such enthusiasm for Roman governors. Its author urges its readers to pray that all in high positions behave themselves decently (1 Tim. 2:1-2). It is not said that they punish only wrongdoers. Here we have something like the fear of Roman authority expressed at Mark 13:9: "You will stand before governors and kings for my sake." All this constitutes evidence that Pilate entered Christian thinking on Jesus only relatively late.

There are admittedly some (albeit very few) statements in Paul's letters that can be construed as corroborating the gospel picture of Jesus as a near contemporary of Paul. For instance, he refers to James, the leader of the Jerusalem Christians whom he knew personally, in a way that is usually interpreted to mean that Jesus and James were brothers. If so, then Paul and Jesus were contemporaries. I have argued elsewhere for a different interpretation.[21] There are also many Pauline passages that are not to the point but are often cited as if they were.[22] Today the historicity of Jesus is so taken for granted that the few passages in Paul that appear to confirm it are regarded as confirmation of the obvious, and alternative exegesis is rejected as weak conjecture and special pleading. On the other hand, the student who denies Jesus' historicity can argue that if Jesus was Paul's contemporary, then not only what Paul says about him, but also the whole treatment of him in the earliest Christian literature is—to say the least of it—not what one might reasonably expect. The real question is which view does better justice to the evidence as a whole?

If Paul, and the earliest Christian writers generally, did not regard Jesus as a near-contemporary preacher and miracle worker, on what could their view of him have been based? It is not in dispute that many religious ideas among Jews and early Christians originated as a result of musing on older sacred and semisacred literature. The principle involved—of prime importance for religious development generally—can be stated in general terms as follows. Written descriptions in any respected document of some person or event, historical or imaginary, may be read by those who know nothing of the real subject represented, and who may freshly interpret the document in accordance with their own knowledge. In this way they may take the writing to refer to people and events entirely unknown to the actual writers. The Dead Sea Scrolls commentaries on Old Testament books are well-known examples. When Christianity originated, the Jewish Wisdom literature furnished material for musing of this kind. Proverbs 3:19 and 8:22-36 represent Wisdom as a supernatural personage, created by God before he created heaven or earth, mediating in this creation and leading man into the path of truth. In the Wisdom of Solomon (from the Old Testament apocrypha) Wisdom is the sustainer and governor of the universe (Wisd. of Sol. 8:1; 9:4) who comes to dwell among men and bestows her gifts on them. Most of them reject her. First Enoch tells that after being humiliated on earth, Wisdom returned to heaven.

It is thus obvious that the humiliation on earth and exaltation to heaven of a supernatural personage, as preached by Paul and other early Christian writers, could have been derived from ideas well represented in the Jewish background. And it is not just that such ideas could have influenced Paul; they obviously did, for statements made about Wisdom in Jewish literature are made of Jesus in the Pauline letters. First Corinthians 1:23-25 comes very near to expressly calling the supernatural personage that had become man in Jesus "Wisdom." The figure of the Messiah had of course not been equated by the Jews generally with that of Wisdom, but there were points of connection that made it easy for the earliest Christians to merge the two. And there was a large body of literature on which to muse. Even the Jews were then divided as to which books belonged to "scripture," and the Christians reverenced them indiscriminately. There was also no agreement as to which passages were to be interpreted messianically, nor as to what the correct interpretation was.

Admittedly, the Jewish Wisdom literature does not state that Wisdom lived on earth as a historical personage and assumed human flesh in order to do so. The statement is that she was available as man's counselor, but was rejected, even humiliated, and then returned to heaven. However, commentators have shown how easy it would have been for readers to suppose that, when the texts spoke of Wisdom "setting up its tent" on earth, the meaning was that Wisdom had assumed human flesh—since "house of the tent" or, simply, "tent" is used (even by Paul) in the sense of man's earthly existence.[23] Furthermore, in the Wisdom of Solomon there is mention of "the just man," Wisdom's ideal representative, who is not only persecuted but even condemned to a "shameful death" (2:20). God tests him with such chastisements and then, finding him worthy, confers great blessings on him, in the form of immortality (3:5). He will be "counted one of the sons of God" (5:5) and receive "a fair diadem from the Lord himself" (5:16). This just man is said by his enemies to style himself "the servant of the Lord" (2:13). The whole depiction of him may well have been influenced by the account of the servant of Yahweh in Isaiah, who was "exalted and lifted up," even though he was despised and rejected of men and persecuted unto death, humbly bearing their iniquities. What Isaiah says about the shameful but atoning death of this servant could well have suggested that he had been crucified; and the reference in Zech. 12:10 to mourning for an innocent and pious man who had been "pierced" would also have put readers in mind of crucifixion. (In the gospels, the use of Zechariah in connection with the Passion is explicit and extensive.) In sum, musing on the Wisdom and on other Jewish literature could have prompted the earliest Christians to suppose that a preexistent redeemer had suffered crucifixion, the most shameful death of all, before being exalted to God's right hand.

This is not idle speculation on my part. Musing on sacred and semi-sacred literature *was* a well-developed habit at the time; the Wisdom literature *was* there to muse on, and Paul *did* muse on it, because he actually refers to Jesus in Wisdom categories. Furthermore, he and other early Christians must have heard of actual crucifixions of holy men that had taken place in Palestine one and also two centuries before their time. The historian Josephus tells that Antiochus Epiphanes (king of Syria in the second century B.C.) and the Hasmonean ruler Alexander Jannaeus (of the first century B.C.) both caused living Jews to be crucified in Jerusalem.[24] (Josephus expressly notes that in these cases the punishment of crucifixion was not inflicted merely after execution, as it often was.) Both periods of persecution are alluded to in Jewish religious literature (in such works as the Assumption of Moses, the Dead Sea Scrolls, and the Similitudes of Enoch), and Jannaeus's crucifixion of eight hundred Pharisees left a particuarly strong impression on the Jewish world. Paul's environment will, then, have included the knowledge that pious Jews had been crucified long ago, although dates and circumstances will probably have been only vaguely known. Such knowledge will surely have seemed to him confirmation of what he interpreted the Wisdom literature as telling him: that Jesus (a redeemer—Jesus means "Yahweh saves") had come to earth and been killed long ago. This dating is actually represented in *Jewish* thinking, for the traditions on which the Talmud drew persistently place Jesus among these ancient victims by dating him somewhere in the second century B.C.[25]

Paul and his contemporaries will have been more readily persuaded by an interpretation of familiar scriptures and prophecies that seemed to elucidate remote historical events of which he had some (albeit sketchy) knowledge, than by the kind of historical evidence that might impress a modern skeptic.

If the earliest Christians had but hazy ideas about Jesus, how came it that, by the end of the first century, Christians had come to suppose that he had lived as recently as A.D. 30? Any answer to this question must necessarily be speculative, but if the gospels really are untrustworthy, it is not idle speculation; for it is important to show that the idea that he had lived then *could* naturally have arisen, even if it were not true. I have already stressed that one factor that facilitated a radical change in knowledge of the past was the Jewish War with Rome from A.D. 66, culminating in the destruction of Jerusalem in A.D. 70 and the dispersal and reduction to insignificance of the Palestinian Christianity known to Paul. All the first writers to link Jesus with Pilate (1 Timothy, Mark, and Ignatius) were active at a later date in gentile Christian communities that had but hazy ideas about Palestine. Again, Paul had affirmed that God sent Jesus to earth to inaugurate a new era. Such ideas would allow an easy transition to the view that Jesus' life and death had inaugurated the final epoch (however long) of human history prior to his second coming. This idea could be expressed by saying that he lived and died "in these last days," "at the completion of the ages." Such a statement, lacking in Paul, is explicit in Hebrews and 1 Peter. The next stage in a developing tradition would be to interpret "these last days" to mean the relatively recent past, and then to specify exactly when in that past Jesus had lived. Now Christians of the late first century will have known from earlier Christian literature that Jesus has been crucified, and, familiar as they were with crucifixion as a Roman punishment, they could easily have supposed that if his crucifixion had been recent, then it must have happened when Palestine was under Roman rule (i.e., after A.D. 6). They will also have known that "Christ" or "Messiah" was a royal title, and that anyone who made pretensions to it would immediately be charged with sedition by the Roman authorities, whether he understood the title in a political sense or not. There had been rebellion enough since A.D. 6 to justify nervousness on the part of the Romans, and hundreds of patriots had been crucified. Indeed, little is known of some of the Roman procurators of Judea except their severity in the face of rebellion. But on the other hand, Christians of the late first century could not suppose that Jesus had lived and died recently enough for people still living to offer plausible firsthand reminiscences, based on personal acquaintance with him; for such people were very obviously not forthcoming. It will therefore have been easy to infer that he could not have died *very* recently (e.g., in the war of A.D. 66-73), but must have lived at some earlier date after A.D. 6. From this premise, Pilate would naturally come to mind as the person who could appropriately be considered as his murderer: for Pilate was particularly detested by the Jews, and is indeed the only one of the prefects who governed Judea between A.D. 6 and 41 who attracted sufficient attention to be discussed by the two principal Jewish writers of the first century, namely, Philo of Alexandria and Josephus. Furthermore, a Christian who stamped Pilate as Jesus' murderer would not need to fear that such allegation would incur Roman displeasure. Both Philo and Josephus criticized Pilate harshly, but were perfectly loyal to Rome, where Pilate does not seem to have been highly esteemed.

This argument does not impute fraud to the Christians of the late first century. Those who lack understanding of the process whereby myths are formed are apt to argue that either a tradition is true, or else it must have been maliciously invented by cynics who knew the facts to be otherwise available. My argument envisages no such process but is simply honest reasoning from the data.

The reader may find it of interest to compare my views with those of Prof. Morton Smith. He has done a great service in giving substantial additional evidence for a view not in itself new, namely, that sections of early Christian writings—in epistles and even in gospels—originated as liturgies for cultic acts of baptism and communion. This is obviously of importance to proper understanding of the genesis of the texts and, to my mind, makes it unnecessary to attribute much of what is alleged of Jesus in them to a historical Jesus. Here, however, Smith will not agree with me, for he is convinced that Christian baptism and eucharist were instituted by Jesus himself. His view of Christian origins is in essence the opposite of mine because it is based on the gospels. His theory that Jesus was a magician is a reasonable one if, as he supposes, the gospels can be accepted as basically reliable, apart from a few mythological accretions in them. My reasons for questioning this will now be clear: their testimony is only apparently multiple and is totally unconfirmed by—and in part in serious conflict with—what is said of Jesus in earlier layers of Christian tradition. Smith's comments on these earlier layers are revealing. He refers, for instance, to Phil. 2:5-11, where Jesus is said to have been originally a supernatural personage who humbled himself by coming down to earth in a human form. In Smith's view, the "original" view of Jesus as no more than a man has here been "overlain" by "later theories of a pre-existent Messiah."[26] But these theories so permeate the earliest extant traditions that they cannot thus be set aside as later excrescences. Smith finds it necessary to discount the whole thrust of the pregospel traditions. Paul certainly did not believe that Jesus' fame was based on his activities as a magician. And so Smith says, bluntly: "On this, Paul is not to be believed."[27] This implies either that Paul was very ill informed about what, according to Smith, was the most striking feature of Jesus' practices (even though, in the terms of the hypothesis, he wrote within two or three decades of their occurrence) or that he dishonestly misrepresented what he knew to be the facts about them. And Smith gives us the same choice between these two assumptions in the case of the not inconsiderable number of early Christian writers who viewed Jesus as Paul had done.

Smith believes that the traditions that make Jesus a magician on which the evangelists drew go back to pre-Pauline times of about A.D. 50; but I think he would find it difficult to give evidence in support of this view without, among other things, taking for granted the very matter I am putting in question, namely, that Jesus lived about A.D. 30. My standpoint is that none of the four canonical gospels existed before about A.D. 90. Most scholars would concede this except in the case of Mark, which they put some twenty years earlier. I have argued for my later dating elsewhere. Here I will note only that, as Mark simply takes for granted that Christians do not need to follow the Jewish way of life, he must have written substantially later than Paul, for whom this question was still a burning issue. The traditions on which the gospels are based could have been adumbrated in the 80s, but hardly earlier; for there is an enormous disparity between their view of Jesus and that of earlier writers. It is only the epistles of the very late first century that in any way reflect the view of Jesus given in the gospels. What my critics have to explain is not just silence on the part of Paul and of other very early Christian writers, nor even just incompatibility between their Jesus and the Jesus of the gospels, but also the way in which, in later epistles, this silence and this incompatibility change into their opposite, into explicit endorsement of much in the gospel picture. In other words, the later authors write as one would expect of Christians who believed in a preacher and miracle worker executed under Pilate. Only the earlier ones do not, and this is difficult to explain if Christianity began with a teaching and miracle-working Jesus of about A.D. 30.

We posit the existence of Caesar, Mohammed, and Napoleon because we possess so much and so varied yet consistent testimony from independent witnesses near in time to the alleged dates of existence of these personages that their actual existence is the simplest hypothesis to explain it all and to account for its consistency. I have tried to show that, with Jesus, this is not the case to anything like the same extent. The work of Christian New Testament scholars themselves points to this conclusion, and one of their number, the late Prof. Martin Werner, noted in 1967 that, although Jesus' historicity was no longer disputed to the extent that it had been at the beginning of the century, anyone who wished to reopen the question could find from contemporary theologians plenty of material to support a negative view.[28] Yet the generality of theologians still finds it possible to dismiss the very suggestion that Jesus never existed as, in the words of Althaus, "folly beneath discussion."[29] Professor John Hick speaks in this sense (although with his characteristic urbanity) when he advises the reader to eschew theories of this kind, saying that today they command no more of a following than the theory that Shakespeare was written by Bacon (see pp. 212). The analogy is perhaps not as apposite as Professor Hick supposed; for the man who gave the complete and knockdown answer to this latter theory—I refer, of course, to J. M. Robertson and his book *The Baconian Heresy* (London, 1913)—was at the same time the most powerful contender of his day against Jesus' historicity.

Today's unwillingness to reopen the question of Jesus' historicity, typified in Professor Hick's comments, is easy to understand. Nearly every informed writer on Jesus today is a Christian theologian who as such can afford to admit only that part of the gospel record is mythical, and who will fain have even that part to be meaningful myth. Much exegesis has come to consist of a display of ingenuity in this regard. As for the not inconsiderable number of uninformed writers, both clerical and lay, they wish to fantasize about Jesus' character and the nature of early Christianity by picking what suits them from incompatible narratives in the gospels and Acts of the Apostles, and by representing highly conjectural interpretations of these pickings as reasonable inferences. For both groups—the informed and the uninformed alike—the founding of Christianity by a Jesus who lived about A.D. 30 is an indispensable datum.

I shall no doubt be told that my own views are not free from speculation. I would reply that a speculative hypothesis is in place only if it serves to show that a development pointed to, but not conclusively established by reliable evidence is within the bounds of reasonable possibility. The evidence that the hypothesis supplements must be really reliable, and not merely a narrative purporting to be history but quite probably based on conjecture, theological need, or on any one of a dozen things other than historical reportage.

NOTES

I refer to my own three books on Christian origins by the following abbreviations:
JEC = *The Jesus of the Early Christians* (London, 1971).
DJE = *Did Jesus Exist?* (London, 1975).
HEJ = *The Historical Evidence for Jesus* (Buffalo, N.Y., 1982).

   1. A. Robertson's *Jesus, Myth or History?* (London, 1949) gives a good account of this controversy. By far the ablest of those arguing against Jesus' historicity about 1910

was John M. Robertson, author of *Christianity and Mythology*, 2d ed. (London, 1910) and *Pagan Christs*, 2d ed. (London, 1911).

2. On all the pagan and Jewish evidence, see DJE, chap. 1.

3. S. G. F. Brandon, *The Fall of Jerusalem and the Christian Church* (London, 1951), 96-97. Paul Winter, in his survey in volume 1 of the revised English edition of E. Schürer's *History of the Jewish People in the Age of Jesus Christ* (Edinburgh, 1973), 430n, names four scholars who "have doubts" about this shorter passage. It would be easy to extend his list of names. Ellis Rivkin mentions neither passage in his symposium paper on "Josephus and Jesus," but makes the staggering claim that the arrest, trial, and crucifixion of Jesus as depicted in the gospels, and also certain elements in his ministry as portrayed there, are exactly what one would expect from Josephus's portrait of Palestine under Roman rule and are therefore authentic. Rivkin must be aware that generations of Jewish scholars have taken the opposite view; for instance, their objections to the gospel accounts of Jesus' Sanhedrin trial have been set out in detail by D. R. Catchpole in his *The Trial of Jesus: A Study in the Gospels and Jewish Historiography from 1770 to the Present Day* (Leiden, 1971). And, as I show in the present paper, even eminent Christian theologians have found the Passion story almost totally unconvincing. As for Jesus' ministry, Rivkin infers from the way the gospels link Jesus with John the Baptist that the historical Jesus did what Josephus represents John as doing, namely, preach love, repentance, and non-violence. But Josephus gives no support at all to the link that the gospels make between the two men. The one passage where he mentions John is authentic. (If it had been interpolated by a Christian scribe familiar with the gospels, then its account of the motives for John's imprisonment and execution would not, as they in fact are, be entirely different from those specified in the gospel version of these events.) But this passage makes no mention of Jesus. The two passages that do mention Jesus do not mention John and, in any case, are not easy to defend as genuinely from the hands of Josephus. It is not only writers denying Jesus' historicity who have set them aside as interpolations. That the linkage between Jesus and John is an entirely unhistorical Christian construction has been cogently argued by Morton S. Enslin, "John and Jesus," *Zeitschrift für neutestamentliche Wissenschaft* 66 (1975):1-18.

4. A. Schweitzer, *Die Geschichte der Leben-Jesu Forschung*, 2d ed. (Tübingen, 1913), 453, 512.

5. On the fourth gospel, see HEJ, chap. 5.

6. F. W. Beare, *The Earliest Records of Jesus* (Oxford, 1964), 13.

7. On these infancy narratives, see JEC, chap. 1. Even on the Catholic side it is now admitted that it is "quite impossible" to harmonize them (R. E. Brown, *The Birth of the Messiah* [London, 1977], 497).

8. C. F. Evans concedes that "almost all the main factors" in the Passion story "have become problematical" (*Explorations in Theology* [London, 1977], 2:28). H. Conzelmann shows that the Passion narratives are the result of "intense theological interpretation" that, he adds, is apt to be overlooked by commentators not theologically trained, who take as historical fact what really owes its existence to theological motive ("Historie und Theologie in den synoptischen Passionsberichten," in *Zur Bedeutung des Todes Jesu* [by several hands], [Gütersloh, 1967], 37-38).

9. Reasons for doubting the historicity of Jesus' trial by the Sanhedrin have been summarized by D. E. Nineham in his commentary on *The Gospel of St. Mark* (Harmondsworth, U.K.: Penguin Books, 1963), 400ff.

10. For a searching discussion of all this, see E. Haenchen, "Jesus vor Pilatus," in his

Gott und Mensch (Tübingen, 1965), 144-56, and the same writer's "Historie und Geschichte in den Johanneischen Passionsberichten," in his *Die Bibel und Wir* (Tübingen, 1968), 182-207.

11. Both Matthew and Luke betray that they knew of the destruction of Jerusalem in A.D. 70. Luke, for instance, inserts, into the speech that Mark had put into Jesus' mouth about the signs that will herald the end of the world, a reference to this destruction, and at the same time betrays that, for him, it was no longer even a recent event. For details, see HEJ, 113-17. Chapters 4 and 5 of HEJ argue a detailed case for putting all the gospels at A.D. 90 or later.

12. Details in HEJ, 118-19.

13. See Nineham, *Gospel of St. Mark*, 41.

14. For details of the serious mistakes in Mark's geographical references to Palestine, see HEJ, 230, note 2 and references.

15. To give but one example: Mark makes Jesus argue against the Pharisees (7:1-23) by quoting a passage from the Septuagint, the Greek translation of the Old Testament used in gentile Christian communities. The Hebrew original of this passage, however, says something different, which would not have supported his case. As Nineham concedes (*Gospel of St. Mark*, 189), "it is hardly likely that Jesus, teaching in Palestine, quoted Isaiah in Greek." It is still less likely that orthodox Jews would be floored by an argument based on mistranslation of their scriptures.

16. H. J. Cadbury, "Mixed Motives in the Gospels," *Proceedings of the American Philosophical Society* 95 (1951):117-24.

17. First Corinthians 2:8 and my commentary on this passage in DJE, 19-20.

18. On these early Christian prophets, see HEJ, 30.

19. On Paul's Christology and that of his Christian rivals, see DJE, 97-101.

20. On this see JEC, 288-97; DJE, 19-20; HEJ, 34.

21. See HEJ, chap. 8. Paul speaks of James not as *Jesus'* brother, but as "the brother of the Lord." He speaks also not of *Jesus'* brethren, but of "the brethren of the Lord," and this could mean a group or fraternity of messianists not related to Jesus, but zealous in the service of the risen one. Support for this view can be found in the fact that in two gospels (Matt. 28:9-10 and John 20:17) the risen Jesus is once made, in circumstances that are similar, to call a group of his followers who are not his blood relatives his "brothers." John did not draw on Matthew directly, and "brothers" is not used in the same sense elsewhere in either gospel. This suggests that the incident was drawn by both from a common source in which the risen Jesus made some statement about his "brethren" in the sense of his close followers. If so, then the term was used in this sense before the gospels, which correlates well with Paul's use of it in this sense. The James with whom Paul contended, who led the Jerusalem church, will have been (as the *leader* of such a group) what Paul called him, namely, *the* brother of the Lord. This James is not said, even in the Acts of the Apostles that depicts the history of the Jerusalem church under him, to have been Jesus' brother.

These questions—to what extent Jesus' family figures in the records and, when it does, to what extent such references represent historical facts—are obviously relevant to his historicity. In his symposium paper, John Dart argues that certain apocryphal material was really written by Jesus' brothers and gives us a relatively authentic Jesus. But even if some of this material can be dated in the first century, its ascription to a close relative of Jesus may not be as early, and—even if it is—may be merely a device to make it carry conviction. One of the documents purports to be a secret revelation made by Jesus, and a close relative would naturally be regarded as an appropriate recipient of such esoteric teaching.

22. For examples see DJE, 22-24. A great favorite is 2 Cor. 5:15-16, to which Morton Smith, for example, appeals in his *Jesus the Magician* (London, 1978), 3. I discuss it in DJE, 98-99, and HEJ, 24.

23. On this see E. Haenchen, *Das Johannesevangelium*, ed. U. Busse (Tübingen, 1980), 129.

24. Flavius Josephus, *Antiquities of the Jews*, 12:5,4 and 13:4,2.

25. See G. R. S. Mead, *Did Jesus Live 100 B.C.?* (London, 1903), 414-15; and E. Bammel, "Christian Origins in Jewish Tradition," *New Testament Studies* 13 (1967):321. Mead allows that Jewish dating of Jesus at 100 B.C. may have originated as a result of controversy between orthodox Jews and Christians of the Pauline type, whose Christianity comprised what he calls "a minimum of history, a maximum of opposition to Jewish legalism" (pp. 419-20). In other words, if Pauline Christians thought of the earthly Jesus as a holy martyr of 100 B.C., the Jews would have replied that he was a heretic of that time.

26. Morton Smith, *The Secret Gospel* (London, 1974), 110.

27. Smith, *Jesus the Magician*, 15.

28. M. Werner, *Der protestantische Weg des Glaubens* (Bern and Tübingen, 1967), 2:237.

29. P. Althaus, *Der gegenwärtige Stand der Frage nach dem historischen Jesus* (Munich, 1960), 5.

Morton Smith*

The Historical Jesus

Professor Wells and I have two things in common: first, each of us holds a theory that most scholars in the field declare absurd, and second, each of us thinks the majority's opinion about the other's theory is correct.

Professor Wells may have explained in his paper his reasons for his estimate of my theory. He mentioned some in his latest book.[1] However, I had to write this paper before seeing his, and I don't think the arguments in the book deserve detailed refutation.

I should probably explain this judgment. The fact is that he argues mainly from silence. Essentially, he claims that since the New Testament epistles and the Apocalypse say little about the earthly life of Jesus, their authors knew nothing about it; and since their authors knew nothing about it, it never occurred.

This argument is absurd. Silence can be explained by reasons other than ignorance, and ignorance of something does not mean it is non-existent. So Professor Wells tries to strengthen, or perhaps conceal, his case with a great many trivial arguments. Some of these are accurate; I owe him for a couple of corrections. However, many are incorrect, far too many to discuss in this space. So I must go on to other things, but first I want to make one comment.

The strongest element in his argument is the silence. Though it is not total, it is demonstrated.

The weakest element, which, in his book, he wisely keeps in the background, is the attempt to explain this silence by conjecturing that somewhere, in the very dim past, there were unknown proto-Christians who built up an unattested myth, based on inadequate passages in 2 Isaiah and the Wisdom of Solomon, about an unspecified supernatural entity that at an indefinite time was sent by God into the world as a man

---

*Morton Smith is Professor Emeritus of History, Columbia University.

to save mankind and was crucified, by persons unknown, for general righteousness.

When Professor Wells advances such an explanation of the gospel stories, he presents us with a piece of private mythology that I find incredible beyond anything in the gospels.

So let's go back to the silence. It is important. That so many of the New Testament texts should have paid so little attention to what would be called, in medieval terms, "the matter of Jesus"—the stories about him and his adventures—is not amazing, because the fact has long been known, but it does deserve more thought than I, at least, have generally given it. So I hope Professor Wells's defense of this paradox may do something to get attention for his evidence.

That evidence should remind us of what we are always forgetting: that the first-century churches had no fixed body of gospels, let alone a New Testament; that we don't know how, or even whether, they used in their services the texts they did have; and that these texts were probably not closely relevant to the main concerns of the believers. Chief of those concerns, as they appear in the epistles, was to get help from their gods and their fellow members: Christianity was a religion of salvation maintained by a network of mutual-help organizations, the local churches. For both salvation and mutual help the normal requirement was membership, which meant baptism, communion, contributions, and participation in services, socials, sessions of spiritual praise, prayer, prophecy, and possession, etc. Storytelling had its place, but except in the eucharist and the Easter festival, that place was usually peripheral, as are the references in the epistles to "the matter of Jesus." Though this fact will deeply shock the professors of Old and New Testament in our bibliolatrous seminaries, recognition of it will help us evaluate the historical data somewhat better than did Professor Wells.

But what can we learn from the data?

This is where the real battle rages, and has raged ever since Schmidt, Dibelius, and Bultmann destroyed the historical reliability of the Marcan outline, so that the gospels fell apart into piles of little pieces, each of which might be broken by form criticism into yet smaller pieces, and so on. Like the splitting of atoms, this produced much hot air. Fragments of the resultant ruins can be found in the many anthologies and surveys of "the new quest for the historical Jesus."[2]

Not all has been lost. Source criticism, by careful work with controllable data, did demonstrate the use of Mark by Matthew and Luke and the coherence of much of the sayings material. These results have survived the flood of conjectures and are still generally accepted, in spite of persistent pietistic attacks.

Redaction criticism, when it can, sharply determines by synoptic comparisons just what the redactors did do, and can also produce results practically demonstrable. So can even form criticism, when dealing with material preserved in synoptic or Johannine parallels.

Beyond these we are in the realm of plausible guesswork, where different prejudices yield different notions of plausibility. The landscape is a jungle of arbitrary analyses of isolated passages, weeds from which those who cook up theories pick whatever will serve their purposes. Hence skepticism, despair, and finally, Professor Wells. It's no accident that he chose as his academic patron the most extreme of the Bultmaniacs, Schmithals.

That these results are undesirable does not prove them false. The observations made by the form critics were often acute; the conjectures based on them, even when not true, were often plausible. Only when it began to be realized that in many cases an indefinite number of equally plausible but contradictory conjectures could be made to explain the same observations, only then did scholars begin to suspect that the quest had led them into an enormously complicated maze, not to say blind alley. To date, the results of the process cannot be evaluated because the process has yielded no final results, only a free-for-all of conflicting conjectures.

But since the initial observations were correct, the questions legitimate, and the conjectures plausible, how can this result be avoided? I would suggest turning from philological to historical criticism.

Philological criticism normally deals with documents singly or in small groups. It considers questions of text, grammar, lexicography, composition, revision, etc., having as its usual objective the precise determination of the meaning, the author's identity and intention, and related matters. Historical criticism uses the texts provided and the results attained by philology, but tries to treat them as evidence for larger historical problems. For this purpose exact solutions of philological questions of detail may be relatively unimportant. Anonymous texts preserved in bad manuscripts may furnish important historical evidence.

In the case of the gospels, this means that the historian will look, to begin with, not for a precise account of the development of each story, but rather, for what historical information can be obtained from a body of obviously legendary material sometimes handed down through a generation of oral tradition, and shaped by the needs of social groups of which our knowledge is sparse and scrappy.

What can be obtained is what the preserved material says. It is evidence, albeit inaccurate, of the society that formed it and of the figure upon whom that society looked as its founder.

Inaccurate evidence is not always worthless. In fact, almost all historical knowledge of major situations and complex courses of events is somewhat inaccurate, because such matters commonly cannot be known in full detail. History, therefore, commonly has to proceed by approximations, determining the peripheries of the possible and moving inward to estimate within these limits the component elements.

In the case of Jesus the possible is limited, on the one hand, by the hard realities of physical nature and the economic and social order of Roman Palestine, but enormously extended, on the other, by the superstitions of the society. The latter leads us to expect, as the former requires us to discredit, the miraculous and mythological elements of the gospels. These are just what they should be for the time and situation. Consider, for example, the ascension story. All the admired Roman emperors ascended, *de rigeur,* to heaven after their deaths. By the early second century there was a regular ritual to assure the ascension.[3] Augustus's ascension was attested to the senate by the sworn witness of a Roman praetorian.[4] To suppose that such mythological accretions discredit the factual reports is historically naive.

The factual reports, too, must fall within the possibilities of the society; the man described in them must be a variant of some recognizable social type. The gospels easily meet this requirement. Jesus the miracle man is completely credible, as are the independent reports in all the gospels that crowds of people came to him from all over to be cured. These reports are complemented by the gospels' reflections of what his enemies said, and here the gospels are confirmed by the bits of hostile traditions we can pick up from the Talmud, pagan authors, and early Christian writers, especially Origen's quotations from Celsus.[5] His enemies declared him a magician and explained his miracles by saying he "had"—that is, had control of—a demon; his followers said he had the Holy Spirit and was a son of God.

The stories that elicit these comments tell mainly of cures of psychopathic conditions, especially hysterical blindness, deafness, paralysis, and coma mistaken for death. Such conditions are liable to sudden remissions that remain inexplicable. We imagine a mysterious thing called "hysteria" and we say, "The hysteria is broken," without knowing what this means physiologically. The ancients imagined supernatural powers and said "The demon is cast out" or "The disease went away."

That both friends and enemies thus, in different terms, described the same sort of man and the same sort of phenomena, is strong evidence for the truth of the elements common to the reports, primarily the cures.

Further evidence is afforded by comparison of the reports in the gospels with stories about ancient magicians and directions for magical practices given in the papyrus handbooks that the magicians used. I have made this comparison in my book, *Jesus the Magician* (2d ed. [Harper and Row, 1981]), where one will find chapter after chapter of parallels from magical texts, regarding not only the major elements, but even most of the minor details of the gospel stories. Particularly important are the demonstrations that not only the cures, but also the stories of Jesus' getting a familiar spirit after his baptism, his overcoming hostile spirits in the wilderness, and his transfiguration have close magical parallels. The postbaptismal experience seems to have marked the beginning of his awareness of his unusual power, an experience he projected and understood as the coming of a spirit from outside. Similar projections of similar experiences are reflected in many stories of the shamanic initiations common among primitive peoples.[6] The eucharist, too, is actually a variant form of an attested magical rite for binding the celebrant and the recipient together in love; a number of other forms are found in the magical papyri; the verbal parallels are unmistakable.[7]

How much such magical rituals had to do with Jesus' success is uncertain, as is the issue of the *nature* of hypnotic and psychotherapeutic powers. Without knowing what they are physiologically, I can only say that they seem to be closely connected, and some people seem to have a natural gift for them, as some are naturally inclined to have visions, and others to have "the evil eye"—whatever that is. Such types of powerful individuals should be studied carefully, using modern medical methods. While awaiting such studies, all one can say is that Jesus seems to not only have had such gifts, but also to have used the magical techniques of his time, probably hoping (perhaps rightly) that they would strengthen his abilities.

Once such cures start to occur, crowds come flocking, and a second factor comes into play—mob psychology. This rapidly produces miracle stories that go far beyond the possible. That Jesus was said to have walked on water is not surprising; the amazing thing is that we have no stories of his flying through the air (until, of course, the ascension).

As the mobs spread the stories, the stories increased the mobs. Among the many who came he found a dozen devoted disciples who served as his bodyguards, agents, public relations men, boys Friday—call them what you will. With them he traveled around Galilee, and perhaps occasionally went to Jerusalem, living off those who had been or hoped to be cured. His cures proved him to his admirers a holy man; to his enemies, a magician. "Magician" was a common social category, but of holy men there were as many different sorts as there were different cults in Galilee's mixed population. Accordingly, for different sorts of pagans who admired him, Jesus was a philosopher, or a divine man, or a son of a god, or a god in human form; for different sorts of admiring Jews he was a rabbi, or a prophet, or a messiah (there are several different sorts of messiahs—a fact commonly overlooked by scholars who think that the title carried with it a ready-made career).

What *he* thought he was, he prudently did not say. Perhaps he was not sure. If you were a peasant boy from a Galilean hill town, and found you could do miracles, what would you think you were? Whatever he was, he decided to make the most of it. He mixed with pious and sinners alike, eating and drinking—sometimes too freely—with everybody, doing cures on the Sabbath, associating with sailors and other roughnecks, and scandalizing the small-town notaries (the "scribes") who were the backbone of local Jewish respectability. To their Jerusalem friends and in-laws we owe much of the hostile tradition that the gospels try to answer.

His admirers repeated and probably improved his sayings, but many may have been good to begin with. Did he have a sharp peasant tongue? In any case, the stories of his cures were soon matched by those of his *obiter dicta*. Whether or not he preached is uncertain. The best of the sermons attributed to him seem to be made up mostly of strings of sayings, originally separate, but this is a question of literary form that can safely be left to philology. For historical purposes, the important question is that of the content.

About the source of his moral teaching it is hard to be sure. Much of it consists of familiar precepts like the golden rule, which he may have quoted or others may have put in his mouth. Similarly, he probably shared the common Jewish expectations about a coming end of the world, and he may have taught them, but his followers may have taken them over from their own backgrounds.

Some of his teaching, however, had historical consequences that make its authenticity very likely. He reportedly taught his followers to see him in glory and think him some sort of supernatural being; this prepared them for their visions of him after his death, visions unparalleled in the Palestinian Judaism of the time, and among the most important events in the history of the world. The reports that he violated the Law and taught that it was invalid are supported by the facts that the Pharisees persecuted

Christianity in Jerusalem and that Paul believed conversion to Christianity set one free from the Law. Probably Jesus' libertine teaching and practice are to be connected with his reported declarations that the kingdom of God had already come and was somehow accessible to a chosen few.[8]

Whether or not he thought himself "the Messiah"—an interminably disputed question—is of little historical importance. The important and practically certain fact was that many of his followers thought him so. Their belief was taken up by the crowd at Passover, probably in A.D. 33, and the crowd's welcome of him so frightened the high priests who ran Jerusalem that they had him arrested and turned him over to Pilate, charging him with sedition and, according to John 18:30, magic.[9]

The reports of Pilate's maneuvers to make the high priests and their adherents publicly demand his crucifixion may have some basis in fact. The emperor Tiberius listened to charges of cruelty and undue severity made against his governors. Pilate would later be removed because of such charges; he may have feared that a trap was being set for him by the accusation of this popular healer. When, however, the demands were made he could not refuse them without laying himself open to the charge of *maiestas*. Thus John's story of the trial, though obviously fictional (report of Pilate's private conversation with Jesus, etc.), fits amazingly the political facts.

I submit that this account of Jesus' life is completely credible: it is given, with relatively minor variations, by four different texts, written between fifty and seventy years after the crucifixion and based on earlier documents of which form-critical analysis pushes the primary elements back at least before the year 50. Undoubtedly the stories as they now stand are full of traits of popular folktales. But those who cannot distinguish between such accretions and the basic facts reported simply cannot see the wood for the trees. The social type pictured and his consequent career perfectly fit the circumstances of first-century Palestine, and those who wish to deny the basic truth of the account must show substantial reasons for rejecting it, not mere conjectures of unknown circumstances that could possibly have produced it. We have a credible account attested by multiple witnesses, all of them writing within two or three generations of the events. Historically, the most probable and economical explanation of these data is to suppose the account true.

NOTES

1. G. A. Wells, *The Historical Evidence for Jesus* (Buffalo, 1982), 24, 130f., 174, 210ff., 236.

2. Anthologies (e.g., H. McArthur, *In Search of the Historical Jesus* [New York, 1969]); surveys (e.g., the papers of the Society of Biblical Literature's *Historical Jesus Consultation* [1982], especially that of J. Baird).

3. E. Bickermann, "Die römische Kaiserapotheose," *Archiv für Religionswissenschaft* 27 (1929):1-34.

4. Suetonius *Augustus* 100.4; Dio Cassius 56.46.2

5. See M. Smith, *Jesus the Magician,* 2d ed. (Harper and Row, 1981), chap. 4.

6. M. Eliade, *Shamaniasm,* Bollingen Series, no. 76 (New York, 1964), 33-66, 88-95, 106, etc.

7. Smith, *Jesus the Magician,* 102f.

8. See M. Smith, *Clement of Alexandria and a Secret Gospel of Mark* (Harvard University Press, 1973), 212f., for a collection of the sayings and pp. 213-51 for my attempt to discover how his followers were thought to get in.

9. The Greek term "a doer of evil" meant, in common parlance, "magician," as comments in the Roman law codes indicate; see Smith, *Jesus the Magician,* 33, 41, and the notes to 33 on p. 174.

Robert S. Alley*

Render to Jesus the
Things That Are Jesus'[1]

At the close of the nineteenth century Shailer Mathews offered an appropriate introduction to our current inquiry. He wrote:

> No one will be apt to expect from Jesus an historical study of the conception of the state. He was a student neither of history nor of politics. But there is no lack of facts that go to prove that men since his day have looked to him as furnishing an ideal of statecraft almost as much as of morals and religion.[2]

In a fit of wit Mathews added that the song "'God's in his heaven, All's right with the world,' would come far nearer expressing the attitude of Jesus [to the state] than the sermons of Bishop Berkeley."[3] In 1985 the United States is confronted with highly organized efforts to establish Jesus as a source supporting a theory of the Christian state. The Bible is being used as a text for frontal attacks upon the secular state. Because this newest wave of prooftexting is not only a serious challenge to the democratic republic, but also a successor to a long tradition of biblical abuse, we will examine historical evidence that demonstrates Mathews' observation to be thoroughly accurate. Indeed, not only have men looked to Jesus for an "ideal of statecraft," they have found that ideal to be strikingly flexible, depending upon the prevailing political climate.

In 1925, commenting upon the words attributed to Jesus in Luke 14:31-32,[4] the eminent scholar C. J. Cadoux wrote in his classic volume *The Early Church and the World,* "We are not likely to be troubled by such a non-committal reference."[5] Obviously Professor Cadoux had not

---

*Robert Alley is Professor of Humanities at the University of Richmond, Virginia.

anticipated Ronald Reagan as president of the United States. Speaking to a gathering of business leaders at the White House, the president referred to that biblical passage and, "calling for a continued military buildup, Mr. Reagan said the Bible story meant that 'the Scriptures are on our side.'"[6] Challenged in a news conference on the appropriateness of such usage of the Bible, Reagan expanded:

> I was actually speaking to some clergymen. I checked that with a few theologians, if it was appropriate. Well, what I meant about "appropriate," [was] was I interpreting it correctly, was it a warning that you should be prepared and otherwise ask for peace because you were outnumbered and out—well, now we would say outgunned—on the other side. And they seemed to think that it was perfectly fitting. It was a caution to those people in our own country who would, if given the opportunity, unilaterally disarm us.[7]

President Reagan, in checking with "a few theologians," might well have taken the advice of a former resident of the White House, Thomas Jefferson: "I not only write nothing on religion, but rarely permit myself to speak on it, and never but in a reasonable society."[8]

To be sure, the remarks by Mr. Reagan are not unique among holders of the office. For example, Harry Truman, in 1950, speaking to a group of Lutherans, said that the Sermon on the Mount was governing American policy in its leadership role over the moral forces of the world.[9]

What we learn from these absurdities is the degree to which our political leaders take cues from theological mentors who have few qualms about the integrity of the text. And they, in turn, have a long heritage of such biblical usage, two millennia to be precise. It is this continued effort to turn Jesus into a first-century equivalent of Machiavelli, using long-employed but dubious methods of text interpretation, that has determined the direction of the presentation.

In the foreword of his 1956 volume *The State in the New Testament*, Oscar Cullmann comments: "Interest in the problem of Church and State usually becomes really vital only when open conflict between the two arises."[10] There is, however, at least one other reason for such interest to become "vital." We observe this same raised consciousness on the subject on those occasions when the church, or some portion thereof, seeks to make common cause with the state in the areas of domestic and foreign policy. Today there are numerous evidences in the world that such coalitions are prepared to employ Jesus as the shaper of theories supportive of particular forms of statecraft. The willingness to manipulate Jesus to specific political ends has not been confined to the fundamentalist enclave.

Reinhold Niebuhr took his fellow supporters of American involvement in World War II to task in 1940.

> Nothing is more futile and pathetic than the effort of some Christian theologians who find it necessary to become involved in the relativities of politics, in resistance to tyranny or in social conflict, to justify themselves by seeking to prove that Christ was also involved in some of these relativities, that he used whips to drive the money-changers out of the Temple, or that he came "not to bring peace but a sword," or that he asked the disciples to sell a cloak and buy a sword. What could be more futile than to build a whole ethical structure upon the exegetical issue whether Jesus accepted the sword with the words: "It is enough," or whether he really meant: "Enough of this"? . . . [We] are very foolish if we try to reduce the ethic so that it will cover and justify our prudential and relative standards and strategies. To do this is to reduce the ethic to a new legalism.[11]

This "futile and pathetic" effort is experiencing a current revival in a hundred television pulpits, and it has roots deep within the Christian tradition, dating to its earliest days.

From the initial accounts contained in Acts we know that the institution of the church found itself concerned for matters of state. The Roman authorities had seen fit to involve themselves in the death of Jesus, thereby creating the seeds of future tension. However, the peculiar political conditions that prevailed in Palestine in the first century delayed severe conflict with Rome for nearly a century. The empire allowed considerable latitude to Jewish religious leaders in matters of law. The early church found itself the object of persecution by those religious leaders who directed the course of that community of which Christians were a part. Luke indicates that the "heresy" espoused by this new sect could be dealt with directly as, for example, in the case of Stephen.[12] By the same token, Christians had a degree of recognition from Roman authorities because they were a part of Judaism. The entire tone of the thirteenth chapter of Romans is a reflection of this condition. Paul, a citizen of Rome, found the empire often more charitable than his former employers. Passive acceptance of authority is encouraged in both 1 Tim. 2:1-2, "I urge prayers . . . thanksgivings be made for all men, for kings and all who are in high positions, that we may lead a quiet and peaceful life, godly and respectful in every way"; and in 1 Pet. 2:13-15, 17b, "Be subject for the Lord's sake to every human institution, whether it be to the emperor as supreme, or to governors as sent by him to punish those who do wrong and to praise those who do right. For it is God's will that by doing right you should put to silence the ignorance of foolish men. . . . Fear God, honor the emperor." We observe this same attitude of cooperation in Clement of Rome: "And grant that we may be obedient to your almighty and glorious name, and to our rulers and governors on earth."[13]

As the book of Revelation makes clear this sentiment soon changed. As early as A.D. 70 Christians were confronted with a new problem. As they expanded their influence they attracted the direct attention of Roman authorities. As we are well aware, the state became the personification of evil as Christians began to experience the persecutions made famous in our time by *Quo Vadis, The Robe,* and the twelve-hour NBC drama "A.D.," an event so "impressive" that Anthony Burgess could write, "But above all, the series should reawaken admiration at the exploits of a handful of tough Jews and Christians who tried to convert a pagan empire to a sense of love and tolerance. At length they succeeded, and a day would come when the emperor Constantine would march against his enemies under a Christian banner."[14] Mr. Burgess does not inform us whether that Christian banner bore the words love and tolerance.

In the following centuries the writings of the church fathers are clear evidence of a running struggle with the state. From Justin Martyr to Tertullian to Origen there is serious attention devoted to the problems created by the empire. But even as these conflicts mounted, there was the anticipation that the state might serve the purpose of the church. "So we ask that you [emperor] should punish those who do not live in accordance with his teachings, but merely say that they are Christians."[15]

In the third century Cecius (249-51)[16] and in the fourth Diocletian (284-305)[17] made certain that all Christians would have to grapple with their relation to the state. As we know, Galerius, Licinius, and Constantine altered the course of history by issuing, in 311, an edict of toleration to Christians "on condition that nothing is done by them contrary to discipline."[18] Two years later, 313, the Edict of Milan gave full freedom to Christianity. It was effective and the church found itself free at last. But the price was high. Williston Walker commented: "In winning its freedom from its enemies, it had come largely under the control of the occupant of the Roman imperial throne. A fateful union with the state had begun."[19]

The Council of Nicea in 325 set the boundaries. To a large extent it was the empire that would establish theological norms. This is even more evident at Chalcedon in 451.

As the non-Christian citizenry accused the church of causing the decline of the empire in the fifth century, Augustine made his classic response. At the same time he offered a philosophical justification of the state without resorting to biblical passages: "The father of the family ought to frame his domestic rule in accordance with the law of the city, so that the household may be in harmony with the civic order."[20]

He laid the foundation for the "two-cities Christianity"[21] that has so pervaded the thinking of the Christian community since then. By the time of Charlemagne every effort was expended to give biblical support to politics. Arguments abounded seeking to establish the role of the church in this dual situation. The typical argument used Luke 22:38: "And they said, 'Look, Lord, here are two swords.' And he said to them, 'It is enough.'"[22] The outlandish conclusion was that with this "one-liner" Jesus endorsed the need for both a spiritual and a temporal head for the state. By the eleventh century this theory was a given, leaving only the question of supremacy unresolved. The conflict raged as confrontations such as that between Henry IV and Pope Gregory VII (1073-85) brought forth appeals to Jesus as the source of royal authority. The pope claimed that Peter had been given both swords and therefore that he could "depose Emperors." Gregory argued: "I am set to rule over the Christian world which was specially entrusted to thee [Henry IV] by Christ. . . . God has given to me the power to bind and to loose in heaven and in earth."[23] Henry had made a counterclaim earlier that same year. "Our Lord Jesus Christ has called us to the government of the empire, but he never called you [Gregory] to the rule of the church. . . . [I] have yet been anointed to rule among the anointed of God, and who, according to the teaching of the fathers, can be judged by no one save God alone, . . ."[24] Obviously, the popes also used Matt. 16:19 in claiming authority over the state. The end result was a power struggle in which the inevitable victor was the state. But if the church seldom reached the pinnacle of power exercised briefly by Gregory, it nevertheless found satisfaction in claiming a kind of international theocracy. Catholicism emerged from the era championing a theory of the supranational church. In contrast, the state argument was advanced:

> Every passage was seized upon when submission to the powers that be is enjoined, every instance cited where obedience had actually been rendered to imperial officials, a special emphasis being laid on the sanction which Christ himself had given to Roman dominion by pacifying the world through Augustus by being born at the time of taxing, by paying tribute to Caesar, by saying to Pilate, "Thou couldest have no power at all against me except it were given thee from above."[25]

By the time of Aquinas the political state was accepted as a necessary part of the life of the world. The Augustinian notion of the state as necessitated by the fall was mitigated.

Meantime the split between east and west provided an alternative style for Orthodoxy. As the term Caesaropapism suggests, the Byzantine emperor was clearly dominant over the chief ecclesiastical official, the patriarch. While recent studies by scholars such as Deno John Geanakoplos [26] provide sound arguments against the oversimplified notion of the "all-pervasive imperial control," nevertheless the history of the Orthodox movement offers considerable evidence that the church leadership was effectively subjugated by the ruler in most instances. The twentieth-century example of the Russian Orthodox Church actively supporting the most extreme social repressions of the tsars is but one example.

Time constraints require that we move quickly to the sixteenth century and the Reformation. Here we find the emerging nation states of Europe becoming the seedbed for Protestant growth. Then came the Reformation and its identification with the nation-states of Renaissance Europe. While Martin Luther was developing a state/church policy that essentially smothered the church's social role, John Calvin was devising the most elaborate theocratic system since Ezekiel. Alongside these two experiments was the "left wing" of the Reformation that caught the spirit of the age of Renaissance and reason respecting the church/state question. But the powerful juggernauts—Lutherism and Calvinism—failed to be ignited by the spirit that would affect most areas of intellectual inquiry. The commonly accepted version of this period of reform makes much of the return to the Bible as authority. A closer examination of the evidence suggests a shattering difference between the dominant sixteenth-century reformers and their contemporaries in other fields of knowledge. During and following the Renaissance a new spirit engulfed Western civilization, one that would produce enlightened approaches to science, literature, art, philosophy, and government. The mistake historians have frequently made is to assume that the Reformation did the same thing for religion. To be sure, the phrases sound impressive—*sola scriptura,* salvation by faith alone—but the reality was far different. Neither Calvin nor Luther adhered to the new humanism, aptly described by Roland Bainton.

> This was the age of the Renaissance. One of the strains in that movement is called humanism. It was in part an attitude to life, aspiring to fulfillment rather than renunciation. . . . Nothing was alien; all learning, all systems, and even all religions should be studied and sympathetically understood. . . . Christianity tended to be expressed in terms of the Fatherhood of God, the leadership of Christ, and the brotherhood of man. These were of course later the slogans of the Enlightenment and of liberal Protestants. Another

aspect of humanism was free inquiry, particularly with regard to historical documents, including those on which rested the claims of the Church and of the Christian religion itself. . . . Humanism, whether within Catholicism or Protestantism, was one of the great strands in the fabric of liberty.[27]

Most of the Christian church, Protestant and Catholic, never participated in such a reformulation. The Protestant Reformation, in its main course, was a gloss supplied by intolerant practitioners of religious exclusivism. These reformers merely recast Roman Catholic theology of the state into nationalist terms. Christian ecclesiologists, obsessed with questions about statecraft, encouraged cultural conformity. And the anomaly is that today these same "doctors" of the church continue to provide the backbone of Protestant biblical interpretations.

The problem the reformers confronted was a massive one. They had set the Bible loose to become the single religious authority, but they dared not allow free interpretation lest institutional strength be undermined. This was particularly a dilemma for a man like Luther, who needed to demonstrate his ability to speak for the German church. Thus the affirmation about the deity of Jesus became, for Protestants, a means to systematize the Bible on the ground that it was the Word of God revealing the truth about the God/Man. The reformers took away with one theory (divine inspiration) what they had proffered with another (salvation by faith alone). And since, thereby, every word or phrase in the Bible took on God-ordained meaning, requiring appropriate interpreters, it was possible to spin grotesque theories in the name of God. The Reformation set forth what I would term a bifurcated notion of sola scriptura. Martin Luther and his successors never really meant to free the Bible for individuals, they merely required a weapon to attack papal authority. In fact, they all relished that authority, merely desiring to exercise it themselves. An exclusivistic religious claim demanded a divinely ordained seer. In the twentieth century the legacy of this logic falls on the shoulders of television evangelists who glibly speak of God's will under the rubric of "The Bible says." It is as if Matt. 16:18-19 had been democratized, made available to whoever will claim the keys.

Martin Luther, the champion of *Here I Stand,* offers a fascinating study of a man constructing a theology to fit political reality. I make this observation with the full awareness that the enormous scholarly output of Luther includes profound insights respecting the Christian faith. Nevertheless, once set on his public course Luther, standing firm on his principles and with the full protection of a German prince, became every bit as repressive as the papacy he attacked. The proof of this expediency lies in his 1525 rhetorical attack on the peasants. The corruption of his moral character is best seen in his convoluted, biblically based attack on the Jews in 1543.

First let us examine the way in which Luther utilized the Bible, and Jesus in particular, to support his political position on the peasant revolt.

> The peasants have taken upon themselves the burden of three terrible sins against God and man; by this they have abundantly merited death in body and soul. In the first place, they have sworn to be true and faithful, submissive and obedient, to their rulers, as Christ commands when he says "Render to Caesar the things that are Caesar's" [Luke 20:25]. And Romans 13 [:1] says, "Let every person be subject to the governing authorities." Since they are now deliberately and violently breaking the oath of obedience and setting themselves in opposition to their masters, they have forfeited body and soul, as faithless, perjured, lying, disobedient rascals and scoundrels usually do. St. Paul passed this judgment on them in Romans 13 [:2] when he said that those who resist authorities will bring a judgment upon themselves. This saying will smite the peasants sooner or later, for God wants people to be loyal and to do their duty.[28]

> It does not help the peasants when they pretend that according to Genesis 1 and 2 all things were created free and common, and that all of us alike have been baptized. [The peasants had claimed that serfdom is un-Christian.] For under the New Testament, Moses does not count; for there stands our Master, Christ, and subjects us, along with our bodies and our property, to the emperor and the law of this world, when he says, "Render to Caesar the things that are Caesar's." . . . We are bound to live according to this teaching of Christ, as the Father commands from heaven, saying, "This is my beloved Son, listen to him" [Matt. 17:5].[29]

> Thus, anyone who is killed fighting on the side of the rulers may be a true martyr in the eyes of God, if he fights with the kind of conscience I have just described, for he acts in obedience to God's word. On the other hand, anyone who perishes on the peasants' side is an eternal firebrand of hell, for he bears the sword against God's word and is disobedient to him, and is a member of the devil. And even if the peasants happen to gain the upper hand (God forbid!)—for to God all things are possible, and we do not know whether it may be his will, through the devil, to destroy all rule and order and cast the world upon a desolate heap, as a prelude to the Last Day, which cannot be far off.[30]

Luther then made the astounding observation: "If anyone says that I am being uncharitable and unmerciful about this, my reply is: This is not a question of mercy; we are talking of God's word. It is God's will that the king be honored and the rebels destroyed; and he is as merciful as we are."[31]

He continued: "Therefore, as I wrote then so I write now: Let no one have mercy on the obstinate, hardened, blinded peasants who refuse to listen to reason; but let everyone, as he is able, strike, hew, stab, and slay. . . .It is better to cut off one member without mercy than to have the whole body perish by fire, or by disease [Matt. 5:29-30]."[32]

On the subject of war, Jesus was enlisted without question. "When Christ stood before Pilate he admitted that war was not wrong when he said, 'If my kingship were of this world, then my servants would fight that I might not be handed over to the Jews' [John 18:36]."[33]

Luther had no intention of allowing divergent interpretations of the Bible. He arrogated to himself the function of God's spokesman. And granted his restricted knowledge of biblical criticism, his exegesis was suspect even for his own age. The Bible was a political weapon.

When the reformer turned to the Jews some two decades later, he employed the identical style of interpretation and similar vehement language as he, on that occasion, quoted Jesus in support of genocidal behavior.

What will the eternal wrath of God in hell be like toward false Christians and all unbelievers? Well, let the Jews regard our Lord Jesus as they will. We behold the fulfillment of the words spoken by him in Luke 21 [:20, 22f]: "But when you see Jerusalem surrounded by armies, then know that its desolation has come near . . . for these are days of vengeance. For great distress shall be upon the earth and wrath upon the people."[34]

For wherever the Seed of the woman is or appears, he (serpent) causes strife and discord. This he says in the Gospel: "I have not come to bring peace on earth, but a sword and disunity" [cf. Matt. 10:34].[35]

What shall we Christians do with this rejected and condemned people, the Jews? . . . I shall give you my sincere advice:

First, to set fire to their synagogues or schools and to bury and cover with dirt whatever will not burn, so that no man will ever again see a stone or cinder of them. This is to be done in honor of our Lord and our Christendom, so that God might see that we are Christians, and do not condone or knowingly tolerate such public lying, cursing, and blaspheming

of his Son and of his Christians. . . .
Second, I advise that their houses also be razed and destroyed. For they pursue in them the same aims as in their synagogues. . . .
Third, I advise that all their prayer books and Talmudic writings, in which such idolatry, lies, cursing, and blasphemy are taught, be taken from them.
Fourth, I advise that their rabbis be forbidden to teach henceforth on pain of loss of life and limb.
Fifth, I advise that safe-conduct on the highways be abolished completely for the Jews.[36]

Luther completes this 1543 diatribe with a claim that Jesus endorsed such treatment. He notes: "We will believe that our Lord Jesus Christ is truthful when he declares of the Jews who did not accept but crucified him, 'You are a brood' of vipers and children of the devil' [cf. Matt. 12:34]."[37]

John Calvin provided a quieter model of exegetical excess in his condemnation of Michael Servetus. In formulating his theory of the state Calvin set forth biblical justifications that were heavily weighted in favor of the Old Testament. In the *Institutes*, chap. 20, "On Civil Government," he had thirty-five references to the New Testament, only six of which were to the Gospels. In contrast, he offered fifty-eight references to the Old Testament. Among the more significant references Calvin offered the following:

> The Lord has not only testified that the function of magistrates has his approbation and acceptance, but has eminently commended it to us, by dignifying it with the most honourable titles. We will mention a few of them. When all who sustain the magistracy are called "gods" [Ps. 82:1, 6], it ought not to be considered as an appellation of trivial importance; for it implies, that they have their command from God, that they are invested with his authority, and are altogether his representatives, and act as his viceregents. This is not an invention of mine, but the interpretation of Christ, who says, "If he called them gods, unto whom the word of God came, and the Scripture cannot be broken" [John 10:35].[38]

Again, Calvin spoke of the state in terms of force.

> Paul says of the magistrate that "He beareth not the sword in vain; for he is the minister of God, a revenger to execute wrath upon him that doeth evil" [Rom. 13:4]. Therefore, if princes and other governors know that nothing will be more acceptable to God than their obedience, and if they desire to approve their piety, justice, and integrity before God, let them devote themselves to this duty.[39]

Modern parallels to this type of biblical use are easy to find. And it would be an error if one assumed that what appears to be toying with the text were evidence of biblical ignorance. Certainly Calvin and Luther were thoroughly versed in the Bible, knowing its content from Genesis to Revelation. It is not ignorance that is at work here, it is a basic theological style. "For any man ultimate authority is in what he takes to be ultimate reality, and this reality he must formulate for himself."[40] Every individual's faith is determined by him or her, not by the Bible. Of course, faith may be assigned to the Bible and that in turn may lead to fanciful excursions through Jesus' words. In point of fact, Luther admitted as much when he asserted that "faith precedes Scripture." And with the reformer's penchant for defining what God meant, reason often seemed to be in the far distant land. For instance, listen to Luther as he admonished the peasants for daring to contradict his views. "Here I do not want to hear or know about mercy, but to be concerned only about what God's word requires. On this basis, my little book was and remains right, even though the whole world take offense at it."[41] Using this device Luther, or any interpreter, may combine a totally irrational presupposition with the most carefully reasoned arguments based upon a bible, the author of whom has confided its meaning to the "man of God." The "Render to Caesar" remark suddenly develops a rich texture for such self-identified experts on "what God's word requires."

Modern biblical scholarship certainly has intended to avoid such subjective manipulation of the text. While the critic may never be objective, he or she can certainly strive for fairness. Yet on occasion the critic, with perhaps the best of motives and without any clear pre-agenda, becomes caught up in that same effort to find "meaning" in every biblical phrase. I am satisfied that such behavior stems from the critic's failure to suspend judgment on the nature of the Bible. As long as it is perceived as the "Word of God," even the best of critics will be tempted to presume more for the text than it can reasonably support. A case in point is Oscar Cullmann, distinguished theologian and critic. In his book *The State in the New Testament,* mentioned earlier, he constructs an involved thesis concerning Jesus and the Zealots based upon the events surrounding the trial. In setting the context for this discussion he offers an extensive commentary on the "Render to Caesar" passage. "Because Jesus' position on this question was not simple but *had* to be complex, men could mischievously distort his point of view, and they certainly did. Thus they distorted also his critical attitude toward the temple, representing it as a revolutionary intention to destroy it."[42]

An examination of alternative interpretations reveals striking disagreements on this subject. Using the same verse, Ernst Troeltsch insisted "There is no thought of the State at all" for Jesus.[43] Shailer Mathews agreed: "Jesus nowhere gives systematic teaching in regard to politics. His attitude towards the state and political relations is to be seen, if at all, in his own life, in scattered statements, and in general comparisons and implications."[44]

According to Mathews the key passages Matt. 22:18-22, 17:27, and John 19:11 offer no real definition of the state.

The divergence on this issue is significant. Cullmann appears to be telling his readers that Jesus' attitude toward the state is so complex that it is nearly impossible to understand. Thus Jesus chose to explain the entire matter in one sentence, a sentence that has led to innumerable efforts to incarcerate, maim, and slay fellow believers and infidels alike. Instead of taking these few words assigned to Jesus as an isolated reference that provides no real clue to a theory of state, all too often biblical interpreters have misconstrued the words to imply some elaborate scheme.

At this juncture I would like to insert a modern analogy taken from the press. We know there are highly competent reporters in the field of religion to whom we can speak with the full expectation of being understood. Yet I would imagine that not one of us has failed to experience the frustration of being quoted out of context. Even more frustrating, however, are those times when fragments from an interview that seemed to us insignificant bridges to major concepts were included in the article, while the heart of the argument was omitted altogether. That it is a natural process of evidential attrition makes it no more pleasant to endure. For years it has puzzled me that no such process is presumed in the case of the New Testament when key passages are on the line. Cullmann builds his entire case for Jesus' final week on the assumption that Jesus was "condemned to death as a Zealot by the Romans."[45] Small wonder, since Cullmann is convinced that Jesus' disciples totally misunderstood his mission even in the final hours. "The words Jesus spoke at the Last Supper must have been a great disillusionment to all his disciples, who even at that time had not yet grasped the sense in which Jesus understood his Messiahship."[46] In that case, how could those reporters of Jesus' messages have been reliable in retelling earlier remarks about the state? Or, more to the point, what may they have omitted in their failure to understand? If Jesus was as complex as Cullmann suggests then we certainly need a carefully drawn essay by Jesus to explain his position on church and state. And, in fact, this is precisely what the church has always assumed. Just this need for authoritative statements on critical issues caused the church leadership to establish and rely upon the label "Word of God." This move established immediately that while complex, the position of God on the issues of the day were contained within a single volume. There remained only the problem of unlocking the text, first with the "keys of the kingdom" and later with the battle cry "sola scriptura." By this method snippets of remembered comments are given divine authority, thereby allowing later interpreters to identify the Christian answers to all questions. The remaining task was to select the criteria for such interpreters, a thorny problem for Protestants as the Servetus case indicates.

Unfortunately, as indicated earlier, in far too many instances even the critic has found it difficult to escape this confining dogma about the nature of the Bible. In many cases biblical scholarship has been the source of unending speculation about meanings because of this backdrop of divine revelation. Honest scholars, within the confessional traditions, have often been oblivious to the nature of the problem that exists between biblical criticism and the faithful. Van Harvey, in his fine study of *The Historian and the Believer,* addressses this situation. "The problem was not, as so many theologians then believed, that the Biblical critics emerged from their libraries with results disturbing to believers, but that the method itself, which led to those results, was based on assumptions quite irreconcilable with traditional belief."[47]

Harvey continues by reminding his readers that the "unspoken issue" between historians and believers is that of the morality of knowledge.[48] He concludes that orthodox belief "corrodes the delicate machinery of sound historical judgment."[49]

All too often the failure to recognize this conflict has led to a kind of multiple-choice fundamentalism that merely eliminates the most noxious forms of dogmatism. In large measure this is the overwhelming burden that theologians and biblical critics bear in the main-line Christian seminaries today. They are bombarded with the absolutes of rigid orthodoxy, absolutes that remain within their own tradition. My own theological education took place under the guidance of talented and gifted scholars who were effectively incarcerated by a so-called "Abstract of Principles" to which each had to adhere.

One can observe the restrictive nature of this legacy in recent scholarly treatments of the subject of Jesus and the state. Encumbered by a theology that may include a belief in a cosmic encounter between God and Satan, the final hours of Jesus' life have been construed as a God-ordained confrontation between Jesus and the powers of darkness. In a desperate effort to give substantial meaning to every scene in the closing act, actions of Jesus randomly recalled by his friends are assigned profound theological meaning. The numbing effect of this method is to turn attention from the overwhelming humaneness of the crucified Jesus and supplant that with elaborate theories of atonement, reconciliation, the eschaton, justification, and salvation.

Jesus called for rejection of rigid orthodoxies. When he addressed religious laws Jesus applied a common measure, the law of love. If the church takes Jesus seriously it is called to iconoclasm in every century, attacking obscure and irrelevant institutions. To his last days in Jerusalem Jesus is presented as decrying religious dogmatism. His opponents, no matter their particular religious or political convictions, were organization men who could only view Jesus as heretic.

> There is a haunting loneliness about the role of the heretic as he passes through the valleys of shadow, often with unspeakable burdens. Can it not be said that he, more than any other, enters into the mysticism of Gethsemane suffering? It is not then strange to observe that the interrogation of Jesus on that last morning was the "prototype of all heresy trials"![50]

The trial of Jesus involved him with a secular state and an irreducible minimum of local religio-political leaders. The evidence suggests that the state authority accepted a coalition that involved him in collusion with self-styled religious leaders. The power of such a minority to wield influence was and is dependent upon two factors: (1) a fanatic dedication to the translation of dogma into statecraft by that minority; and (2) a willingness or eagerness on the part of the state to use religion to achieve secular goals. Harvey Cox wrote recently of that trial and came to this interesting conclusion:

> Through the ages, Christians have given Jesus' death a variety of theological meanings. But on the historical plane, he was one more victim of a cynical power play. His death tells us nothing in particular about Jews or Romans, but it speaks volumes about the human propensity to prop up teetering positions of privilege with the pain of innocent people.[51]

As we return to the theme of this paper, the search for answers concerning Jesus and the state is encumbered with at least three serious difficulties. First, the tradition about Jesus is rife with exegetical fantasy on the subject. Second, the myth of the divine Christ coupled with abnormal attitudes toward the Bible make the historical task extremely difficult. Third, Jesus is the victim of successive waves of acculturation that effectively cloud any insights he may have had.

The largest problem that I see in the analysis of Jesus and his views of the state centers on the seeming necessity to find a consistent philosophy of government that can pass muster in every generation. This quest is made necessary by the inherent nature of the God/Man theology. That is not to say that this problem is unique to Jesus.

If we can view the Gospels divested of centuries of theological overlay, I think Troeltsch was correct: Jesus neither had a theory of state nor did he organize a church. "This is the reason why the sociological thought of the Gospel has been able to react again and again against ecclesiastical tyranny."[52] The paucity of evidence concerning Jesus' view of the state has provided a vacuum into which interpreters of Romans 13 have moved with vigor to co-opt the state for their God and his purposes. Generation after generation of Christians has sought to extrapolate from the Bible support for political systems. The popes did it, Luther did it, Calvin did it, the Massachusetts Puritans did it, Jerry Falwell does it. But so did Constantine and Henry and James I and Frederick and dozens of other political figures. There have been notable exceptions, among them that remarkable theologian of Rhode Island, Roger Williams. Listen for a moment to him in his own peculiar style:

> . . . the cry of the whole earth, made drunk with the blood of its inhabitants, slaughtering each other in their blinded zeal, for conscience, for Religion, against the Catholics, against the Lutherans, etc.[53]

> But oh what streams of the blood of the Saints have been and must be shed by the unmerciful most bloody doctrine. . . . Is not this to take Christ Jesus, and make him a temporal King by force? (John 6:15).[54]

> He that reads the Records of Truth and Time with an impartial eye, shall find this to be the lancet that hath pierced the veins of Kings and Kingdoms, of Saints and Sinners, and filled the streams and Rivers with their blood.[55]

> The unknowing zeal of Constantine and other Emperors, did more hurt to Christ Jesus his Crown and Kingdom, than the raging fury of the most bloody Neroes.[56]

> All these lived under the Government of Caesar, being nothing hurtful unto the Commonwealth, giving unto Caesar which was his. And for their Re-

ligion and Consciences towards God, he left them to themselves, as having no dominion over their souls and consciences.[57]

We would all admit that Jesus knew nothing of the cultural, economic, social, and political conditions prevailing at the time of any of these later propounders of church/state philosophy. The continuing practice of seeking Jesus' endorsement reminds me of a person trying to charge something to his account by seeking an authorization number from central theology. The ultimate in the use of the Bible to endorse public policy may be found in the nineteenth-century writings of southern churchmen supporting slavery.

> The Fuller theory (silence in the New Testament is tantamount to sanction) was especially useful in aligning Jesus on the side of human bondage, since in all four gospels he was entirely silent on the subject. The fact that Jesus in his parables made pedagogical use of the master-slave relation [as in Luke 17:7-10] without ever condemning slavery, signified to Bishop John England . . . that he did not regard it as sinful in principle.[58]

This same line of thought considered Jesus' endorsement of the centurion's faith noted in Luke 7:2-10 as a demonstration that Jesus saw no inconsistency between slaveholding and Christianity.

The bankruptcy of the type of biblical inquiry that I have described is not confined to fundamentalists or biblicists, as Niebuhr reminded us. Is there an alternative? I believe so. We need to inquire concerning the long tradition of ethical theory associated with the Bible. Have ethicists been correct in identifying concepts of love, compassion, freedom, justice, and mercy with the biblical writers? If so, then we might ask what form of government best accommodates these principles? This quest should constantly bear in mind the fact that questions about church and state have always been posed by men. . . . The long history of bloody persecutions and wars in the name of Jesus may well be, in part, the result of a totally male-oriented context. Even the effort to interpret kingdom is encumbered with a legacy of male images. We might get some glimmer of understanding of Jesus' sense of just government in his relationship with women, particularly the tragic scene surrounding the planned stoning of the "woman taken in adultery." Male theologians need to examine their presuppositions in more than a cursory fashion and to believe that only radical surgery on theological traditions will suffice.

My own personal conviction is that it may be time for the churches to re-examine the Social Gospel. In proposing this I am aware that I am referring to a type of Christian biblical study that has been ridiculed by much of the past fifty years of male scholarship. Norman Perrin insisted that: "As an interpretation of the teaching of Jesus the Social Gospel movement's understanding of the Kingdom of God is unacceptable for the simple reason that it is not an interpretation of the teaching of Jesus at all."[59] Perrin continues by describing what he terms the "fundamental and total weakness" in the work of the Social Gospel. It is the next step that he takes that has me fascinated. He quite forthrightly affirms:

> That the Social Gospel movement has made a tremendously significant contribution to American church life and work, and to American society at large, is not to be denied. In this respect its understanding of Kingdom of God is important. But concerning the interpretation of the Kingdom of God in the teaching of Jesus, the fact that its insights were not derived from an exegesis of the teaching of Jesus really precluded it from making any significant contribution to the discussion.[60]

The great moment for Perrin came in 1927 when a conference in Canterbury dismissed the older ideas of the kingdom as an ethical concept, as something that evolves, as concerned with political or social reform. In its place came the kingdom as apocalyptic in nature, which cannot be established by human exertions, "but only by the interference of God from heaven."[61] We are all to feel much better because proper exegesis has informed us that Jesus cared only for divine inbreaks, which, unless I am sadly mistaken, have not been all that frequent. Can Perrin say with as much assurance that the last fifty years of eschatological speculation have made a "significant contribution" to the church or American society?

I rather like Walter Rauschenbusch's assessment. He pointed out the discrepancy between an "aristocratic attitude to authority in theology" and the spread of democracy in "modern ethical life."[62] One British humorist suggested that democracy involved belief in "the plenary inspiration of the odd man."[63] In some respects the biblical scholar is no more prepared for that democratization than is the theologian.

Did Jesus offer a pattern of statecraft for future readers? On the basis of the evidence in the Gospels the answer must be negative. In spite of all the efforts by Christian interpreters to provide a clue to the meaning of the "Render to Caesar" utterance, it remains an enigmatic one-liner, probably best understood as a device to avoid a prolonged, debilitating debate. Indeed, most of those who go on to offer elaborate explanations admit that this was the likely intention of Jesus. The rather extensive array of references by Jesus to kings, armies, rulers, laws, and the like, serves to remind the reader of the political context in which Jesus operated. Jesus' use of such illustrations can no more be used to pinpoint a theory of statecraft than may a modern physicist's comment on the sunrise be employed to determine his view of the universe. As we have noted, most of the biblical writers, and in particular Paul, were pro-Roman. This, of course, poses the question of the sayings of Jesus. But I am satisfied that there is so little evidence of the imposition of a calculated state theory on Jesus by the writers, that a careful dissection of each word or phrase referring to the state would prove nonproductive. The Gospels offer no evidence of a philosophy of state either on the part of Jesus or those who remembered his words. If one wishes to enlist Jesus in support of any form of government, that person must appeal not to specific sayings, but to a spirit manifest in the Gospels.[64]

In our day the tendency to employ the Bible as a text for domestic and foreign policy is evident from the words of the president to his congressional supporters and to his theological advisors. Grandly parading Jesus as the authority, the state is encouraged in political directions upon which there is no consensus among citizens. In the name of Jesus America is encouraged to assume the messianic mantle. I think it was Gary Wills who remarked that he would rather face a herd of angry, charging elephants than one dedicated Calvinist armed with the word of God.

In the final analysis it is not what Jesus had to say about the state that is important. No serious student of political philosophy would likely turn to those scant words of the Galilean for insight on the subject. The problem arises when Jesus is identified as an absolute authority who must, perforce, be obeyed. All of the speculation as to whether Jesus was a Zealot, or if his disciples thought he was one, becomes important beyond the scholarly community only when it provides yet another alternative authoritarian model for state policy. It may have taken Jefferson only two or three nights to abstract "what is really his [Jesus'] from the rubbish in which it is buried," because it was "easily distinguished by its luster from the dross of the biographers, and as separable from that as the diamond from the dunghill."[65] But the modern practitioners of fundamentalist evangelism take far less time to enlist Jesus in holy crusades against fellow citizens. And unlike Jefferson, they turn their proclamations into dogma in the name of God. If we were to apply "Jefferson's Razor" to those dogmatic assertions concerning Jesus and the state, I believe we would experience Jefferson's results.

In my way of thinking, the best use of Jesus respecting the arena of statecraft is developed through the Social Gospel, with its rejection of a deterministic view of sin. Indeed, it is the obsession with the "sin of Eden" that generates a lack of optimism regarding social action. The church really likes its sin. "Every generation tries to put its doctrine on a high shelf where the children can not reach it."[66] Rauschenbusch insisted, I believe correctly, that his theology takes the human condition seriously. He noted, "Any religious tendency or school of theology must be tested by the question whether it does justice to the religious consciousness of sin."[67] However, he reminded his reader that

> It is possible to hold the orthodox doctrine on the devil and not recognize him when we meet him in a real estate office or at the stock exchange.[68]

> If the exponents of the old theology have taught humanity an adequate consciousness of sin, how is it that they themselves have been blind and dumb on the master iniquities of human history? During all the ages while they were the theological keepers of the conscience of Christendom, the peasants in the country and the working class in the cities were being sucked dry by the parasitic classes of society, and war was damning poor humanity.[69]

One of the by-products of the all-male theological establishment proclaiming on "sin" was an inherent sexism. When Niebuhr spoke of moral man and immoral society he created what Rosemary Ruether terms an "essential dichotomy between the home and public life."[70] She observes that religion and morality became feminized, "unrealistic" in the public sphere. There justice was defined as "a balancing of competitive egoism." While Niebuhr, I am certain, never intended to make such a division, in many cases misapplication has emptied civic life of human values while sentimentalizing the private home life as feminine.[71] Normally a function of fundamentalist theology, one sees the epitome of this in the pious preachments of Richard Nixon.

The Social Gospel appears to have had a greater capacity to avoid this pitfall, even as it was largely oblivious to sexist implications of the entire Garden of Eden scene. The charge leveled against the movement was to the effect that it failed to take sin seriously. The evidence suggests another reading. These theologians redefined sin in nondoctrinal terms, removing the determinism that is associated both with Marxism and traditional Christianity. The advocates of the Social Gospel, armed with a rational, reasoned optimism, never neglected the darker side of human nature. Their optimism was ever tempered with the knowledge that, as President Franklin Roosevelt observed: "The fight for social justice and economic democracy is a long, weary, uphill struggle." But, dedicated to the hope for human progress, they recognized that the biological explanation of "sin" offered only a bleak human future. Rauschenbusch and his contemporaries chose to think of sin in another dimension:

> There is the moral inducement to teach clearly on the social transmission and perpetuation of sin because the ethical and religious forces can really do something to check and prevent the transmission of sin along social channels, whereas the biological transmission of original sin, except for the possible influence of eugenics, seems beyond our influence.[72]

A human community invigorated with the challenge to change the social order in terms of the ethic of love and justice will not be nearly so attached to legalistic doctrines that place all hope beyond grasp. Thus we may strive to create a social order consistent with justice and mercy, rather than be enslaved to rigid loyalty to the "governing authorities."

In 1985 our secular republic is being accosted by the vigorous descendants of Calvinistic exclusivism, armed with selected words of Jesus. Denigrating the humanity of Jesus, these self-styled spokesmen for God insist upon belief in an inerrant Bible that they alone understand. In their hands, as they touch political power, the words of Jesus concerning the state, coupled with Paul, become a blueprint for international diplomacy and domestic dogma.

In the face of this obscene abuse of the literature some have abandoned the document. This is tragic, for it allows the dogmatists to lay claim to a profound thinker. If we are careful in our examination of the ethic of Jesus, it remains reasonable to respond to his humanism as a touchstone for statecraft. Jesus' comments, to the extent that there were any on the state, come from a person basically ignorant of political forces, even of his own time. But if we ask what kind of social system will allow justice to roll on like a river and righteousness like an ever-flowing stream, then we have a point of reference for making judgments focused on human freedom.

It is that passion for justice born of love that we see looming large in the biblical record, particularly in an Amos or a Jesus. We may differ on our definition of justice. We may differ over our interpretation of Jesus on the subject. We may differ over the degree to which Jesus is accurately recorded. But those differences will respond to a rational exploration once we have been freed from the myth of the divine Jesus and the inerrant Bible. We will then be free to allow Jesus to make sense, not doctrine.

Is there, then, a form of government *consistent* with the thrust of Jesus' approach to love and justice? Karl Barth was of the opinion that "There certainly is an affinity between the Christian community and the civil communities of free peoples."[73] Roger Williams stands as that lone seventeenth-century prophet who demonstrated how the Gospel message supported only the freedom of religion and conscience. No blueprint from Jesus, to be sure, but there is a wealth of evidence that the faith espoused in the Bible presumes a free conscience. If this be the case, then every effort to establish religion either by church or by state contradicts the Christian ethic, and any plan to prohibit the free exercise of conscience is an affront not only to the citizen, but to the God of Christianity as well. James Madison sensed this in his *Memorial and Remonstrance* as he claimed for true Christianity the high ground of absolute religious freedom in the civil society.

All of the evidence I have presented here from nearly two thousand years of history makes clear that any form of government that restricts the mind ends in outrage against the body, both of which deny the essence of the Jesus ethic. Any tendency toward theocracy is a denial of the freedom of the will. And, as Williams notes, any other will than a free one is an abomination to the God who Williams believed offers grace to the believer. Without such freedom belief is without meaning.

NOTES

1. Copyright by the author, 1985.
2. Shailer Mathews, *The Social Teachings of Jesus* (London: Macmillan, 1897), 107.
3. Eighteenth-century British philosopher who espoused a form of theistic idealism.
4. "Or what king, going to encounter another king in war, will not sit down first and take counsel whether he is able with ten thousand to meet him who comes against him with twenty thousand? And if not, while the other is yet a great way off, he sends an embassy and asks terms of peace." It should be noted that this is followed immediately by the words, "So therefore, whoever of you does not renounce all that he has cannot be my disciple."
5. Cecil J. Cadoux, *The Early Church and the World* (Edinburgh: T. & T. Clark, 1955), 36.
6. Kenneth A. Briggs, "Theologians Fault Reagan on Bible Arms Lesson," *New York Times,* February 6, 1985, D14.
7. *New York Times,* February 22, 1985, A14.
8. Thomas Jefferson to Charles Clay, January 29, 1815.
9. "Mr. Truman's Spiritual Blindness," editorial, *The Christian Century* 67, no. 26 (June 28, 1950): 782.
10. Oscar Cullmann, *The State in the New Testament* (New York, 1956), vii.

11. Reinhold Niebuhr, *Christianity and Power Politics* (New York, 1940), 8-9.

12. Whether or not the speech of Stephen in Acts 7 was composed by Luke, the story, culminating in Stephen's death (7:58), and consented to by Saul (8:1), makes plain that in the mind of the early church the persecution was at the hand of the religious establishment.

13. "Clement's First Letter," chapter 60 in *Early Christian Fathers,* vol. 1 of The Library of Christian Classics (Philadelphia: Westminster, 1953), 72.

14. Anthony Burgess, "Darkest Villainy! Divine Humor! An Empire Under Siege," in *TV Guide,* March 30-April 5, 1985, 5.

15. "The First Apology of Justin," in *The Library of Christian Classics,* vol. 1 (Philadelphia: Westminster, 1953), 252-53.

16. Decius instituted the first universal and systematic persecution in 250.

17. The Edicts of Diocletian began in 303 and included destruction of books, torture of clergy, and required "pagan" sacrifices.

18. Eusebius *Church History* 8.17.9.

19. Williston Walker, *A History of the Christian Church* (New York: Scribners, 1959), 102.

20. Augustine, *The City of God,* book 19, chap. 16.

21. Cf. Don Cupitt, *Crisis of Moral Authority* (London: Butterworth, 1972), 102.

22. See the papal bull *Unam Sanctam* by Pope Boniface VIII.

23. Gregory VII, "First Deposition and Excommunication of Henry IV" (1076).

24. "The Disposition of Gregory VI by Henry IV" (1076).

25. Bryce, *Holy Roman Empire,* p. 113 as quoted in Mathews, *Social Teachings of Jesus,* 114.

26. Deno John Geanakoplos, *Byzantine East & Latin West* (New York: Harpers, 1966).

27. Roland Bainton, *The Travail of Religious Liberty* (New York, 1951), 56-57.

28. Martin Luther, "Against the Robbing and Murdering Hordes of Peasants," in *The Christian in Society,* vol. 46 of *Luther's Works,* ed. Robert C. Schultz (Philadelphia, 1967), 49-50.

29. Ibid., 51.

30. Ibid., 53-54.

31. Luther, "An Open Letter on the Harsh Book," *Works* 46:65-66.

32. Ibid., 73-74.

33. Luther, "Whether Soldiers, Too, Can Be Saved," *Works* 46: 97.

34. Luther, "On The Jews and Their Lies," *Works* 47: 139.

35. Ibid., 219.

36. Ibid., 268-70.

37. Ibid., 277.

38. John Calvin, *The Institutes of the Christian Religion* (Philadelphia), Book 20, p. 774.

39. Ibid., 783.

40. Edwin Lewis, *The Biblical Faith and Christian Freedom* (Philadelphia: 1953), 154.

41. Luther, "Open Letter," *Works* 46:66.

42. Cullmann, *State in the New Testament,* 37.

43. Ernst Troeltsch, *The Social Teaching of the Christian Churches,* trans. by Olive Wyon (London: George Allen & Unwin Ltd., 1950), 59.

44. Mathews, *Social Teachings of Jesus,* 115.

45. Cullman, *State in the New Testament,* 48.

46. Ibid., 38-39.

47. Van Austin Harvey, *The Historian and the Believer* (New York: Macmillan, 1966), 5.

48. Ibid., 47.

49. Ibid., 119.

50. George H. Shriver, ed., *American Religious Heretics* (Nashville: Abingdon, 1966), 16.

51. Harvey Cox, "The Trial of Jesus," *New York Times,* April 5, 1985, A27.

52. Troeltsch, *Social Teaching of Christian Churches,* 58.

53. Roger Williams, "The Bloudy Tenent of Persecution," in *The Complete Writings of Roger Williams,* vol. 3 (New York: Russell and Russell, 1963), 309.

54. Ibid., 145.

55. Ibid., 182.

56. Ibid., 184.

57. Ibid., 213.

58. H. Shelton Smith, *In His Image But . . .* (Durham, 1972), 133.

59. Norman Perrin, *The Kingdom of God in the Teaching of Jesus* (Philadelphia: Westminster, 1963), 47.

60. Ibid., 48.

61. Ibid., 56. Perrin is quoting K. L. Schmidt.

62. Walter Rauschenbusch, *A Theology of the Social Gospel* (New York: Macmilllan, 1917), 5.

63. Charles E. Raven, *War and the Christian* (New York: Macmillan, 1938), 80.

64. Cf. Mathews, *Social Teachings of Jesus,* 129-30.

65. Thomas Jefferson to William Short, letter dated October 31, 1819.

66. Rauschenbusch, *Theology of Social Gospel,* 10.

67. Ibid., 32.

68. Ibid., 35.

69. Ibid., 34.

70. Rosemary R. Ruether, *New Woman, New Earth* (New York: Seabury, 1975), 199.

71. Ibid.

72. Rauschenbusch, *Theology of Social Gospel,* 68.

73. Karl Barth, *Against the Stream,* 44.

George E. Mendenhall*

The Palestinian Grass-roots Origins
of New Testament Christology

W. Lambert has observed that we know next to nothing about the submerged 80 percent of the population of ancient Assyria and Babylonia. To
that we can certainly add ancient Egypt and Canaan. One of my colleagues
in the classics department years ago announced to my surprise a graduate
seminar on Roman popular religion. When I asked him why he didn't
offer it as an undergraduate course his response was, "I don't know enough
about the subject."

These observations drawn from recent cultural phenomena certainly
justify the conclusion that we are dealing with a polarization that is a
constant in complex societies, but little attention has been paid to the
historical constancy, probably because scholars unconsciously identify with
the ancient population groups who produced the written materials that
constitute their *metier,* and have never had firsthand experience of village
life; or if they had, they have been eager to forget it as soon as possible.
Except for the thousands of pre-Islamic Arabic inscriptions, virtually all of
our excavated written sources stem from the elites of political, business,
and priestly specializations. We can easily see from the condescending
dismissal of the prophet Amos by the priest of Bethel that such elites had
little regard for the country-bumpkin upstarts who presumed to preach to
them. Indeed, such preaching was doubtless received with the same attitude
illustrated in one dictionary definition of preaching: "the giving of un-
wanted advice in an offensive manner."

The Bible seems so strange and foreign to most of the modern political
and educated elites in part simply because much of it, and the mainstream

---
*George E. Mendenhall is Professor of Ancient and Biblical Studies at the Uni-
versity of Michigan.

79

at that, stems precisely from those elements of the population of ancient Palestine that we know next to nothing about in other societies. In other words, the popular religion of the villages was the real *Sitz im Leben* of the prophetic Yahwism during the monarchy. For this reason all of the prophets except Isaiah came from small villages, some of which were heard from neither before nor after. At the same time, the evidence is now massive that the ruling elite in Jerusalem and Samaria was thoroughly assimilated to the common political paganism of the ancient Near East. The representation of "Yahweh and his Asherah" at Kuntillet Ajrud is merely the latest artifact that illustrates the process that had become complete during the reign of Solomon. It was necessarily so: no political regime of whatever nature can continue to exist in a complex society without creating a politically based hierarchy of power, beginning with the army and its chain of command, and culminating in the collectors of internal revenue, in New Testament times known as publicans.

These constants in the human historical process are not usually valued highly as means for understanding ancient texts and documents, but it takes only a minimum of historical imagination plus hints in the texts to realize that issues and factors in modern political and religious life differ from those of antiquity only in scale, specific cultural forms, and to some extent in value systems. It is one of the purposes of the present paper to suggest that many of the ancient biblical texts were responses to such real-life situations or predicaments, to the kinds of social conflicts and tensions that were then and are now escalating to an intolerable degree. The escape into purely academic pursuits, as well as into the ascetic life of monastics, is again a predictable reaction to the increasingly felt imminence of the apocalyptic doom. In view of the long-continued fashionableness of apocalyptic literature, it must be considered that this category of writing was actually a literary genre that had long been emancipated from the concrete historical situations in which it arose, and had become simply a usual means by which persons with pretensions to creative writing could obtain a temporary audience and some hope of literary immortality.

Over and against this fashionable literary genre were occasional persons who had the effrontery to suggest that the *oikumene,* as it was known, was actually to come to its appropriate end. The Old Testament prophets were almost certainly the first of this category, and it is well known how most of them were received, even though the traditions about the killing of the prophets seem to have been exaggerated in later tradition, to judge from the meager evidence we do have. Prophecy was never a high-prestige occupation, except when it produced results that coincided with the official policies of the political powers that were, and certainly it entailed a high insurance risk. What does not seem to have received much attention is the fact that the prophets' oracles were associated with a very profound conviction of the predictable long-range relationships between cause and effect; or in modern conceptual terms, a historical process that was not an automatic social-science predictability (and the successes of modern social science since the production of the Edsel have not been overwhelmingly superior to those of the ancient diviners). Instead, the predictions were based upon the conviction of the eventual operation of a value system represented by Yahweh/God, the transcendent creator of the physical and historical universe, that was beyond normal human control or predictability. It is perhaps one of the most delicious ironies of cultural history that at the present time the concept of "acts of God" has important social status only in courts of law, and it must be admitted that even there it is not much more than a legal fiction, albeit a necessary one, though the same concept exists in most legal systems under another verbal label.

It is in the context of village communities, over against political organizations, that the characteristic motifs of both Old Testament prophecy and the New Testament teachings of Jesus of Nazareth find their historical origin and operational significance. As mentioned above, it is here also that the original community of the Yahwist religious faith and social reality had its beginnings and its first realization in a social and cultural system that can only have been regarded as the "Kingdom of Yahweh/God." This ancient and very diverse society that called itself Yisra'el/Yeshurun (it did not always have the same name!) was a village and pastoral society in which *all* of the characteristic functions of a king/state—war, law, and economic well-being—were attributed to the deity who, like any other "national hero" king, created the political and social entity by a process that inevitably entailed warfare; but it was not warfare that created the society—quite the contrary. It was the existence of the covenant-bound community that made possible the warfare that, for a time at least, enabled the far-flung village populations of Palestine and northern Transjordan to become independent of the politically ambitious imperial epigones of the old Hittite and other empires of the late Bronze Age that had recently transferred their theater of operations into most of the eastern and parts of the western Mediterranean littoral regions. Historically, this unification of village populations is perhaps the least-believable aspect of biblical history to the modern academician (or even to the Marxist theoretician), but there is no plausible alternative at present available. I assume that in the academic world of the post-World War II era racial theories of historical processes need not be taken seriously.

Unfortunately, the submerged 80 percent of ancient populations is not often accessible to us, and therefore the modern scholar who knows nothing but modern political processes must inevitably view the biblical sources within his own limited range of experience. On the other hand, the traditional conservatism of village societies does make it possible to engage in some generalizations that are directly applicable to the New Testament sources, though I would be the first to agree that these observations are not provable in any legal or logical sense.

The traditional conservatism of village society is usually grotesquely misunderstood by urban elites. As we are experiencing today, the agricultural village has always been the economic bottom of the social hierarchy and, at the same time, the foundation of the entire social system, if only because the king's bureaucracy cannot function if the farmers cannot produce. Village conservatism is the product of necessity: change of almost any sort requires diversion of economic resources that are too scarce to waste on unpredictable ventures. Even apart from the political organization whose only contribution to the producer was the internal revenue agent, the well-being of the typical Syro-Palestinian farmer or shepherd was completely beyond his control—but it was also beyond the control of whatever gang of robbers or politicians happened for the time to have a superior ability to commit murder with impunity.

In village society political processes and political controls are irrelevant and even evil. The village community typically has as little as possible to do with central government, though, as Ramsey MacMullen has observed with regard to villages of the Roman Empire, they can protect themselves against little but stray dogs.[1] As in traditional China, and in many other parts of the world, the appeal to government legal processes for the settlement of disputes is regarded as shameful, just as it was in the early Christian churches, according to Saint Paul.

If the village is the locus of conservatism, it follows also that it is here that are to be found very archaic traditions, practices, and even language. It is this constant of ancient societies, and to a lesser degree today, that needs to be explored and taken much more seriously than it has been in the recent past. As some anthropologist has correctly observed, it is not cultural continuity that needs to be explained, it is cultural change and innovation.

"Can anything good come out of Nazareth?" is the typical attitude of urban sophisticates concerning villages that no one ever heard of before. It is well known that the rabbis had nothing but hostility and contempt for the *'am ha-'aretz*, who were "ignoramuses" who did not know and refused to study the rabbis' Torah. It needs to be considered as an important historical probability that the *'am ha-'aretz* returned the compliment: another characteristic of village life, whether in Palestine or Montana, is the fact that literacy is irrelevant to the normal needs of village farmers and shepherds. But that by no means implies an intellectual vacuum in the villagers' noggins: quite the contrary. Characteristically the village ethos is intimately integrated into their entire environment, social and material; for Palestinian villages of the early Roman Empire period, that ethos was inseparable from the contents of the Hebrew Bible that no doubt many knew from memory, either in whole or in part, in Hebrew or informal Aramaic or even Greek translation. To judge from more accessible processes of historical linguistics known in other times and places, it is entirely predictable that a considerable segment of village population was at least bilingual. This is demonstrated, for example, in the third-century villages of southern Syria, where village carpenters (builders) left behind inscriptions in Greek.[2]

What I am suggesting, then, in this depiction of the normally inaccessible, i.e., the 80 percent of the unknown populations of antiquity, is the fact that the written materials preserved from the literary elites of antiquity are only accidentally relevant to the understanding of the early Christian origins and early Christian literary productions such as the Gospels. They sprang from the same diversity of cultural and also biblical tradition. The very fact that there was no canonical form, that the teachings of Jesus were not preserved in their original language, that the traditions varied in minor details—all are exactly what should be expected from the social location and processes for which I am arguing. The community of the early church in Palestine had a body of common knowledge both of events and of the contents of Jesus' teaching, but no need or motivation for translating that body of common knowledge into a literary form. The idea that it was the later church that created the common knowledge is the sort of thing that would be plausible only in theological circles, and certainly attributes to the early church a creativity that is contrary to what evidence we have in such works as the Didache, where the difference between the true believers and the hypocrites is the selection of the days on which to fast.

To come to the Christology, then, of the Palestinian grass-roots church: many times through the past couple of decades I have painfully worked through some problem of the theology of the Hebrew Bible only to find that it is already in the New Testament. The concept of the "humble king" is already deeply ingrained into the prophetic stratum of the Hebrew Bible, though dismissed with contempt by Rehoboam and his ambitious young political advisers. It is so emphasized in the deuteronomic depiction of the king that it is difficult to figure out from that source what the king is supposed to do—another typical village attitude toward government bureaucrats. But it is with 2 Isaiah that the process reaches its culmination, and it is no accident that the Christology of early New Testament times is astonishingly similar to the content of this work.

Isaiah 40-66 and especially the "Servant Songs" of chapters 40-56 are derived to a large extent from the language or, perhaps better, the ideology of kingship: the light to the nations, the nations bringing tribute, the servant as the interface between God and the existing community, even the servant as the prime target of pagan powers who suffers as a consequence of the mistakes and sins of the community as a whole. Even the constant designation of the figure as *bāḥir*, "chosen," is most specifically a kingship term, and its parallel "servant" indicates both the role of the king as servant of Yahweh (as well as "son"!) and his role as servant to the people that is implied strongly in the narrative of Rehoboam's disastrous policy at Shechem. The entire corpus presupposes the prophetic attitude toward kingship that derives from the experience and needs of village societies from time immemorial. That includes a recognition of the need for governance and leadership in a complex society, but also a bitter hostility to the unscrupulous manipulation and ruthless exercise of power and authority reckless of the legitimate expectations of the powerless, and the equally legitimate obligations of the power-holders to standards of behavior that transcend their temporary self-interest. Rather than being "visionary" as Hanson would have it,[3] it is ultimately a necessity for the well-being of any complex society that has unfortunately not been successfully realized for long periods of time.

But most important is the fact that the Messiah, the anointed *political* power, was Cyrus, king of Persia, who is not designated as "chosen," though he is "called by name" and his hand is "grasped" by Yahweh, in accordance with the age-old pagan[4] terminology used to designate the "religious" legitimation of imperial power. The distinction between political power of war and law and the religious tradition was not only complete and systematic, it was a fact of daily life for half a millennium before Jesus of Nazareth. The refusal to admit that religion and politics are two different areas of experience and reality is based merely upon the age-old pagan conviction that there is no important factor in human life other than the socially organized operation of coercive force: army, police, and the atom bomb. Nothing could be further from the truth, especially in a complex society.

The problem of New Testament Christology is absolutely inseparable from the centuries-long dilemma of the concern for the value system represented by Yahweh, and the inevitability, if not the necessity, of socially organized force for the exercise of war, law, and economic controls. It is much too easy to ignore the fact that regardless of the particular political structure, all of these functions are ultimately dependent upon the total of customary patterns of behavior and the attendant ideologies (value systems) of the populace. Even more important for religious faith is the fact that what is central to the biblical tradition—love, justice, and mercy—is almost totally irrelevant to the political process: "Justice is a topic for meditation in a monastery" is the quip proceeding from law schools. The same is true of "peace."

Behind the Christology of the New Testament lay not only the centuries-long Yahwist and prophetic vision, but also a couple of centuries characterized by a very complex power struggle, first, between internal and external forces (Ptolemies, Seleucids, Romans), and second, between internal factions themselves, that several times resulted in civil war. The powerful tendency on the part of the religious elite to assume that their particularisms would usher in the millennium if only the political powers would enforce *their* "law" presupposes precisely that ancient Near Eastern pagan ideology that God is merely the symbol of socially organized force. The ideology breaks down with the observation that enforced "law" has little or nothing to do with justice. As a matter of fact even the Wisdom literature of the Old Testament had already observed the fact that "justice" is an "act of God": "Many seek the favor of a ruler, but from Yahweh a person obtains justice" (Prov. 29:26).

A considerable part of the exceedingly complex issue of early Christianity and especially its Christology is the confusion concerning the nature and function of law. On the one hand, Torah, identified as "law" in English language, is a corpus of literature that includes a considerable number of normative imperatives. On the other hand, those imperatives remain mere literary forms until something drives their translation from archaic language to behavioral reality. This contrast corresponds exactly to the often-drawn distinction in modern jurisprudence between the "substantive law" and the "adjective law." The confusion is compounded by the fact that there is a very considerable coincidence between the content of the "substantive law" and the content of religious obligation in the biblical tradition—one need only note the content of the Ten Commandments. It is thus easy to think that if murder, theft, perjury, and adultery are action-able in law courts, that therefore all of the religious definitions of obligation can and ought to be similarly enforced by socially organized means. This naive simplism is rejected in the teachings of Jesus, following the earlier observations of the Old Testament prophets. An enormous amount of substantive law has to do with the social concern for maintaining reciprocity in economic dealings—the law of contracts, for example. But the Sermon on the Mount already quite rightly dismisses reciprocity as a secular matter that has nothing to do with religious life: "They have received their reward." Thus early Christianity not only secularized en-forced law, it at the same time refused to identify any political system with the rule of God. Instead of formally defined obligations enforced by socially organized force, the religious ethic centered upon the root problem of all legal systems: the character of persons in society. The "adjective law" had nothing to do with police, armies, and weapons, but with those aspects of personality that produce behavior in community "against which there is no law": "love, joy, peace, patience, goodness, gentleness, meekness, kind-ness." These things cannot be produced by the combination of law courts and language, but only through personality. This is why Christ is the "end" of the Torah.

NOTES

1. Ramsey MacMullen, *Roman Social Relations* (New Haven, 1974), 27: The village had "no real power to protect itself at all, save against another village or a passing traveler. Any force, economic or administrative, easily penetrated its defenses, abused it, and drained off its resources."

2. Henry I. MacAdam, "Epigraphy and Village Life in Southern Syria during the Roman and Early Byzantine Periods," *Berytus Archaeological Studies* 31 (1983):103-15. Under "Professions and Occupations" he notes that "The builder . . . partly out of pride and partly as free advertising, often notes his native village" (p. 112).

3. Hanson, *The Dawn of Apocalyptic* (Philadelphia, 1975).

4. Some clarification of the use of the term "pagan" is necessary in view of the fact that I have frequently been attacked in print for the use of this term. Granted, it is ironically inappropriate etymologically since the term originally designated peasantry, exactly the opposite to the biblical contrast that underlies the usage of *goy* in the Old Testament and or *'ethnos* in the New Testament. That these terms designated a value contrast as well as a social one is beyond question. However, it is necessary to emphasize that the terms had nothing to do with nineteenth-century racial theories. They had every-thing to do with the bitter hostility to foreign political entities that were characterized precisely by the obsession with power and the ensuing affluence that stemmed from "near-ness" to the political holders of power. Cf. Matt. 20:25.

II

Historical Problems

John M. Allegro*

Jesus and Qumran: The Dead Sea Scrolls

INTRODUCTION

The very category under which this paper is included, "Historical Problems," assumes the self-evidential thesis that there are elements in the
Gospel narratives that do not ring true to social and religious conditions
as we otherwise know them to have existed in Palestine at the turn of the
era. Much of what we have heard and shall hear during the course of this
symposium supports this point of view. But any constructive analysis of
the New Testament records cannot rest content with a simple arithmetical
equation: "Fact" = "the possible" minus "the less likely and downright
impossible." That is, if we go on peeling away the skins of improbability
from the onion we shall end eventually with a small kernel of historical
fact on which to build some new theory about the historical Jesus: who he
was, who his parents were, where he was really born and lived, how he
spent his formative years, whether he was a well-meaning if somewhat
ineffective political subversive, or just a religious reformer who annoyed
the Roman and Jewish authorities and paid the price of nonconformity. It
has all been done before, and there never seems to be a year that passes
without the publication of some fresh, fanciful reconstruction of Jesus' life
and death. That kind of speculative exercise may be commercially profitable, but is of no real consequence. For the impact made by Christianity
and the church in two thousand years of Western culture owes little to the
comparatively trivial circumstances of its supposed founder's birth, life,
and death, but much to the strangely compulsive nature of a faith that can
turn sinners into saints, and charming old men into "born-again" politicians not entirely averse to blasting the rest of the world into a philosophic

---

*John Allegro taught at the University of Manchester and was the first British
representative on the international scroll-editing team.

conformity in the name of the Lord. The importance of this symposium seems to me that we are able to look at the Christian story in this larger perspective, and to discuss the wider issues that take us beyond the minutiae of textual and historical criticism.

THE CONTRIBUTION OF THE DEAD SEA SCROLLS

The discovery of Essene texts from the Qumran caves presents us with a rather similar dual perspective. Donning our short-focus spectacles, we can for the first time clarify the Semitic background of some technical religious phraseology in the Greek testament; appreciate hitherto unrecognized specific doctrinal allusions; trace the extracanonical sources of some elements of Christian teaching; and match the manner and substance of certain kinds of biblical interpretation. In the sectarian rules of conduct we can even see clear patterns for the organizational structure and discipline of the early Christian communities, like the institution of the presbytery and bishopric, disciplinary procedures, standards of communal behavior, methods of joint funding, attitudes toward women and sex, the theological basis for the practice of spiritual healing, and so on. But to appreciate the main importance of the scrolls for an understanding of Christian origins we need to raise our eyes to a much wider perspective. As never before it is becoming possible to understand how an exclusive, nationalistic movement like postexilic Judaism could combine with an alien, dualistic philosophy to produce a kind of Jewish gnosticism; and then in due course, under the heat and pressures of certain sociopolitical events over the turn of the era, be transformed into the even more unlikely Hellenistic hybrid of a messianic mystery cult, a scandal to any decent-minded Jew, and sheer nonsense to an intelligent Greek.

JESUS AND QUMRAN

On such a long view, can the scrolls help us to understand the person of Jesus of Nazareth? Well, not much, I think. In those early, heady days after the public became aware that caves in the Judean wilderness had turned up really ancient Jewish documents dating from around the supposed time of Christ, popular speculation centered on the person of the man Jesus and his relationship to the Essenes. Had he perhaps been a member of the Qumran community at some time? Had those "forty days" in the wilderness been spent in the monastery by the Dead Sea? Were the parallels between some aspects of his teaching and Essene thought due to such direct contact, or came they by way of that mysterious prophet of the wilderness, John the Baptist?

Alas, the scrolls make no mention of the Nazarene Teacher by name. Indeed, the gospel tradition of a wine-bibbing associate of whores, pimps, and quislings, a friend of Roman officers, and an advocate of paying taxes to the enemy has no parallel at all in what little we can glean from the scrolls about the manner of life of Jesus' Essene counterpart, the so-called Teacher of Righteousness. But then, the Qumran writings have no literary parallel to the synoptic Gospels, nor do the Essenes seem to have shown any interest in recording events in such narrative form. For them the experience of their forefathers chronicled in the Bible was all the history they needed; their own situation was but a repetition of what had gone before. In taking up their station on the outskirts of the Promised Land, they believed they were reenacting the events of Joshua more than a millennium earlier, when he led the Chosen People across the Jordan to prepare them for their entry into the land God had promised them. The Essene sojourn in their so-called House of Exile was for these latter-day Covenanters merely the turn of the circle, the foreordained rehearsal for the establishment of the New Israel and the institution of God's kingdom on earth.

In other words, where there are parallels in the scrolls to the Christian story they are, for the most part, more likely to be in the nature of a common mythology; and to seek in the documents detailed correspondences of time, place, and persons is to misunderstand the nature of the Qumran texts and their authors' attitudes to history. The events that had affected them in their past were significant only so far as they could be related to biblical prophecy: they then served as "signs of the times," to be noted sometimes—though rarely recorded—and then interpreted by their seers to determine their place in the eschatological time scale, factors in the cosmological almanac by which men of understanding could recognize the proximity of the End-time and the appearance among them of the Messiah, or Christ, "him who is to come." The question we now have to ask is whether the New Testament traditions, despite their easily read narrative style, are not to be understood similarly: whether our onion peeling in search of the kernel of the historical Jesus is not itself misconceived. I believe it to be so. Even if there was a sectarian Jewish teacher living in Palestine during the first part of the first century called Joshua, or Jesus, he had nothing at all to do with the crucified *Christos* of Paul's theology, and thus had no part to play in the formation of that distinctive amalgam of faiths that eventually swept the world. I believe that the innocent collection of tales and sayings that was apparently allowed to pass freely among the beleaguered cells of believers, in hourly danger of discovery and execution, was but a cover story.

From that highly improbable account of a gentle rabbi, friend of little children, Roman tax collectors, and ladies with gynecological problems, could be distilled by skilled interpreters, well versed in the art of rabbinic exegesis as well as the *abracadabra* of gnostic mysticism, secret passwords and sayings, the formulae for medicaments and hallucinatory drugs, the therapeia in practice and prescription that had earned them their reputation and name of *Asayya*, Essenes, "physicians." In the stories and adventures of the Master and his followers may also be found more day-to-day reminders of communal regulative disciplines, and of the titles, qualifications, selection, and duties of their administrators, the bursars, presbyters, and bishops. As I have tried to show in my recent book, *The Dead Sea Scrolls and the Christian Myth*, the stories of Peter in particular are nothing but a dramatized mnemonic of the credentials and responsibilities of the Essene *Mebagger*, "guardian." Peter's activities can be paralleled at practically every point by the regulative manuals among the scrolls. The guardian of the scrolls community was early on recognized by scholars as the exact counterpart in name and function of the church's *episkopos*, "bishop." The small parchment scrap from the Fourth Cave whose *editio princeps* I publish in an appendix to that book seems to me to offer the first real evidence we have yet seen for the technical meaning of the title *Cephas*, "physiognomist, scrutineer," by which alone Paul refers to the first "pillar" of the Jerusalem Church. And that in turn helps us understand the underlying significance of the story in Matthew 16 of Peter's power of spiritual discernment by which he could recognize the Master's messianic status and special relationship to God. That story alone should have given us pause before dismissing verbal puns and "nicknames" in the gospel narratives as examples of the trivial banter to be expected among friends, particularly when, as in the case of the brothers Boanerges, the name is accompanied by a patently false "translation." We have been too ready to shrug off such solecisms as mere faults in transmission by linguistically incompetent scribes. And once we begin to treat those "onion skins" more seriously we shall begin to recognize beneath their surface other meaningful concepts, and to find their source in key biblical texts whose manner of interpretation is now explicable in terms of the Essene *pesharim*, or commentaries, from the Qumran library.

In several recent books, I have tried to demonstrate something of the multilayered structure of the gospel narratives and teachings. Their "decipherment" is difficult and was intended to be so, just as the Essene secrets were not for the eyes of the uninitiated: even their written works were wrapped up and hidden in caves or, in the final emergency, simply wrenched apart and thrown into a secret underground chamber. Their most vital mysteries were never committed to writing, as Josephus makes clear (*War* 2.141), but passed only by word of mouth under awful oaths of silence, and we have found fragmentary documents among their scrolls that were encoded in ciphers of their own devising.

Similarly, the inner councils of the church were aware of secret writings which were not to be promulgated, even among the faithful. As the second-century Church Father Clement of Alexandria said in a letter recently recognized and published by Prof. Morton Smith (*The Secret Gospel*, 1974), "not everything that is true needs necessarily to be divulged to all men." That was in connection with part of the Marcan Gospel whose circulation the church's elders had deemed wisest to restrict to "those who had been initiated into the great mysteries." It had to do with the story in the Second Gospel of the rich young man who approached Jesus and who we now learn was initiated by the Master into "the mystery of the Kingdom of God" during the course of a secret nocturnal ceremony. Once we can bring ourselves to admit that early Christianity, like Essenism, was an esoteric faith offering access to the divine mysteries, and never the open, evangelistic gospel of the church's defensive propaganda, we can begin more realistically to probe the depths of the New Testament writings, and to set the faith in its proper historical and religious perspective. As far as the gospel narratives of Jesus are concerned, we may free ourselves forever from the need to lay bare a reality on which to base a more historically convincing portrait of a first-century teacher who, in three short years, was supposed to have founded a new religion, or so transformed an existing messianic faith that it could become almost immediately acceptable to a gentile world. We are dealing with myth, not history.

JESUS, THE LAMB, THE WORD OF GOD

The question we have now to ask is what was the nature and purpose of that myth? And for the answer we must turn our attention away from the more immediately comprehensible and popular accounts of the synoptics, to the abstruse interpretations offered by the Fourth Gospel and the related

Johannine works. And it is significant that it is just here that we come closest to Qumran, as was very early on recognized by scholars. The Dead Sea Scrolls have completely upset the accepted view of the place of the Johannine witness in Christian tradition. Far from its being thought the least representative of early Christian thought and the most alien to the Palestinian homeland, we have had to recognize that it is among the earliest, and firmly rooted in native soil.

For the writer of the Fourth Gospel, Jesus was the Logos, the Word (1:1). And when he has John the Baptist proclaim, "Behold, the Lamb of God" (1:29), he symbolizes, in what is probably the most significant verbal pun in the New Testament, the whole essence of the transformation of the Jewish substitute ritual of the Passover sacrifice and the concept of the Messiah, into the self-immolation of the Savior-god of the Hellenistic mystery cults and Pauline Christianity. And *that* was the faith that won the allegiance of the Western world. The pun itself was no more than the interdialectal homonym of the Hebrew *imerah*, "word," with the Aramaic *immera*, "lamb." Its graphic representation assumes the nature of the bizarre when the Apocalyptist has the Lamb marrying into the church (19:7-9), leading the white-robed martyrs as a shepherd to the Throne of Grace (7:13-17), having seven horns and seven eyes (5:6), able to break open documentary seals (6:1) and to terrify the world's rulers with its wrath (7:16), and so on. But the myth's imagery is no more important than the stories of Jesus' conjuring tricks with water and wine, or his demonstrations of water walking and levitation. What is vital to our understanding of the Christian revelation was that the Jewish Passover victim was identified in this extraordinary mixture of traditional Judaism and Hellenistic mysticism with the Logos, Divine Wisdom, the Essene and Christian "Knowledge of God," whose mysteries initiates were invited to share in the secret rituals of the gnostic cults.

THE CRUCIFIXION

The second element in the Jesus myth, his crucifixion, was equally significant. Now whether there ever was a Jewish messianic pretender named Joshua or Jesus who was crucified at the instigation of his fellow countrymen in the procuratorship of Pontius Pilate, we shall probably never know. It hardly matters. For the "Christ crucified" of Pauline theology has little to do with the fate of some poor wretch in or about A.D. 33. The highly developed theology expounded by Paul on the theme of the crucified Savior was surely the fruit of much longer pious speculation than the intervening decade or two allowed by traditional chronology, and the product of a continuing school of thought rather than the inspired deliberation of one man. If we seek a more suitable point of historical reference, it might be a century or so earlier, when the hated Jewish priest-king Alexander Jannaeus took a terrible revenge against the Jews who had rebelled against him and had some hundreds of them crucified in Jerusalem. An Essene commentary on Nahum refers specifically to that revolt and its terrible outcome, and this seemed to me particularly significant when I first published the manuscript some thirty years ago. I suggested then that such an unusual historical reference in Essene literature implied some very special eschatological interest in the event, and that this could best be explained if the community's own beloved Teacher of Righteousness had been caught up in that rebellion and had shared the fate of the other victims of the so-called Lion of Wrath. Be that as it may; it is important to note that the later Essene commentator shows himself fully aware of the theological significance of that particular form of execution when he speaks of the victim as "the one hanged alive upon a tree," a clear reference to the deuteronomic curse that the hanged man shall be "accursed of God" (21:22-23), and one that is taken up in the New Testament (Gal. 3:19).

When we examine the history of the practice in the Old Testament its theological importance becomes clear. For "hanging before the Lord" was not just another barbaric form of execution: it was regarded as a propitiatory offering to the deity to allay the divine displeasure that had manifested itself in some inexplicable natural calamity or other affliction. Its essential feature was that it exposed the body of the victim to the elements and clearly goes back to a very old fertility concept of substitutionary sacrifice to the creator god. So, to bring an end to a punitive famine, the Gibeonites requested that the seven sons of King Saul be given them "so that we may hang them before the Lord" and they were duly put to death "in the first day of the harvest, at the beginning of the barley harvest" (2 Sam. 21:6, 9). The Israelites on their journey to the Promised Land had flirted with local cults encountered on their way and suffered plagues as a result. In an expiative ritual Moses had the tribal chiefs, as representatives of the nation, executed by exposure to the sun's heat, "that the fierce anger of the Lord might turn away from Israel" (Num. 25:4). The Hebrew word used in these passages means properly "dislocate, be torn away" and is variously translated in the ancient versions as "impale," "expose [in the sun]," "make an example of," "put to shame," or "crucify."

The execution of the teacher might have been viewed by his followers at first as a mere tragic accident, a temporary setback to the progress of the movement, but later reflection must have brought home to their interpreters its theological significance, particularly when, as would appear from their use of common titles, the idea suggested itself to them that the historic Teacher of Righteousness, the Priest, the Law Interpreter, would reappear at the End-time as the Messiah, that second Joshua/Jesus who was to lead his people to the New Jerusalem. It was but a step then for their Christian successors to identify that messianic figure who had once been offered as a propitiatory sacrifice to God by the crucifixion ritual, with the self-immolated Savior-god of gnostic theology who afforded the means by which the initiate could mystically apprehend the Knowledge of God, or Logos, or, as Paul puts it, "be crucified with Christ" and thereafter have the Christ "live within him" (Gal. 2:20).

If, then, we project the Essenism of Qumran forward in time and place from the Dead Sea Scrolls to the New Testament, we can see a clear line of theological speculation that transformed an exclusive Jewish sectarianism into a Hellenistic mystery religion that could attract the allegiance of all men, Jew or gentile, bond or free. But the kind of Christianity we arrive at is not that of a faith committed to the historicity of Jesus and the Gospel tradition and the imposition of a single canon and a tyrannical creed, but that gnostic "heresy" whose essential individualism was so abhorred by the so-called Great Church and that became the target of a persecution no less ruthless than that of the movement's first political and religious enemies. And to judge from the church's subsequent history as well as the illegitimacy of its claims to primacy, one cannot help feeling that the wrong side won.

David Noel Freedman*

Early Christianity and the Scrolls
An Inquiry

The thesis of this paper is that the differences between Essenes and Christians are much more numerous and significant than their similarities, that what they held in common was part of the biblical tradition and of the faith and practice of Judaism generally. Their differences reflect the true nature of the two movements, in light of accumulated evidence that they were diametrically opposed to each other in most critical matters. To put it a little differently, the Essenes were ultraorthodox conservatives while the Christians were radical revolutionaries and innovators, at least those whose Christianity survived and is recorded and reflected in the New Testament.

Before we proceed, a digressive word may be in order. There was no direct contact of which we have knowledge between the two groups. This was partly a matter of time and partly of space. Their period of overlap was relatively short, i.e., 30-70. The Essenes were a spent force when Christianity was beginning to be a force in Judaism and the world. Additionally, Christians were widely spread but were apparently centered in Galilee, while the Essenes were in Qumran. But there is a larger point: the Essenes were secretive and reclusive. They kept away from outsiders, including Christians. The chances of contact between the two were limited from the start: a Christian Essene was a contradiction in terms.

This leads to the following points. One, Essenes were essentially a closed and secret society while Christianity was essentially an open one. To illustrate the point we mention the subect of personal names. To this date we cannot be sure from the Dead Sea Scrolls of the actual name of a single Essene, although there are some plausible guesses and a few names

---

*David Noel Freedman is Professor of Biblical Studies at the University of Michigan and Editor of the Anchor Bible.

from other sources such as Josephus. Contrast this with Christianity, with hundreds if not thousands of personal names, many of which are only that. We do not know the name of the founder of the Essene movement, or of his principal disciples. We do not even know the names of their enemies. There are many different possible reasons for this passion for anonymity. The contrast with Christianity is extraordinary. There may be an apocalyptic and cryptic element in it, especially where identifying the enemy as in Daniel and Revelations. But this is a controlling factor among Essenes, in stark contrast with Christians. The Christians were real people with real pedigrees. The Essenes, no doubt, were real people too, but they were shadowy and cloaked in secrecy.

That consideration leads to point two: curiously enough it is a matter of language. The New Testament is written in Greek. This is not amazing in itself, but it is significant, especially since the language of the Bible at that time was Hebrew with a small admixture of Aramaic. It is not hard to explain the use of Greek in the New Testament, but contrast that circumstance with the Essenes and their writings. They preserved and copied the Hebrew Bible, whereas the Bible of the church from almost the beginning was a Greek Bible and remained so, a partial explanation of the New Testament that imitates and is influenced by the Septuagint. It is fair to say that the Essenes avoided Greek; there are some scraps and fragments but there is no new literature in Greek. It is part of their isolation and secrecy and their tendency to look inward (i.e., in on themselves). Not only did they keep the Hebrew Scriptures, but they imitated biblical Hebrew in their own writings. They knew Mishnaic Hebrew and, doubtless, Aramaic and Greek but the overwhelming emphasis is on Hebrew, biblical Hebrew at that. The contrast is dramatic and stark. One is pushing the world away and making a closed world of its own, while the other is pushing out into the world, making the world its own. One can hardly imagine Essenes using Greek for any purpose while certainly, the church of the New Testament would rarely use anything else. Even though the movement led by Jesus was Semitic speaking at first, and Jesus himself doubtless used Aramaic and probably some Hebrew, practically nothing of that stratum of Christianity has survived. Just a word or phrase here and there, painstakingly translated and not always correctly explained.

Point three is essentially the same, but adds a critical element to the mix: the gentiles. Whatever the intention or expectations of Jesus and his intimate followers, there is no question that by the end of the first generation (ca. 70) there was a very large influx of gentiles into the church, and by the end of the second generation, ca. 100, the church was predominantly if not overwhelmingly gentile. The contrast with the Essenes could not be greater. It is so difficult to imagine the categories of Essene and gentile overlapping or conjoining at any point as to make the terms ultimately, if not a priori and from the beginning, mutually exclusive. To begin with the Essenes were traditional Jews, and they were highly exclusive about their membership. While there were some superficial similarities in terms of membership in the group, the real correspondences come later with elitist and superexclusive monastic and gnostic groups. In general that is true of the correlation and correspondences when dispute develops later, which is typical of groups interested in preserving their identity and assuring their continuity.

The radical nature of the Christian movement is brought into focus by comparison with the Essenes. After 150-200 years the Essene community remained closed, totally ingrown and totally Jewish. By contrast Christianity moved out into the world and in the same length of time became totally gentile, totally Greek (and other languages), and totally other. There must have been extraordinary differences built in from the earliest days.

Consider the approach to and treatment of Torah or Law. In a recent paper E. Landers of Oxford argued that Paul's attitude toward the Jewish Law was essentially positive and perhaps upbeat, but there were three areas in which Paul parted company with the legalists of either Christianity or Judaism.

Circumcision. Paul's passionate statements that go beyond the bounds of propriety can be explained on a variety of grounds, including the problem of recruiting gentiles in the face of Roman legal restrictions. But there can be little doubt that Paul believed firmly and passionately in his assertion that circumcision in itself had no religious value any more than did uncircumcision. Furthermore, he argues the case using Abraham as the model. Abraham was saved by faith before he was circumcised, hence circumcision is of no value with regard to salvation; it is a mere work the church has been only too happy to embrace. The assertion and the argument, which is itself a model of casuistry, are correct in particulars and totally irrelevant to the point at issue, namely, compliance with the law of God as recorded in Torah. No wonder Paul exasperated people everywhere. It is bad enough to annul a law at the heart of the faith, that has been in place and observed for a thousand years, but how much worse to claim the authority of the same Scripture for abrogating or abolishing such a law. Anyone who can read can tell that the law of circumcision is a simple, divine command imposed on Abraham and his male offspring through all their generations. The applicability to Jews certainly is hardly in question, although Paul's statement about Christians would seem to contradict the plain statement of Genesis. The only point I wish to make is that it would be as inconceivable to the Essenes to suspend or abrogate such a requirement as it would to most other Jews. And if it were conceivable for a gentile to become an Essene, then the requirements for membership would surely have included circumcision. The contrast could hardly be greater.

Sabbath observance. Here again Paul seems to have little patience with a basic law of Torah. To him one day is like another, and people may observe any day they wish or none. While he may be thinking of gentiles, it is clear that for Jews too the same reasoning must apply. Obligation became *adiophora,* hence dispensable.

It is difficult to imagine any Jewish group, least of all the Essenes, abandoning a rule imposed in the Decalogue, the fundamental charter of the Bible and Judaism. Nevertheless, in spite of this, judging by what must have been serious arguments in the early church, especially when there were Jews around, the direction Christianity took admits of no confusion on this point. Only much later did Christians create their own Sabbath (on a different day) or devise a rite of initiation to match circumcision.

Food laws. Here again we can see the extraordinary difference between Christianity and Essenism. It was almost impossible for Essenes to eat with anyone other than Essenes because of restrictive rules, which excluded table fellowship with most Jews, let alone gentiles. Again, there were struggles on this matter in early Christianity, but Pauline doctrine triumphed and the food laws were successfully abolished; observing them became a matter of prudence and consideration, not of mandate and law.

On all these counts the Essenes were more severe and strict than most Jews. On the same points the church moved in the opposite direction.

It was also argued that in the main points and the major issues, Paul agreed with Jesus and with Jewish tradition: the great commandments to love God and one's neighbor, and on essential ethical behavior. All too true, but agreement here hardly means anything since everyone paid lip service to these idealistic utterances. What does that show? There was, however, a radical difference with regard to the understanding of the command to love one's neighbor.

The function of this command was to identify the people whom one should love and at the same time separate out those whom one need not, indeed should not love. The Essenes incorporated this commandment in their elaborate and precise eschatological system. Just as it was mandatory to love one's brothers, those in the community, it was equally mandatory to abhor all those outside the home group. This is a universal concept of human beings, but Jesus generally opposed such restriction on love, and Paul agrees that this is the church teaching, which would abolish any restriction on love of one's neighbor. Love creates and defines neighbor, not the other way around. Difficulty with this point arose very early, and it is not surprising to find people like Paul and John, who are most eloquent on the subject of love, nevertheless denouncing their enemies, precisely the ones they are required to love, with language that the Essenes especially would have appreciated. What has survived in Christianity, with few exceptions, is the duplicity and hypocrisy of proclaiming love of enemy and practicing the same old hostility.

We will pass over the numerous and obvious theological differences concerning which the Essenes are much closer to traditional Judaism than the Christians, with doctrines concerning the nature of the Christ and the personality of the Holy Spirit leading ultimately to the doctrine of the Trinity. While the formulas are not explicit, the seed and roots were already present and visible in New Testament Christianity but largely absent from Essenism. We can look at related areas for overlap and contrast.

The Essenes subscribed to fairly traditional doctrine on messianic hope and expectation: two anointed figures, one royal and one priestly, from the lineages of David and Zadok respectively, preceded by the eschatological prophet in the line of Moses and Elijah. Some of these elements are to be found in the New Testament as in Judaism generally, but there are significant divergences as well. In Christianity the priesthood has been radically reinterpreted because there is only one Messiah, of the house of David. Christians could not qualify for the Aaronic priesthood. But there was another also invoked by the Essenes in a drastically different way, that of Melchizedek. While Jesus is compared with that thought and mysterious figure, for the Essenes the eschatological point would have that added qualification. In fact the priesthood may reflect the fundamental and overriding difference between the two groups. Christianity from the beginning was essentially a laymen's movement whereas Essenism was predominantly a movement led by priests, namely, the Zadokites. The very word *priest* is a misnomer and comes out of Christianity (and Judaism) and designates a layman, that is, elder = presbyter. Only later were priestly functions and responsibilities attached to this position. We must distinguish between *zaken* = elder (presbyter) and *kohen* = the Aaronic and Zadokite priesthood. The origins of the Essenes lie in a bitter controversy between a dissident group of priests and the high priest and his associates. The essence of the struggle we will learn from an unpublished epistle apparently written by the righteous teacher, the leader of the dissidents, to the incumbent high priest. In it the grounds for their complaint and the threat of secession are presented; it is the matter of purity and holiness in practice, true meticulous observance of Torah, compared with the laxity of the leadership.

Contrast this with the story of Jesus and his confrontation with his own wicked priest, whether Annas or Caiphas. The wicked priest, so far as we can tell, is never named in the Essene documents, although I have a theory against the prevailing ones. I cannot quite imagine that the righteous teacher could ever have accepted any of the Maccabees as a legitimate high priest, since they were clearly not Zadokites, and thus, not qualified for that office. I think the break came with the last great paragon of the high priests, Onias III mentioned in Ecclesiasticus.

We may mention in passing that the points on which Christianity broke with Judaism, and most clearly with the Essenes, were precisely the issues at the time of the beginning of the Maccabean movement. The hellenizing Jews were specifically charged with not practicing and even revoking circumcision, and with not observing the Sabbath or the dietary rules. It is difficult to imagine that the Essenes, who like the Maccabees so vehemently opposed such innovations and accommodation, would sit still for or approve in any way what in their eyes could only have been a replay of the earlier effort to subvert Judaism from its essential traditions and practices.

We should talk about messiahship and what it meant to Essenes on the one hand and Christians on the other. No doubt the dramatic reinterpretation of royal messiahship (of the Davidic lineage of Jesus that is affirmed by several New Testament writers) as that of suffering, dying, and rising servant must have astounded the Essenes at least as much as other Jews since there is no hint of it in their writings. The interweaving of messiah and suffering servant is uniquely Christian, so far as I am aware, and effectively nullifies one of the most powerful of Jewish doctrines, one that led to the extraordinary upheaval and military struggles of the three hundred years of the Maccabean revolt until the defeat of Bar Cochba, 165 B.C. and A.D. 135.

In a word we must look elsewhere for the original or the congenial environment in which Christianity came to birth, and not among the Essenes.

Ellis Rivkin*

Josephus and Jesus

I

The quest for the historical Jesus has been as alluring as it has been illusory. It has been alluring because the prize is well worth winning. It has been illusory because the only sources on which we can draw for a portrait of the historical Jesus render our quest hopeless. The Gospels, by blending as they do features of the historical Jesus with features of the risen Christ, leave the scholar with no sure method for separating the one from the other. Nonetheless, the quest goes on, in the hope that in another re-reading of the Gospels the long-sought-for road to the historical Jesus will be found.

But if this is a road that will never be found—because, in principle, it cannot be found—by focusing on the Gospels, perhaps another road can be found that can lead us, however indirectly, to the historical Jesus. Such a road, I suggest, may be found in the writings of Josephus. For though he barely mentions Jesus either in *The Jewish War* or in the *Antiquities,* he does provide us with a highly reliable framework of time, place, structure, and circumstance that can be used as a filter for separating out the histori-cal Jesus from the resurrected Christ in the Gospel stories.

I am aware, of course, that Josephus's credibility has been challenged on the grounds of his pro-Roman bias and his antipathy to the Jewish revolutionaries. But, as I shall seek to demonstrate, this challenge to Josephus's credibility is based on very shaky ground. For it fails to take note of the fact that Josephus's account of the road to war, as against his account of the war itself, is a devastating indictment of the way in which Roman emperors and procurators drove the Jewish people to such des-

---

*Ellis Rivkin is Adolph Ochs Professor of Jewish History at Hebrew Union College-Jewish Institute of Religion.

peration that they preferred to perish together than to perish by degrees. What we find in Josephus's account is Roman animus, not Roman bias. By heaping unrestrained praise on Vespasian and Titus, who waged a war they did not cause, Josephus was able to tell the bitter truth about how the Romans provoked the Jews to a suicidal revolt by the harshness of their rule.

Josephus's searing indictment of the emperors and the procurators is bold and blatant. Once seen, it is difficult to comprehend how it could have gone unnoted for so long a time, for Josephus has painted for us a rogues' gallery of ruthless Romans. Consider, for example, the portrait of Pontius Pilate, who began his procuratorship by provoking the Jews to the edge of martyrdom by flaunting both their autonomous rights and their religious insensitivities. This he did by sneaking the Roman standards bearing the effigies of the emperor into Jerusalem under cover of night, arousing the Jews to immense excitement. Josephus tells us,

> Those on the spot were in consternation, considering their laws to have been trampled under foot, as those laws permit no image to be erected in the city; while the indignation of the townspeople stirred the country-folk, who flocked together in crowds.
>
> Hastening after Pilate to Caesarea, the Jews implored him to remove the standards from Jerusalem and to uphold the laws of their ancestors. When Pilate refused, they fell prostrate around his house and for five whole days and nights remained motionless in that position.
>
> On the ensuing day Pilate took his seat on the tribunal in the great stadium, and summoning the multitude with the apparent intention of answering them, gave the arranged signal to his armed soldiers to surround the Jews. Finding themselves in a ring of troops, three days, the Jews were struck dumb at this unexpected sight.
>
> Pilate, after threatening to cut them down, if they refused to admit Caesar's images, signalled to the soldiers to draw their swords. Thereupon the Jews, as by concerted action, flung themselves in a body on the ground, extended their necks, and exclaimed that they were ready to die rather than transgress the law.
>
> Overcome with astonishment at such religious zeal, Pilate gave orders for the removal of the standards from Jerusalem. (*Jewish War* 2. 172-174)

Josephus likewise exposes Pontius Pilate as a deliberate provocateur of the people's wrath when, in his account of Pilate's filching moneys from the temple treasury to build an aqueduct, he tells us that Pilate, foreseeing tumult, "had interspersed among the crowd a troop of his soldiers, armed but disguised in civilian dress, with orders not to use their swords, but to beat any rioters with cudgels. He now from his tribunal gave the agreed signal. Large numbers of the Jews perished, some from the blows which they received, others trodden to death by their compatriots in the ensuing flight. Cowed by the fate of the victims, the multitude was reduced to silence" (*Jewish War* 2. 175-77).

Or consider Josephus's portrait of Albinus:

> The administration of Albinus, who followed Festus, was of another order; there was no form of villainy which he omitted to practise. Not only did he, in his official capacity, steal and plunder private property and burden the whole nation with extraordinary taxes, but he accepted ransoms from their relatives on behalf of those who had been imprisoned for robbery by the local councils or by former procurators; and the only persons left in gaol as malefactors were those who failed to pay the price. (*Jewish War* 2. 273-74)

Or his portrait of Florus:

> Such was the character of Albinus, but his successor, Gessius Florus, made him by comparison a paragon of virtue. The crimes of Albinus were, for the most part, perpetrated in secret and with dissimulation; Gessius, on the contrary, ostentatiously paraded his outrages upon the nation, and, as though he had been sent as hangman of condemned criminals, abstained from no form of robbery or violence. Was there a call for compassion, he was the most cruel of men; for shame, none more shameless than he. No man ever poured greater contempt [unbelief] on truth; none invented more crafty methods of crime. To make gain out of individuals seemed beneath him; he stripped whole cities, ruined entire populations, and almost went the length of proclaiming throughout the country that all were at liberty to practise brigandage, on condition that he receive his share of the spoils. Certainly his avarice brought desolation upon all the cities, and caused many to desert their ancestral haunts and seek refuge in foreign provinces. (*Jewish War* 2. 277-79)

And to these frightening features of Florus, etched in the *Jewish War,* Josephus adds another frightening feature or two in his *Antiquities:*

> So wicked and lawless was Florus in the exercise of his authority that the Jews, owing to the extremity of their misery, praised Albinus as a benefactor. For the latter used to conceal his villainy and took precautions not to be altogether protected; but Gessius Florus, as if he had been sent to give an exhibition of wickedness, ostentatiously paraded his lawless treatment of our nation and omitted no form of pillage or unjust punishment.

Pity could not soften him, nor any amount of gain sate him; he was one who saw no difference between the greatest gains and the smallest, so that he even joined in partnership with brigands. In fact, the majority of the people practiced this occupation with no inhibitions, since they had no doubt that their lives would be insured by him in return for his quota of the scrolls. There was no limit in sight. The ill-fated Jews, unable to endure the devastation by brigands that went on, were one and all forced to flee, for they thought that it would be better to settle among gentiles no matter where.

What more can be said? It was Florus who constrained us to take up war with the Romans, for we preferred to perish together rather than by degrees. (*Antiquities* 20. 253-57)

Thus when we lift the Roman veil from Josephus's countenance, we discover that he has a Jewish face, lined with anger, pain, and resentment at the tragedy that emperors and procurators have inflicted on his people. For with the exception of Petronius, Josephus gives us no Roman governor with any redeeming features; and, with the exception of Augustus and Claudius (abetted by Agrippa) there is no emperor who does not border on the monstrous, with Caligula, who directly flaunted his omnipotence of God, in the van. Read without an anti-Josephus bias, his account of the road to war is one that is penned with vitriol and written with bile.

But Josephus gives us not only an indictment of Roman rule, but a remarkably balanced evaluation of those violent revolutionaries who rallied around Judas of Galilee and his proclamation of a fourth philosophy. On the one hand, Josephus blames them for unleashing the violent passions of the people and holds them responsible, alongside the emperors and procurators, for the outbreak of the war against Rome. On the other hand, he bespeaks their passion for liberty with an eloquence that their own leaders might have envied. He dignifies Judas of Galilee's battle cry of "God alone is Emperor [*despotes*]" by elevating it to the level of a fourth philosophy, alongside the other three philosophies of Judaism that forswore any direct challenge to Roman sovereignty, and he calls Judas of Galilee a sophist, a sage, and not some mere rabble-rouser. So, too, far from penning a diatribe against Eleazar the son of Yair for holding out to the death against the Romans at Massada, and for poisoning the Roman victory with martyrs' blood, Josephus puts into the mouth of Eleazar a panegyric of liberty, which would have done any Greek or Roman orator proud: "Let our wives die dishonored, our children unacquainted with slavery; and when they are gone, let us render a generous service to each other, preserving our liberty as a noble winding sheet." Eleazar, the Jew, is

portrayed by Josephus as having been the most noble Roman of them all.
    Likewise in Josephus's rendition of Eleazar's final plea to his followers
to take their lives and the lives of their wives and children rather than to
fall alive into Roman hands, Eleazar directs the eyes of his listeners on
high to glimpse the immortality awaiting their souls when they free themselves from the prison house of the body. He implores them to quit this
life together, unenslaved by the foe, as free men. "The need for this is
God's ordering, the reverse of this is the Romans' desire, and their fear is
lest a single one of us should die before capture. Haste we, then, to leave
them, instead of their hoped-for enjoyment at our death, an admiration of
our fortitude" (*Jewish War* 7.377-78).
    And this admiration, Josephus tells us, was forthcoming: "Encounter-
ing the mass of slain, instead of exulting as over enemies, [the Roman
soldiers] admired the nobility of their resolve and the contempt of death
displayed by so many carrying it, unwavering, into execution" (*Jewish
War* 7. 406).
    Virtually the last word and the last deed recorded by Josephus of the
war against Rome immortalize not only those who like himself sought
accommodation with Rome, but those followers of Judas of Galilee and
Eleazar the son of Yair who, in preferring liberty to death and life eternal
to life enslaved, cheated the Romans out of the joys of victory by living up
to the highest Roman ideals in their show of noble resolve and contempt
for death.
    Josephus's demonstrated capacity for portraying the enemies of Rome
in so noble a light, along with his readiness to place the ultimate responsibility for the revolt of the Jews on the Roman Empire and procurators,
requires us to take a new look at Josephus's claim to have written his
history with such grand historians as Thucydides as his models. When we
take such a look, we see that Josephus has indeed woven together the din,
the tumult, the turbulence, and the provocations that marked the road to
self-destruction, from the seedlings sown by the first of the procurators, a
Roman, and by Judas of Galilee, a Jew, till its flowering in the razing of
Jerusalem, the destruction of the temple, and the fall of Massada, into an
awesome tragedy foreshadowed from the very beginning. By weaving this
tapestry of tragedy, Josephus has achieved the most that any historian can
hope to achieve when he seeks to make some grand event, such as a war
or a revolution, intelligible, by making it seem, in retrospect, to have been
inexorable—even as Thucydides did when he chronicled his immortal
tragedy of the rise and fall of Athens in his *Peloponnesian Wars*.

II

Now that a case has been made for putting Josephus into the first rank of historians, we can draw upon his writings for an objective framework of time, place, structure, and circumstance for that frame of time during which the historical Jesus traced his trajectory from life to life. Such a framework would reveal two structures distinguished by features that, though alien to one another, interacted in a complementary way. The first of these would be the structure of Roman imperialism, while the second would be the structure of Judaism.

The Roman imperial structure was designed to achieve two ends: the flow of tribute and the maintenance of law and order. All those who exercised authority in the system, whether Romans or provincials, did so in the interest of achieving these ends.

In the time of Jesus, the imperial structure consisted of the emperor who appointed the procurator who in turn appointed the high priest whose legitimacy was grounded neither in the written nor in the oral law, but in the Roman imperium. Finally, a sanhedrin or privy council was appointed by the high priest. Its legitimacy, like that of the high priest's, was political, not religious.

Alongside the Roman imperial structure, we find the structure of Judaism that, though consisting of three highly divergent "philosophies" of Judaism, was unified by the belief that there was one God who had chosen Israel to be His people and who had revealed to them His will on Sinai's mount. For this belief, Jews of all three forms of Judaism were ready to bare their necks to the Roman sword rather than allow a Pontius Pilate to parade the icons of the emperor through the streets of Jerusalem, or Gaius Caligula to set up images of himself in the temple. Drawn together by this shared belief, the Sadducees, Pharisees, and Essenes appeared to the Roman authorities as a mosaic in which the inserts were subordinated to an overall design that imposed a unity upon them.

For the Jews, however, the differences between these three forms of Judaism were of great consequence. The Sadducees, who were the vestiges of that Aaronide Judaism that had flourished under the high priests who traced their lineage back to Zadok, Phineas, Eleazar, and Aaron from the time of the canonization of the Pentateuch till the eve of the Hasmonean Revolt, affirmed that God had given only one law, the written law, and that God's rewards and punishments would be meted out in this world.

Josephus refers to the Pharisees as the most accurate expositors and interpreters of the laws and the leading school of thought in Jesus' day.

They taught that God had given two laws, the written and the oral, and that God allotted to the souls of those individuals who had internalized and obeyed the twofold Law "the most holy places in heaven whence in the revolution of the ages, they would return to find in chaste bodies a new habitation" (*War* 3.374-75), while He consigned the souls of sinners "to the darker regions of the world" (*Antiquities* 18.14; *War* 2.163) where they will undergo eternal imprisonment.

The third philosophy, namely, that of the Essenes, taught that the soul was imprisoned in a corrupt body from which it is freed by death and to which it never returns. In contrast to the other two forms of Judaism, Essenism demanded an ascetic code of life, which appealed to only a handful of Jews.

In the Hasmonean period the religious differences that separated the Pharisees from the Sadducees had led to a violent civil war during the reign of John Hyrcanus, but by Jesus' day these differences were confined to verbal onslaughts. A policy of "live and let live" had come to be accepted by both schools of thought, since the alternative, continual civil war, was recognized as suicidal. Hence while Josephus makes it clear that the teachings of the Pharisees were normative for all Jews insofar as matters affecting the public expressions of religion were concerned, they were not normative insofar as religious beliefs were concerned, except for those who voluntarily adhered to them.

The differences between the three forms of Judaism were very real and they were taken very seriously, but insofar as the Roman authorities were concerned, they carried no weight as long as the principle of "live and let live" guaranteed that these religious differences would not disturb the peace. For the Romans, it was the mosaic that counted, not the individual parts.

And this mosaic counted for them because all three philosophies of Judaism acknowledged that there was one realm that belonged to Caesar and there was another realm that belonged to God. So long as Caesar did not violate God's turf by setting up images in the temple, or by parading icons of the emperor through the streets of Jerusalem, or by prohibiting Jews from adhering to their philosophies and the way of religious life they enjoined, the Sadducees, Pharisees, and Essenes could recognize Roman sovereignty as legitimate, and the payment of tribute to Rome as mandatory. This compact was confirmed by the Sadducees, Pharisees, and Essenes when they sanctioned the taking of the census by Quirinus for the determination of the tribute that the Jews would have to pay.

Had the framework of time, place, structure, and circumstance been limited to the interaction of the Roman imperial system and the mosaic of Judaism, there would have been neither a violent revolt against Rome nor a historical Jesus. But these two fundamentals upholding Roman sovereignty and its law and order cracked in reaction to the brutal provocations of the procurators. Judas of Galilee and Zadok, a Pharisee, were outraged at the levying of tribute, and they called upon the people to take up arms against Rome on the grounds that for a Jew to call anyone other than God Himself *despotes,* emperor, was blasphemous. God would therefore bless their arms and grant them victory. And because their violence was justified on religious grounds, Josephus clothed their ideology with religious respectability by calling it a fourth philosophy.

The emergence of this fourth philosophy proved to be highly destabilizing, precisely because it was a movement that, by appealing to the people to rise up against Rome on religious and not political grounds, blurred the line of demarcation between God's province and Caesar's. This the Romans could not tolerate, since a violent uprising against Rome, however justified in God's name, was a political challenge.

This blurring of the line was further intensified when a breed of nonviolent charismatics, prophets, and would-be messiahs sprang up and confronted the authorities with a far more tricky dilemma. Unlike the men of the fourth philosophy, these charismatics, prophets, and would-be messiahs preached repentance and not violence. Yet, their call for repentance carried with it an implication and an anticipation that God would respond to the penitent by Himself removing the heavy yoke of Rome and ushering in His kingdom. The means were, to be sure, nonviolent, but the end would, in one respect at least, be the same—God, and not the Roman emperor, would be *despotes.* The danger lurking within the call for repentance and the absolute reliance on God's power to save was clearly seen by Josephus when he tells us that

> there arose another body of villains, *with purer hands* but more impious intentions, who no less than the assassins, ruined the peace of the city. Deceivers and imposters, under the pretense of divine inspiration, fostered revolutionary changes and persuaded the multitude to act like madmen, leading them out into the desert under the belief that God would there give them tokens of deliverance. Against them Felix, regarding this as but the preliminary to insurrection, sent a body of cavalry and heavy-armed infantry and put a large number to the sword. (*Jewish War* 2.258-61, emphasis mine)

The fear of the procurator and high priest with respect to charismatics, prophets, and would-be messiahs preaching repentance, but no violence, was the unpredictability of the "multitude driven to madness" by despair. Every crowd was for them a witch's brew, ready to boil over into uncontrollable violence in response to a charismatic's cry of "Repent now, for the Kingdom of God is at hand." It was not the call to repentance or a fevered vision of the end of days that set the teeth of procurator and high priest on edge, but crowds ripe with madness.

It is to this fear of crowds that Josephus attributes the decision of Herod the Tetrarch to put John the Baptist to death. John, he tells us, was a good man, who exhorted the Jews to lead righteous lives, to practice justice to their fellows and piety toward God, and so doing join in baptism.

Yet Herod became alarmed "when others too joined the crowds about him [John] because they were aroused to the highest degree by his sermons. *Eloquence that had so great an effect on mankind,* [he reasoned] *might lead to some form of sedition, for it looked as if they would be guided by John in everything they did.* [Whereupon] *Herod decided that it would be much better to strike first and be rid of him before his work led to an uprising, than to wait for an upheaval, get involved in a difficult situation and see his mistake,"* and had John put to death—a death that so stunned the Jews at large that they attributed the defeat of Herod's army as "a vindication of John, since God saw fit to inflict such a blow on Herod" (*Jewish War* 17.117-19, emphasis mine). In this judgment, Josephus acquiesces, for he, too, considered John to be a good man, exhorting the people not to take up arms against Rome, but against the power of sin within themselves.

When, therefore, we construct from the writings of Josephus the framework of time, place, structure, and circumstance, we find that this framework is tottering on the edge of collapse. It displays all those features that we associate with a society that is on the verge of a revolutionary shakedown. It is a framework that narrowed down the options that were open to the rulers to such a point that only repressive violence remained. Caught between the need to exact the tribute and the need to maintain law and order, the procurators could achieve the one, the collection of tribute, only by compelling law and order. Yet, though repressive violence may stave off a full-blown revolution, it not only does not guarantee tranquility, but frequently hastens the day when even violent repression can no longer hold back the flood tide of revolution.

III

With this tottering framework in mind, let us turn to the Gospels and focus first on the trial, condemnation, and crucifixion of Jesus. It is here that we come most directly into contact with the fear and desperation of those charged with the responsibility for exacting the tribute and maintaining law and order, and most directly in contact with a historically verifiable procurator, Pontius Pilate, and a historically verifiable high priest, Caiphas.

As for Pontius Pilate, since Josephus has already taken his measure, we can turn to Caiphas. What is striking about Caiphas is that he is the only high priest who was able to satisfy a procurator for more than a year or so. Caiphas's ears were so keen and his eyes so penetrating that he not only satisfied the demands of one procurator, but two. He outlasted even Pontius Pilate by a few months. What more eloquent testimony can there be of Caiphas's determination to snuff out the sparks of dissidence before these sparks could be fanned into raging flames than his long tenure as high priest. Like Herod the Tetrarch, Caiphas was concerned with one question only: Was the eloquence of this or that charismatic attracting crowds? What the charismatic was preaching was not the nub, but how many were listening. A call for violence could be overlooked if it was a voice crying in the wilderness. However, a call for repentance that attracted crowds was no less than a call for revolt. Crowds were unpredictable and, once let loose, uncontrollable. Better, Caiphas reasoned, to execute an innocent and politically naive charismatic than to have a violent eruption on one's hands that might require a bloody massacre to put down.

It is this grip of fear that explains Caiphas's role in the arrest, trial, and crucifixion of Jesus as portrayed in the Gospels. Here we find Jesus' eloquence, wonder working, and preachments attracting crowds; and it is here that we read of Jesus' entry into the city of Jerusalem, attracting excited onlookers. It is here that we read of Jesus turning over the table of the money changers in the temple at festal time when the area teemed with crowds highly susceptible to mass hysteria and rioting. Prompted by the dangers inherent in the situation, Caiphas takes decisive action, arrests Jesus, brings him before his council and, having been persuaded along with his privy councilors that Jesus' eloquence, ministrations, and preachings had indeed attracted crowds, turns him over to Pontius Pilate for final judgment.

But through it all Caiphas was acting as an instrument of the procurator, and not as an instrument of God. *He held high-priestly office by imperial, not divine right.* In God's eyes, Caiphas could only have been a renegade who had usurped an office to which he had no claim other than a lust for power. Caiphas's decisions were prompted not by the prescriptions of the written or the oral law, but by his role as a Jewish surrogate of the procurator, striving to hold on to his office by snuffing out sparks before they burst into flame. His judgment was thus a political, not a religious, judgment. The charge that Jesus was proclaiming that he had been chosen by God to be king of the Jews was a charge focusing on the main issue of Jesus' loyalty to the emperor and not on his loyalty to God.

And what held true for the high priest held true for the high priest's council, his sanhedrin. This council had no more religious legitimacy than the high priest who appointed it. Its members, as we know from Acts, consisting of Sadducees and Pharisees, could hardly have judged Jesus on religious grounds, since they looked on each other as rank heretics.[1]

And when we move from the trial and condemnation to the crucifixion itself, we are struck not only by the titulus reading "King of the Jews," but by the picture the Gospels give us of the two revolutionaries, [2] one on either side of Jesus, being crucified with him. We have portrayed before our very eyes the two major threats to Roman rule. In the center is Jesus, a charismatic, whose only offense against Rome was that his call for repentance and his anticipation of the coming of God's kingdom attracted crowds. On either side of Jesus are two revolutionaries, presumably followers of Judas of Galilee and adherents of the fourth philosophy, whose offense against Rome was the preaching of divinely sanctioned revolutionary violence. Yet we see that insofar as Rome was concerned, both preachers of violence and preachers of nonviolence were equally deemed to be threats to Roman rule. Both were equally deserving of crucifixion, that cruelest of punishments meted out to traitors and revolutionaries.

When we turn from the arrest, trial, and crucifixion of Jesus to his life and ministry as portrayed in the Gospels, we are no less impressed with how much of what is told seems not only to be compatible with the framework, but, as it were, mandated by it. Consider for example the linkage that we find between John the Baptist and Jesus. It is a linkage between a historically verifiable charismatic, John the Baptist, and his fate, and a charismatic whose historical features have been blurred, if not erased, by the liberties that the early Christians had taken with the original historical portrait transmitted to them by those who had actually known Jesus while he was alive. For Josephus makes it clear that John the Baptist was a charismatic who preached repentance and not violence, righteousness and not rebellion, justice and not vengeance. He was, as Josephus attested, a good man who had had such a marked impact on the people that they were ready to see in the defeat of Herod the Tetrarch's armies a sure sign of God's displeasure with Herod for having put John to death, and were ready, as the Gospels testify, to recognize him as a man of God (*Antiquities* 18.116-19). Yet this nonpolitical, nonviolent charismatic suffered the same fate as those who called for a violent uprising against Rome.

Josephus's vignette of John, by confirming that in Jesus' day there was at least one charismatic who though nonpolitical and nonviolent was nonetheless put to death for no other reason than that his eloquence attracted crowds, allows us to elicit from the Gospels that Jesus, who resembled him—preaching repentance and not violence, love and not hate, forgiveness and not retaliation, hope and not despair, but who was cruci-fied nonetheless because his teachings, his healings, his exorcisms, his acts on behalf of the poor, the wretched, and the sinful, and his vision of the kingdom of God near at hand—had the fatal flaw of attracting crowds. Since crowds struck terror into the hearts of procurators and high priests alike, nothing short of crucifixion could quiet their fears. Thus that framework that gives us a nonrevolutionary charismatic, John, who is put to death for attracting crowds is the very same framework that makes the crucifixion of Jesus for the same crime of attracting crowds thoroughly credible.

Building, then, on the historically verifiable John and his fate, we can filter from the Gospels those features of Jesus that refract the image of John or are compatible with that image. Thus when we read of Jesus healing the sick; exorcising demons; sitting with sinners; raising the dead; turning the other cheek; spinning parables of God's kingdom come; render-ing unto Caesar what is Caesar's and unto God what is God's; preaching love, compassion, and nonretaliation; debating with the Scribes-Pharisees or the Sadducees; teaching the belief in the resurrection and holding out the hope that the kingdom of God was near at hand, we see a John the Baptist writ large.

Those features, however, that are attributed to Jesus in the Gospels but are not reflective of the image of John must be viewed with high skepticism. Thus the violent denunciations of the Scribes-Pharisees at-tributed to Jesus in Matthew 23 are thoroughly incompatible with the Jesus who was slow to anger, sat with sinners, and turned the other cheek, and are for this reason historically suspect. Jesus, finding himself at odds with the Scribes-Pharisees and holding his ground against them is one thing; a Jesus calling them vipers and sons of hell quite another. Similarly, turning over the tables of the money changers in the temple in a fit of righteous indignation at what Jesus considered to be an affront to the Lord's house is a far cry from calling on the people to take up the sword against Rome. Since we have no need to transform Jesus into either an overt or covert revolutionary to make his trial and crucifixion plausible, given John the Baptist's fate, all those passages in the Gospels that have been drawn by scholars arguing that Jesus was plotting a violent overthrow of Roman rule do not hold a candle to the nonviolent, nonpolitical portrait of Jesus so abundantly evident in the Gospels, and so in line with the fate of John the Baptist.

Our framework likewise allows us to extend historical credibility to the accounts given in the synoptic gospels of Jesus' confrontation with the Scribes-Pharisees. Since Josephus makes it clear that the Pharisees were the most exact expositors and interpreters of the laws; that they were the leading school of thought in Jesus' day, enjoying the enthusiastic support of the masses; that they set the norms for temple cultus and public worship in accordance with their interpretation of the Law, we would expect them to loom large in any account of a charismatic who challenged their religious authority. It comes to us as no surprise, therefore, to read in the Gospels that Jesus and his disciples were continually coming into conflict with these authoritative teachers of the twofold Law, even as it comes as no surprise to read in the Gospels (Mark 12:28-34) that a Scribe was pleased when Jesus, in reply to the Scribe's question "Which commandment is the first of all?" responded that "Hear O' Israel; the Lord our God, the Lord is one; and you shall love the Lord your God with all your heart, and with all your soul and with all your mind and all your strength" is the first, and "You shall love your neighbor as yourself" is the second; or when we read of how Jesus parried the Sadducees, supporting the pharisaic belief in the resurrection with a proof text from the Pentateuch; or when we read of how Jesus confounded the Pharisees when, in response to their questions "Is it lawful to pay taxes to Caesar, or not? Should we pay them or should we not?" he asked for a coin with Caesar's likeness and inscription and said to them, "Render to Caesar the things that are Caesar's, and to God the things that are God's" (Mark 12:13-17). Little wonder that they were amazed, for Jesus had phrased their own dicta so succinctly.

We see, too, that Jesus followed the teachings of the Pharisees in all matters of faith and law that did not conflict with his own very special relationship to God the Father, a relationship that allowed him to brush the teachings of the Pharisees aside when they stood in the way of his gospel of kingdom come. Mark succinctly sums it up when he tells us of how astonished the people in the synagogue were with Jesus' teaching, "for he taught them as one who had [singular] authority and not as the scribes [who had collective authority]" (Mark 1:21).

It was his teaching as one who had the authority that was both the nub—and the rub—of Jesus' relationships with the Scribes-Pharisees. They took umbrage at his healing on the Sabbath (Mark 3:1-6); at his exorcising of demons (Matt. 12:22-24); at his forgiving of sins (Matt. 9:1-8); at his sitting with sinners; at his brushing aside the *pardosis,* the oral laws, of the elders (Mark 7:1-8); at his refusing to give a sign (Mark 8:11-13); and at his implying that since his authority, like that of John the Baptist, came from God, he therefore need give the Scribes-Pharisees no further explanation (Mark 11:27-33).

We thus find in the Gospels a portrait of Jesus, a charismatic who sprouted out of the same soil of discontent, desperation, and despair that had seeded a John the Baptist, with this notable difference: whereas John the Baptist was a charismatic whose teachings did not challenge the authority of the Scribes-Pharisees, Jesus was a charismatic whose teachings aroused their hostility because, unlike John, he taught with an authority that transcended theirs. The clashes between Jesus and the Scribes-Pharisees thus bear the indelible mark of historical authenticity because the Scribes-Pharisees would indeed reject any religious teacher who claimed a special relationship to God that bypassed their God-given authority—however much he may have shared their beliefs in eternal life and resurrection, and however much he may have acknowledged their authority in all matters that did not impinge on his special relationship with God the Father.

And finally, even the witnessing of Jesus risen from the dead is utterly credible in the light of the framework of time, place, structure, and circumstance. For the Gospels make it clear enough that Jesus adhered to the pharisaic belief in the resurrection of the dead. Resurrection for Jesus and his disciples was not only possible but inevitable. The question was thus not whether there could be a resurrection, but when and under what circumstances.

When, therefore, Jesus was crucified, his disciples, unable to come to terms that their teacher was gone, were ripe and ready not only to see Jesus risen from the dead, but also to believe what they saw, and not brush it aside as some fantasy or daydream. Utterly believing that their charismatic teacher was indeed God's chosen one, and yet confronted with the stark evidence of the crucifixion that they had been deceived, the followers of Jesus, seeing him resurrected before their very eyes, took this rising from the dead as the sure sign that Jesus was truly the Christ. For here was no mere run-of-the-mill sign that the Scribes-Pharisees could brush aside, but a singular proof; not since Elijah had so miraculous evidence of God's power been seen.

The Gospels' attestation to Jesus' resurrection is thus an attestation to the hold that the pharisaic belief in eternal life and resurrection had on the hearts and minds of Jesus and his disciples. So much so that Paul, who had been "as to the Law a Pharisee and as to righteousness under the Law blameless," was so absolutely certain that the risen Christ was no fantasy that he was transfigured and proclaimed to all who would hear that Jesus must indeed be the Christ because he had seen him risen from the dead. And it should be noted that this certainty was vouchsafed for by one who had never even seen Jesus during Jesus' lifetime.

When, therefore, we read in the Gospels filtered of Jesus' trajectory from life to life, we find ourselves reading an account so conforming to the framework of historical possibility that it gives us almost a sense of *déjà vu*, as though we were witness to a classical tragedy in which not only the fate of the hero is predestined, but also the process by which that fate is sealed—but with this significant deviation: In Jesus' case, the tragedy of the crucifixion by worldly standards is for Christian believers only the prelude to the glorious triumph of Jesus' resurrection, a transmutation of tragedy into glorious destiny, a destiny that, in retrospect, lay dormant in the pharisaic belief in the resurrection of the dead, a belief so fervently taught by Jesus and so tenaciously held to by his disciples that they could see Jesus sitting alongside the Father and believe what they saw.

Thus Josephus has done for us what he had no intention of doing: he has opened up a path to the historical Jesus where no path had been. And he was able to accomplish this only because in waging his own war against Rome, he had drawn up an indictment in both *The Jewish War* and in *Antiquities* that can now serve as building blocks for the construction of a framework of time, structure, and circumstance—a framework that enables us to filter out from those blurred accounts in the Gospels the historical from the nonhistorical Jesus. In a word, Josephus has resurrected for us the Jesus of history, a Jesus who for so long had been entombed in gospel stories inspired far more by Jesus, the risen Christ, than by the Jesus of history.

NOTES

1. There is another subtle bit of information that Josephus supplies for us that is of inestimable value. On two occasions Josephus tells us that there was a building on the

temple mount called the *bouleuterion* (*Jewish War* 5.144; 6.354), but nowhere does he tell us that there was a building on the temple mount called a *synedrion*. The importance of the mention of the one and not the other is that a *bouleuterion* is the Greek word used, as ' for example, in 1 Macc. 8:1, 13-16, to describe the Senate House in Rome. It is a word that refers to the place where a *boulé*, a legislative deliberative body and not a sanhedrin, an appointive privy council, meets. This would seem to point to the likelihood that the *bouleuterion* was where met the *Beth Din Ha-Gadol* of the Pharisees, a deliberative body whose major function it was to discuss, debate, and pass on *halakhoth*, i.e., oral laws, and not, except in rare cases, to sit as a court.

The *Beth Din Ha-Gadol* was a body headed by a *Nasi* and an *Ab Bet Din*. Since we have recorded in the Mishnah the names of every sage who was a *Nasi* and *Ab Bet Din* from the early Hasmonean period till the time of Jesus, and since not one of these was a high priest, the *boulé* that met in the *bouleuterion* on the temple mount would seem necessarily to have been the *Beth Din Ha-Gadol* referred to in Mishnah Sanhedrin 11:2, from which the twofold Law went out for all Israel. Caiphas's sanhedrin that we read of in the Gospels was a thoroughly political body that had no religious legitimacy. The *boulé* of the *bouleuterion* on the temple mount was a body exclusively made up of authoritative teachers of the twofold Law, and was concerned with the transmission of oral laws still operative and with legislating oral laws as circumstances dictated. It was never presided over by the high priest, nor numbered Sadducees among its members as did the sanhedrin, a privy council appointed by a high priest who had been appointed by a procurator to be his eyes and ears. See E. Rivkin, "Bet, Din, Boule, Sanhedrin: A Tragedy of Errors," *HUCA* 17 (1975):181-99.

2. Although the standard versions generally translate *lestoi* as robbers, Josephus uses this term, in appropriate contexts, to mean "revolutionaries."

Tikva Frymer-Kensky*

Jesus and the Law

Writing about Jesus and the law[1] is a little like trying to solve an algebra problem when all that is known is that, perhaps, X has some sort of relationship to Y. As should be clear from the preceding selections, we have trouble knowing exactly what we mean when we talk about "Jesus"; furthermore, it is very difficult to know what the law was that Jesus stood in some relationship to. For this reason, as one reads the literature, one can choose at will from conclusions that Jesus was a revolutionary eschatological figure, an antinomian messianic figure, a pietist, a Pharisee, a Sadducee, a Dead Sea covenanter, a Hillelite, a Shammaite, a proto-rabbi, and a forerunner of Liberal Judaism. Nevertheless, despite these difficulties, we persist in trying to understand Jesus' attitude towards the law, for the law was a matter of great acrimony and dispute for the early church. Christians disagreed on whether the whole Israelite law should be considered in force; whether only circumcision should be abrogated (as necessary for the conversion of the gentiles); whether dietary and Sabbath laws should be considered of the past; whether there should be a distinction between Jewish Christian and gentile Christian so that only the born Jews should observe the law; whether all should abandon the law.[2] The disputes were quite bitter, and ultimately resulted in any observance of the Hebrew law being considered heretical for Christians. In our modern era, which seeks authenticity in the earliest "pristine" time of Christianity, it seems imperative to understand what Jesus may have taught, or what he may have been understood to have taught, before the church fathers, before Paul, and before the Hellenization of the church.

Focusing on Jesus and the law almost seems to do violence to our general impression of Jesus, for law does not appear to have been at the

*Tikva Frymer-Kensky is Lecturer in Religion and Women's Studies at the University of Michigan.

119

center of Jesus' activity. Although Jesus preached in the synagogues, and gave popular lectures (al fresco), the traditions portray him as having spent much of his time healing. He seems to have felt that the presence of God, or the kingdom of God, was manifested through his own ministry, and particularly through his miracles and his healings. In this way, Jesus can be seen as a charismatic figure and compared to such other prominent charismatics as Honi the Circle Drawer and Hanina ben Dosa.[3] Like him they were from Galilee; like him they were considered particularly close to God; like him they effected healings, although usually by the efficacy of their prayer rather than by their personal power. There were, however, significant differences between Jesus and these Galilean charismatics. Unlike them, Jesus did not make rain, which was their most significant achievement. And unlike him, as far as they were remembered, they did not preach, nor did they travel with a coterie of student-disciples. In this, Jesus was like the rabbis, the interpreters and expounders of Torah, and it is legitimate to ask, what was the relationship of the teaching of Jesus to the Torah of Israel?

It is wrong to translate Torah by "law." Torah, literally "divine instruction," included all the teachings of Israelite tradition—all the books of scripture and, in fact, in rabbinic theology, all the teachings about the books of scripture, and all the teachings derived from scripture. It included ethics and prophecies as well as legal prescriptions. One can and should study the ideas of Torah as ideas. In addition, in more practical terms, the urgent task of teachers of Torah was the Halakhah, the transformation of legal pronouncements, ethical statements, and prophecies into practical guidelines for action—in other words, into laws. When we speak of Torah or Halakhah or even of "the Law," we mean the whole system of individual legal prescriptions, the ideology from which they derive, the mechanisms by which this ideology is translated into statutes, and the mechanism by which changing circumstances and changing ideology can be incorporated in the system.

The centuries before and after Jesus were times of great flux in the Halakhah. Changing economic and political fortunes and the impact of Hellenistic ideas and foreign governments had created great changes in the understanding and application of Torah. Arguments raged among various factions about how (or even whether) to adapt the law of the Hebrew Bible to changing times; new concepts were incorporated and various ideas of law underwent extensive development. Much practical Halakhah had been transformed by the "great assembly" (whether or not it existed), during the Hellenistic period, and even greater changes were effected by the rabbis after the destruction of the temple in Roman times. At the time of Jesus there was no unanimously accepted monolithic, immutable law toward which he had to take a stance. There may already have been a conscious ideology (known to us from later rabbinic sources) that the Torah was indeed unchangeable, but even this theology held that the unchangeable Torah encompassed the written scripture, its interpretations, and its methods of continued reinterpretation. In practice there were many alternative ways of living within the law in times and circumstances not envisioned by the written Torah. In trying to understand the relationship of Jesus and the law we have to understand his relationship to the laws he inherited, to the interpretations with which he was familiar, and to the processes of its transformation.

What evidence do we have at our disposal to try to answer these questions? We have an organized presentation of pronouncements about the law presented in the Sermon on the Mount, and we have individual statements of Jesus presented in the form of controversies with the Pharisees and the Scribes. And we have a curious bit of negative evidence: nowhere in the Gospels do we find a statement by Jesus that the law should be abolished, or even that the law belonged to the past; nowhere do we find Jesus even revoking the commandment of circumcision, the first of the commandments to be vitiated by the church. In the world of Jesus, Torah was a given, questioned as to meaning but not as to existence. There is no tale of Jesus actually breaking one of Israel's laws, and despite the concerns of the early church, despite its need to justify abandoning many of the laws, and despite its later desire to declare the law null and void, no one puts the revocation of the law into the mouth of Jesus. Moreover, the synoptics present a rather harmonious picture of Jesus' actions and attitudes vis-à-vis the law, even though the evangelists themselves (we think) were addressing different needs in the developing church and held differing attitudes towards Judaism and toward the law. The Matthean Jesus is a better legal scholar: he is more careful in his debates, he uses more sophisticated legal reasoning, but there are really no major differences between the Matthean and the Marcan Jesus. Despite our necessary skepticism toward our sources, these facts make us more ready to accept these pronouncements of Jesus preserved in the synoptics as at least received tradition (Jesus of history if not Jesus of biography) rather than as tendentious invention.

THE DEBATES WITH THE PHARISEES[4]

Before we can turn to the traditions in which Jesus engages in controversy with the *pharisaio,* we have to state our hesitations and reservations. In the first place, we don't really know who the *pharisaio* are.[5] If they are Pharisees, is the pharisaic movement the same as the later rabbinic? If so, why are their positions so strangely at variance with later rabbinic tradition, so that if we did not know history we would swear that Jesus, and not these "pharisees," was the precursor of Rabbinic Judaism? The agenda that is so important to these Pharisees is the same agenda reflected in the traditions that we have about the great Pharisees (or proto-rabbis) before 70: tithing, purity laws, Sabbath laws, although here too we cannot be absolutely certain that this was truly a pre-70 agenda.[6] Yet the positions held by the gospels' Pharisees do not follow rabbinic lines, not even those of the stricter Shammaite school, and they seem more like the very strict constructions of the sectarians of the Dead Sea Scrolls and the book of Jubilees. For this reason some have attempted to divorce these New Testament characters from the Pharisees of rabbinic tradition, and to identify them with the *perushim,* "sectarians," of whom we occasionally hear in rabbinic sources. But were there really so many Dead Sea-type sectarians in the Galilee, or even table-fellowship Pharisees? As far as we can tell, the Pharisees held no political power until 70, when they became part of the rabbinic movement at Yavneh, and even then they were not the sole voice, and perhaps not even the dominant voice at Yavneh.[8] Yohanan ben Zakkai, the leader of the rabbinic group at Yavneh, spent (according to legend) eighteen years in the Galilee, during which time he was only asked to decide upon two questions of law (as recorded in Jerusalem Talmud Shabbat 16:715d); is it possible that Pharisees were so involved in Galilean practice that Jesus kept encountering them? Or were they sectarians from whom he had broken away, who were trying to prevent him from attracting more disciples?

We also have to ask questions about the controversy form. Did Pharisees really come so often to question Jesus? Did the heathen really come to inquire about the essentials of the law from first Shammai and then Hillel (BT Shabbat 31a, ARN A15, 61)? Did a heathen really come to argue with Yohanan ben Zakkai about the rules of the red calf (Bamidbar Rabbah 19:8; Pesikta deRab Kahana 4 and parallels)? On the one hand, this kind of controversy form is characteristically rabbinic: Jews studied in pairs and in groups and studied (then as now) "dialectically," which means by arguing with each other, sometimes passionately and heatedly. On the other hand, the individual controversy tales about both Jesus and the early rabbis often seem to simply form the background for some pithy and pregnant utterances. It may be that the presentation of a controversy narrative sets the scene for this statement by quickly defining the parameters of the debate. If this be so, the Pharisees of these stories may be a literary foil, and we need not ask if Jesus really encountered them at every turn. One further comment about dialectical tradition: whether the controversies were real or literary, the *pharisaio* of the New Testament, as presented by the evangelists, do not follow one of the basic rules of the convention. If one is bested in an argument, if one's opponent has discovered either a new answer or a new question, the proper response is not anger or plotting revenge (as do Mark's Pharisees), but delight, astonishment, and/or reward. According to the Hillel legend, when Hillel won his disputations with the sons of Bathyra, he was appointed *nasi* (Pes 66a, TJ Pes 6:1). Even though this story may not be historical, it illustrates how the dialogic learning process was understood.

Despite these caveats, we cannot simply dismiss everything in these controversy stories as having arisen in this post-Yavneh period and as totally unhistorical. We should pay attention to the statements of Jesus that form the focus of these stories, and therefore to the lines of his thought on some of the legal issues of his day.

The dispute between Jesus and the Pharisees centers on several important issues: in the straight polemic of Matthew 23, Jesus attacks them on tithing, the preoccupation with which he declares insignificant compared to the weightier matters of the law (Matt. 23:23). In the same place, he attacks them on purity regulations, for he declares that they purify the outside of the cup (Matt. 23:25). In the actual dialogues Jesus attacks them for allowing a son to abandon his financial obligations to his parents by means of a vow (Matt. 15:1-6); they attack him for eating with sinners, they question him about allowing his disciples to eat without washing their hands (Mark 7:14-23, Matt. 15:10-20), and about divorce; they attack him for letting his disciples pluck and eat grain on the Sabbath, and for healing on the Sabbath. The issues in these disputes ring true, for the Pharisees were a group determined to observe a fully holy life in all aspects of life, and not only in the temple. As such, they were scrupulous about tithing, so that they would not be eating food that had not been properly tithed, and they were scrupulous about purity regulations, which they extended to all dietary laws so that they "ate secular food in purity." Like all Jews at the time they were interested in the observance of the Sabbath. In order to maintain this they formed, it appears, a table fellowship, eating only with those whom they could trust to have tithed and observed purity laws. (It should be noted that the Pharisees were willing to eat with Jesus.)

To turn first to the hand-washing stories of Mark 7:14-23 and Matt. 15:10-20. The Pharisees ask him "why do your disciples break the tradition of the elders?" in that they do not wash hands before eating. Here the question of the Pharisees (who thereafter say nothing) seems to point to a real disagreement in practice: Jesus does not demand this aspect of purity regulations. We should of course note that there were many Jews, non-fellows in the Pharisaic fellowship, called "Ammei Ha'aretz," who were not observing the purity rules. (Later one of the five major rabbis at Yavneh, Simeon ben Nathaniel, ate food in an unclean state [Tos. A.Z. 3:10]; there are also pietists, Hasidim, who obey purity rules that are defined differently from those of the Pharisees.)[9] However, Jesus is not said to have mentioned this. Instead, in the form of the dispute that we have, he first goes on the attack, condemning Pharisees on the question of filial vows (about which more later), and then gets to the crux of the story, a pithy statement to the crowd, "What goes into a man's mouth does not make him 'unclean,' but what comes out of his mouth, that is what makes him unclean." Later, the disciples ask him to explain what is obviously a radical statement, and he explains that all that enters the body ultimately exists, but the true uncleannesses are the evil thoughts in a person's heart. It is clear that Jesus is taking the opportunity to deliver a moral lesson about the true purity, that of right action, and the true object of concern, the purification of one's thoughts and utterances. This is also his use of purity regulations in Matt. 23:25, where he accuses the Pharisees of declaring the outside of a cup clean while the inside is unclean: there he uses the language of a real debate about whether cups can transfer uncleanness from outside to inside in order to again illustrate his concern with the interiority of cleanliness. But what about the externals? Does Jesus really mean to abandon all concern about purity regulations? If he does, he is clearly at variance with Pharisees and Qumran, though perhaps not with the ordinary people and not even with the Sadducees, who limited purity considerations to the temple. But does this statement really throw out all purity regulations? A somewhat analogous story is told about Yohanan ben Zakkai (Numbers Rabbah 19:8 and parallels), for an idolator came to him claiming that the laws of the red cow were sorcery-type regulations. He drew an analogy to exorcism and the idolator left, but the disciples demanded a better explanation of the question. Yohanan said "In truth, the dead do not defile and the water does not purify." Yohanan (who incidentally was not a Pharisee, for the traditions about him do not concern purity or tithing),[10] abandons the whole theory underlying the categories of purity and defilement. In this case, however, Yohanan demanded that the law be followed because it is a commandment of the Torah itself. Like Yohanan, Jesus denies the principle of purity; in the case of hand washing, which is not prescribed in the Torah, he feels under no obligation to follow it, or at least to demand that his disciples follow it. What he would have said about those purity regulations that are found in the Torah, we do not know. It has been argued that the fact that Jesus does not object to being touched by the women with a bloody discharge shows that he was not concerned with purity laws of any type, but this is an irrelevant argument. Not all blood, even genital, was considered menstrual; and, more importantly, despite, or perhaps in agreement with the parable of the good Samaritan, Israelite law did not demand that one actively avoid impurity, which would mean not caring for one's sick and dying, not burying the dead, not having sexual intercourse, and not procreating. Israelites were to perform all of these positive commandments and then remove impurity; they were not to avoid them in order to avoid impurity.

THE SABBATH CONTROVERSIES

Keeping the Sabbath holy is one of the ten commandments, but the exact definition of keeping the Sabbath is not mentioned there. From at least the time of Isaiah and Jeremiah there was an increasing tendency to specify the prohibiton of things to be done on the Sabbath. From the intertestamental and later books we know that the prescription of Sabbath laws was an increasing concern, that ultimately there was an attempt to codify all possible activity into permissible and prohibited. Opinion was not unanimous as to what was and was not permissible, and debates occurred, particularly between the Sadducees, who held to the strictest possible interpretation of Sabbath regulations, and Pharisees, who attempted to work within the law to make the Sabbath enjoyable. During the early rabbinic period there was a concern not only with lenient interpretation of inherited rules, but also with the formulation of principles for which the Sabbath should be set aside. The primary—but not the sole—reason was the saving of life. Although this would have seemed self-evident to us, there is some evidence that Qumran did not even consider this cause to set aside the Sabbath. The temple cult certainly set aside the Sabbath. The Pharisee Eliezer ben Hyrcanus of Yavneh is known to have ruled that circumcision set aside the Sabbath, as did the Passover, and as in fact did the Omer (for, according to Pharisees, one could harvest the Omer on the second day of Passover, even if it fell on Sabbath). Ultimately, rabbinic Judaism allows the Sabbath to be overridden for the needs of a mitzvah apostle for any question of the possibility of danger, and even, it seems, in order to make the sick comfortable.

Jesus was confronted with having allowed his apostles to pluck and eat grain on the Sabbath. Although plucking for agricultural purpose is forbidden, we don't know whether stripping an ear would have been considered plucking the fruit, nor whether plucking for the sake of eating would have been considered agriculture at this time. When Jesus was questioned, however, he did not use these arguments, nor the argument that the needs of a mitzvah apostle set aside the Sabbath, which had possibly not been enunciated yet. Nor did he argue from danger to life, for presumably the apostles were not starving. On the other hand, he also did not say that the Sabbath was irrelevant to him, despite the attitude of the later church. Jesus counters with two arguments, both of which state the same thing. He relates that David had eaten holy food on his journey, even though he was neither a priest nor even in a state of impurity. If, therefore, David had eaten something set aside for God, how is it wrong that the disciples set aside the Sabbath for their purposes? Matthew adds another argument, that in the temple the priests profane the Sabbath, and that something greater than the temple is here. Therefore, if the Pharisees had known the true meaning of "I wish for mercy and not sacrifice" they would not have condemned the disciples. He then concludes with a pithy statement of which the Marcan form is "the son of Man is lord even of the Sabbath" and the Matthean form, "Man is lord of the Sabbath." The two forms of the logion mean much the same, for Mark seems to be reflecting a literal translation of Aramaic *barnash,* i.e., everyman. This pericope has often been misunderstood to mean that Jesus considered himself greater than the temple, and that as the "son of man" (taken as an eschatological term) he could supersede the Sabbath. However, if this were the case, what would be the purpose of quoting Hosea's "I desire *hesed* and not sacrifice"? That which is greater than the Sabbath, holier than the temple, is precisely *hesed* (see Sigal). In a sense, this is a more radical statement than the eschatological, for Jesus is saying that the well-being of humans is more important than literal interpretation of Sabbath restrictions. He repeats this theme when asked why he healed the bent-double woman on Sabbath when she could have been healed on the other six days of the week, having already been crippled for eighteen years (Luke 13:10-17). He again brings up the theme when he asked (Mark 3:1-6; Luke 6:6-11) whether it is lawful to do good or to do evil on the Sabbath, or when he was asked whether it is lawful to heal on Sabbath (so Matt. 12:9-13). In Matthew's version Jesus again used a *qal vehomer,* this time by claiming that people would pull a sheep out of a pit on Sabbath (which, incidently, seems to have been forbidden at Qumran) and that humans are more valuable than sheep, thus proving that "it is lawful to do good on Sabbath."

Jesus' prime principle is that doing good, i.e., *hesed,* must supersede the Sabbath, and in support of this he attests Hosea, "I desire mercy and not sacrifice," an attestation that he also uses to justify eating with sinners. Each time he prefaces the prooftext with a statement about his special exegesis of it—in the Sabbath episode, "if you had known . . . you would not condemn the guiltless"; in the case of the sinners, "go and learn what this means" (Matt. 9:13). This passage from Hosea does not have to imply that *hesed* should become the prime motivating factor in the law. Nevertheless, this interpretation of the passage is not unique to Jesus. In Avot deRabi Nathan, the story is told about Rabbi Yohanan ben Zakkai that, when asked about what could take the place of the temple for the expiation of sins, he responded that the mechanism for this was already known, that it was doing good, *gemilut hasadim,* i.e., *hesed.* As support for his opinion he used the same verse from Hosea, "I desire *hesed* and not sacrifices" (ARN A4 B8). Was Jesus the first to enunciate this principle, which was transmitted and adopted before the parting of the ways between Judaism and Christianity? Or did Matthew learn this tradition from the rabbi of Yavneh and then put it into the mouth of the earlier Jesus? Or are Jesus and Yohanan both part of a contemporary tradition that, rather than being concerned with purity and tithing, concerns itself more with *hesed* and with the love commandment of Lev. 19:18? We, of course, cannot answer this question, but it should be clear that Jesus has no intention to abolish or even to violate the Sabbath, but rather to set it aside if necessary in favor of the holy principle of *hesed,* just as the earlier law had set it aside in favor of the holy principle of sacrifices.

The fourth issue on which the Pharisees question Jesus is the issue of divorce. And here, for the first time, we find a substantive difference in the evangelical accounts. In Mark, the Pharisees ask the question. Jesus points out that Moses permitted but did not command divorce, then follows with a *binyan ab* from the fact that God created male and female (Gen. 1:27) and man is to cleave to his wife (Gen. 2:24), declaring that they are therefore no longer two but one, and therefore "what God has joined together, let not man separate." Jesus further explains to his disciples that if anyone divorces his wife and marries another woman he commits adultery, and if she divorces (some say deserts) her husband and marries another, she commits adultery. This would seem to be an absolute prohibition on divorce. Matthew however (19:2-8) says that divorce is forbidden except in cases of *porneia* (horrendous sexual practice, such as adultery or incest); furthermore, he states the more Judaic view that if anyone divorces his wife (except for adultery) he causes her to commit adultery. The implication in Matthew seems to be that adultery destroys the marital bond, so divorce can follow (and in the view of the Hebrew Bible, it seems must follow). We do not know which position was Jesus', but we know that both positions stand along a continuum in the contemporary debate over divorce.[11] The Hillelites permit divorce for any wrongful act of the wife, sexual or not; Akiba ultimately allowed divorce on demand (of the male, of course). The Shammaites allowed divorce if the wife committed sexual indecency, which included public bathing or wearing loose hair or sleeveless clothes. At Qumran it appears that they never allowed remarriage, whatever the opinion on separation and divorce. In Rabbinic Judaism there were two tendencies: a desire to find divorce lawful, and a desire to find it wrongful. Although the rabbis could not find reason to forbid it, they made it difficult by establishing stiff financial penalties in the Ketubah. Jesus, it seems, was content to prohibit it not on the basis of exegesis of law, but by arguing legally from the Genesis narrative, something that Christianity continues to do that Judaism has always been reluctant to do. We should note that in this case also, although Jesus certainly innovated over biblical statute, he did this within the frame of law as an ongoing reinterpretive process.

There is one controversy in which Jesus attacks the Pharisees. In the hand-washing debate, he accuses them of violating the law themselves. According to Jesus, they violate the fifth commandment, the command to honor one's father and mother, in that they allow a son to vow his goods as a *qorban,* thus making his goods inaccessible for the support of his parents. This statement may reflect a discussion of that time, for the problem is addressed by the Yavnean Pharisee Eliezer ben Hyrcanus, who declared that the honoring of one's parents would be sufficient reason to annul such a vow of *qorban.*

A serious question arises with this charge against the Pharisees. Is Jesus the pot calling the kettle black? Jesus, after all, is not portrayed in the Gospels as very kind to his own parents. He was impatient with his mother (as we all are) at Cana (John 2:1-4). Furthermore, when told that his mother and brothers were outside and wished to speak to him, he embarrassed them in public by saying that his disciples were his real mother and brethren (Mark 3:31-35, Matt. 12:46, Luke 8:19). When an anonymous woman who heard him speak proclaimed, "Blessed be the womb that bore you and the breasts that gave you suck," Jesus answered, "No, say rather 'blessed be he who hears the word of the Lord and follows.'" Jesus is depicted as calling for the division of families (Luke 12:52-53) and as requiring people to hate their families in order to follow him (Luke 14:26). We must ask what is going on here. Is it possible that Jesus (or the early church) is abrogating one of the six commandments of the Decalogue that he is elsewhere held to have proclaimed (Mark 10:17-19)?

The answer to this question lies in the nature of the Decalogue, which was always treated as charter ideology, rather than as statute. It was therefore frequently reinterpreted. Deuteronomy uses laws to interpret the Decalogue; Jeremiah and Ezekiel changed the principle of divine retribution to the third and fourth generation. So here too we have a particular interpretation of the commandment to honor one's parents. This interpretation is reflected in the Mekiltah to Ex 20:2, which states, in a form somewhat reminiscent of the Sermon on the Mount, that one might think that the commandment means to honor with words, and therefore Ex 20:2 teaches that it means honor with substance by providing for food, drink, and clean garments. If one construes the commandment to mean only material provision, then Jesus fulfilled it by commending his mother to another's care at his death.

There is a reason that Jesus (and the early church) chose to follow such a narrow interpretation of the commandment. The demands of their situation as creators of a new way demanded that children sometimes reject the ways of their parents and go against the wishes and demands of their parents in order to follow Jesus. Similarly, at the time of the Babylonian exile, Jeremiah and Ezekiel declared an end to divine cross-generational retribution in order to meet the need of the exilic generation to know that they would not continue to be punished for the sins of preexilic Israel.

This brings us to the Sermon on the Mount, with its statement of fidelity to the "least of the commandments" and its statement of intent to fulfill the law, followed by the six antitheses in which Jesus "fulfills" the law. The general scholarly opinion is that the completed Sermon on the Mount is a Matthean construction in which he presents his image of a new Moses and a new Sinai. However, the components of this sermon, the individual pronouncements of Jesus, may have been part of the tradition that Matthew received.

To turn to the antithesis. Jesus deals with six topics: murder, adultery, divorce, oaths, talion, and love of neighbor. In the first two, Jesus extends the prohibitions to include emotions that might lead to them. He forbade divorce (except in cases of adultery) and oaths, he counseled against using the legal revenge of talion, and he extended love of neighbor to include love of enemy.

Is any of this radical? Certainly, Jesus went beyond the literal interpretation of the prohibitions of the ten commandments to call for inner purity. He went beyond the call of the law to forbid things that had not been previously permitted. To find out how a Pharisaic Rabbi would have handled some of the same topics that Jesus considered, we can look at Eliezer ben Hyrcanus, who held that Sabbath could be put aside for circumcision and for Passover, who pronounced on the tithing of dill, who held on the purity of the outside of the vessel, and who annuled the vow children might make to the detriment of parents. He also dealt with oaths and vows, not forbidding them, but addressing himself to the question of how to declare such oaths null and void. Similarly, neither the Pharisees nor the rabbis forbad divorce, but they did seek ways to make it harder. The rabbis had a practical task: they were concerned to set forth practical parameters and guidelines to action. In other words, they acted to establish laws that people could live by. They established the laws *(din)* and the parameters of the law *(shurat hadin),* even while they exhorted people to go beyond the parameters of the law *(lifnim mishurat hadin)* into the realm of the counsels of perfection.[12] In the collection of pronouncements presented as the Sermon on the Mount, Jesus offers only counsels of perfection. Counsels of perfection are not practical law, and demanding that people be perfect beyond the requirements of the law does not abrogate the law.

Even if Jesus had intended to abolish one of the laws of Israel which he mentioned, this would not mean that he intended to abrogate the Law. There is a fundamental misconception in attempts to find an antinomian Jesus here: you can abolish a given law without revoking or abrogating the whole system of Torah. Yohanan ben Zakkai, who was so instrumental in both preserving the Torah after the destruction of the temple and in placing the study and observance of Torah at the center of the Jewish faith, did not hesitate to do away with large portions of the law. He abolished the trial of the suspected adulteresses (Num. 5:11-31), and he presided over the dissolution of the entire sacrificial system after the destruction of the temple. Yet he is regarded as the savior rather than the destroyer of the law. As far as we can tell, Jesus not only had no wish to destroy the law, he did not even go as far as Yohanan ben Zakkai. But if Jesus was law abiding and law accepting, we must ask, "what happened here?" How could Christianity have moved so quickly to abrogate the laws? Although we know the many reasons that it was advantageous to the church to abolish the law in order to attract the gentiles, how could it have taken the license to do so? There is an inherent domino effect in any counsels of perfection, for if perfection cannot be reached, there is little to guide one as to where the practical person should make a stand. An emphasis on interiority also gives no guide to action. *Hesed* is a dangerous principle of law, for how can *hesed* be legislated? As Jesus became the center of Paul's faith, the way was open for Paul and others to abolish the law, or at least any laws detrimental to the spreading of Jesus' teaching to the gentiles, i.e., circumcision, Sabbath, and dietary rules. Rabbinic Judaism took a different path, for although the rabbis also adopted *hesed* as a major principle, they used the rest of the same verse of Hos. 6:6 to show that knowledge and study of the law were required by God. In Judaism, then, the study of the law and its doing became the operative center of religion.

NOTES

1. For some of the more important works, see Robert J. Banks, *Jesus and the Law in the Synoptic Tradition* (Cambridge University Press, 1975); Donald Hagner, *The Jewish Reclamation of Jesus: An Analysis and Critique of Modern Jewish Study of Jesus* (Zondervan, 1984), 87-132; John P. Meier, "Law and History in Matthew's Gospel: A Redactional Study of Mt. 5:17-18," *Analecta Biblica* 71 (1976); Geza Vermes, *Jesus and the Jew: A Historian's Reading of the Gospels* (Macmillan, 1973), and *The Gospel of Jesus the Jew* (Fortress, 1983); and Stephen Westerholm, *Jesus and Scribal Authority,* Coniectanea Biblica New Testament Series 10 (Lund, 1978). Other suggested readings are Joseph Baumgarten, *Studies in Qumran Law* (Leiden, 1977); Bruce Martin, "Matthew on Christ and the Law," *Theological Studies* (1984): 53-70; and Benedict Thomas Viviano, *Study as Worship: Aboth and the New Testament* (Leiden, 1978).

2. On the different groups, see Raymond Brown, "Types of Jewish/Gentile Christianity," *CBQ* 45 (1983).

3. See particularly the works of Geza Vermes: "Hanina ben Dosa," *Journal of Jewish Studies* 23 (1972): 28-50; 24 (1973): 51-64; and *Jesus the Jew* and *Gospel of Jesus* in note 1.

4. For general information about the Pharisees, see Louis Finkelstein, *The Pharisees,* 2 vols., 3d ed. (Philadelphia, 1962); and Jacob Neusner, *The Traditions about the Pharisees,* 3 vols. (Leiden, 1971), and *Early Rabbinic Judaism* (Leiden, 1975). For discussion about the relationship between Jesus and the Pharisees, see John Bowker, *Jesus and the Pharisees* (Cambridge, 1973); Michael J. Cook, "Jesus and the Pharisees—The Problem As It Stands Today," *Journal of Ecumenical Studies* 15 (1978): 441-60; Asher Finkel, *The*

Pharisees and the Teacher of Nazareth (Leiden, 1964); and Phillip Sigal, "The Halakha of Jesus of Nazareth according to the Gospel of Matthew" (Ph.D. diss., University of Pittsburgh, 1979).

   5. See Sigal, "Halakha."
   6. See in particular Neusner, *Traditions.*
   7. So, particularly, Sigal, "Halakha." Note that "Pharisees" itself means "Separatists," as far as we can tell.
   8. This is stressed by Neusner, *Eliezer ben Hyrcanus: The Tradition and the Man,* 2 vols. (Leiden, 1973). He points out that Eliezer ben Hyrcanus seems to represent the Pharisee tradition, but that Yohanan does not.
   9. For the *'am ha'aretz,* see Aharon Oppenheimer, *The 'Am Ha-retz* (Leiden, 1977).
   10. See Jacob Neusner, *Development of a Legend: Studies on the Traditions concerning Yohanan ben Zakkai* (Leiden, 1970).
   11. For a discussion on this continuum, see Sigal, "Halakha."
   12. For an excellent discussion of *lifnim mishurat hadin,* see Sigal, "Halakha."

III

The Development of Christology

Randel Helms*

Fiction in the Gospels

Northrop Frye has categorized fictions as either mimetic or self-reflexive; mimetic fictions "reflect the actual world, sustaining an illusion of reality, life as it is lived," while "Self reflexive fictions describe worlds governed primarily by an internal logic, so they reflect life much less insistently than they reflect themselves or other fictions."[1] Frye has written about the self-reflexive aspects of the Gospels in another work:

> How do we know that the Gospel story is true? Because it confirms the prophecies of the Old Testament. But how do we know the Old Testament prophecies are true? Because they are confirmed by the Gospel story. Evidence, so called, is bounced back and forth between the testaments like a tennis ball; and no other evidence is given us. The two testaments form a double mirror, each reflecting the other but neither the world outside.[2]

I want to discuss this self-reflexive aspect of three fictional episodes in the Gospels: the miracle stories of the raising of the widow of Nain's son (found only in Luke), the feeding of the five thousand (found in all four Gospels), and the stilling of the storm (found in the Synoptics, Matthew, Mark, and Luke).

That the Gospel miracle stories are indeed fictional is no longer a live question, according to Ernst Käsemann:

> Over few subjects has there been such a bitter battle among the New Testament scholars of the last two centuries as over the miracle-stories of the Gospels. . . . We may say that today the battle is over, not perhaps as yet in the arena of church life, but certainly in the field of theological science. It has ended in the defeat of the concept of miracle which has been tradition in the church.

---

*Randel Helms is Professor of English at Arizona State University. He has written extensively on the fiction of J. R.R. Tolkien.

135

Käsemann's judgment is that the "great majority of the Gospel miracle stories must be regarded as legends."[3] I shall quarrel only with Käsemann's terminology, using Frye's term "self-reflexive fiction" rather than legend, because I think it much better expresses the literary methods of the authors of the miracle stories. First-century Christians believed that events in the career of Jesus occurred, in Paul's words in 1 Cor. 15:3 "according to the scriptures"; that there should be stories about Jesus performing miracles was virtually a requirement, given such an understanding of the Old Testament. Matthew made this quite clear:

> John, who was in prison, heard what Christ was doing, and sent his own disciples to him with this message: "Are you the one who is to come, or are we to expect some other?" Jesus answered, "Go and tell John what you hear and see: the blind recover their sight, the lame walk, the lepers are made clean, the deaf hear, the dead are raised to life, the poor are hearing the good news."[4]

In these verses (according to Matthew), Jesus lists what are in fact the signs of the incoming of the New Age, as Isaiah had predicted them: "the eyes of the blind shall be opened, and the ears of the deaf shall hear. Then shall the lame man leap as an hart" (Isa. 35:5 LXX). Isaiah had also declared that "the dead shall rise, and they that are in the tombs shall be raised" (Isa. 26:19). With this, Matthew combined Second Isaiah's declaration that he had been appointed to "preach good news to the poor" (*euangelisasthai ptōchois*—Isa. 61:1 LXX), using that prophet's very words from the Septuagint. Sayings taken as prophecies from Jesus' own time required that he be represented doing these things.

The scripture cannot be broken: the prophecy necessitated the narrative. As it happened, scripture contained not only the prophecy, it also contained the narrative. The miracle stories of Elijah and Elisha in 1 and 2 Kings provided the basis for many of the stories of Jesus' miracles. Noting the theory that early Christians turned the Old Testament into a book about Jesus, we can trace the literary lineage and grasp the literary structure of the Gospel miracle stories. Both Elijah and Elisha mediate two striking miracles: the creation of quantities of food from little and the resurrection of a dead son. One should not be surprised to discover these familiar stories in the Gospel.

The raising of a dead child or loved one is perhaps Jesus' most characteristic miracle. Lazarus (in John), Jairus's daughter (in Matthew, Mark, and Luke), and the widow of Nain's son (in Luke) are all depicted as raised from the dead in order for the evangelists to present typical themes.

Since Luke's account of the raising of the widow of Nain's son so clearly betrays its literary lineage, we shall begin with it:

> And it came to pass [*kai egeneto*] afterwards that Jesus went to a town called Nain, accompanied by his disciples and a large crowd. As he approached the gate of the town he met a funeral. The dead man was the only son of his widowed mother; and many of the townspeople were there with her. When the Lord saw her his heart went out to her, and he said, "Weep no more." With that he stepped forward and laid his hand upon the bier; and the bearers halted. Then he spoke: "Young man, rise up!" The dead man sat up and began to speak; and Jesus gave him back to his mother. Deep awe fell upon them all, and they praised God. "A great prophet has arisen among us," they said. (Luke 7:11-16)

Either Luke or some unknown Greek-speaking Christian behind Luke composed this story on the basis of the account in the Septuagint version of the book of Kings depicting Elijah's raising of the dead son of the widow of Sarepta:

> And it came to pass [*kai egeneto*] that the word of the Lord came to Eliu, saying Arise, and go to Sarepta of the Sidonian land: behold, I have there commanded a widow-woman to maintain thee. And he arose and went to Sarepta, and came to the gate of the city. . . .
> And it came to pass afterward, that the son of the woman the mistress of the house was sick; and his sickness was very severe, until there was no breath left in him. . . .
> And Eliu said to the woman, Give me thy son. And he took him out of her bosom. . . .
> And he breathed on the child thrice, and called on the Lord, and said, O Lord my God, let, I pray thee, the soul of this child return unto him. And it was so, and the child cried out, and he brought him down from the upper chamber into the house, and gave him to his mother. (3 [1] Kings 17:8-10, 17, 19-23 LXX)

Both stories begin with the Septuagint's favorite formula, "And it came to pass" (*kai egeneto*); Luke characteristically wrote in "biblical-sounding" (i.e., Septuagintal) Greek. Both stories concern the dead son of a widow (*chēra* in both). In both stories the prophet "went" (*eporeuthē*) to the town, where he met the widow at the "gate of the city" (*ton pylōna tēs poleōs,* LXX; *tē pylē tēs poleōs,* Luke), even though archeological study has shown that the village of Nain in Galilee never had a wall; Nain's fictional gate is there for literary reasons, Sarepta's gate transferred. In both stories, the prophets speak and touch the dead son, who then rises and speaks. Then in both stories it is exclaimed that the miracle certifies the prophet ("Behold, I know that thou art a man of God," LXX; "A great prophet has arisen," Luke). And both stories conclude with precisely the same words: "and he gave him to his mother" (*kai edōken auton tē mētri autou*).

Just as Luke's account of the resurrecting of the widow of Nain's son is consciously modeled after the story of the raising of the widow of Sarepta's son, so are the Gospel stories of the creation of much food from little modeled after the accounts of similar miracles of Elijah and Elisha in the books of Kings in the Old Testament. In this case all four of the Gospels have versions of this story. Let us compare Mark's versions in chapters 6 and 8 with its source in 2 Kings 4. In both stories the prophet— Elisha or Jesus—wishes to feed a large number of people with an inadequate amount of food. Both stories specify the number of hungry persons (one hundred in the Old Testament, five thousand and four thousand—a much greater miracle!—in the New). Both stories specify the amount of food available (twenty loaves in the Old Testament, five and seven—again a greater miracle—in the New). In both stories, the prophets instruct their disciples to feed the people, and in both the disciples protest the inadequate amount of food: Elisha's disciple complains "I cannot set this before a hundred men" (2 Kings 4:43), while Jesus' disciples ask "How can anyone provide all these people with bread?" (Mark 8:5). Finally, in both stories, the inadequate amount of food is miraculously amplified to feed all present, so much so that there are leftovers: "and they ate, and left some over" (2 Kings 4:44); "they all ate to their hearts content, and seven baskets were filled with the scraps that were left" (Mark 8:9). Mark's two stories, in chapters 6 and 8, about the miraculous increase of food, clearly stem from the story of Elisha's miracle in 2 Kings 4. In Mark's accounts, however, there are no direct verbal relationships with the source story; but there is such a direct literary connection between John's version and the Greek Septuagint translation of the book of Kings, the version of the Old Testament usually quoted by the New Testament writers. The miracle of the loaves and fishes is one of the very few synoptic miracle stories also found in the Fourth Gospel, and John's version shows specifically its source in Septuagint 4 Kings. In Mark's account, it is the disciples who have the loaves of bread, but in John's version, it is a "boy" *(paidarion)* who holds the five loaves of barley *(artous krithinous),* just as in the Septuagint it is the servant or boy *(paidarion)* of Elisha who has the barley loaves *(artous krithinous).* John's story was clearly composed by a Greek-speaking Christian who based it directly on a copy of the Septuagint open before him as he wrote. The story was either composed directly from the Greek, thence entering John's Gospel, and was corrupted in oral tradition before reaching the Synoptics, Mark first; or else it was composed in the Aramaic tradition out of the Old Testament and "corrected" on the basis of the Septuagint by John or his source. In either case, the story of the miracle of the loaves and fishes is a self-reflexive fiction, based on the New Testament understanding of the mirroring of Jesus' career in the Old Testament.

The miracle story of the stilling of the storm, found in the three synoptic Gospels, shows not only the formative power of an Old Testament story—the book of Jonah—but also the fictional creative power of one evangelist, Matthew, in correcting and improving his written source—in this case, the Gospel of Mark—to make it align more closely with what he regarded as historical reality. As it happens, that "historical reality" is in fact Mark's unrecognized source in the Old Testament, which Matthew reads *through* Mark in order to correct Mark.

The two stories about the stilling of the storm—in Jonah and the synoptic Gospels—begin in Psalm 107.

> At his command the storm-wind rose
> > and lifted the waves high.
> Carried up to heaven, plunged down to the depths,
> > tossed to and fro in peril,
> they reeled and staggered like drunken men,
> > and their seamanship was all in vain.
> So they cried to the LORD in their trouble,
> > and he brought them out of their distress.
> The storm sank to a murmur
> > and the waves of the sea were stilled.
> They were glad then that all was calm,
> > as he guided them to the harbour they desired.
>
> > > > > (Ps. 107:25-30)

From this famous and imaginatively fruitful passage we can trace the development of two separate fictional narratives, one about Jonah, one about Jesus.

When the author of Jonah wanted to present a narrative about the stilling of a storm, he consulted this psalm for some of his details. In Jonah, the Lord sends a great storm and a high sea (1:4), as in the psalm, at the Lord's "command the storm-wind rose and lifted the waves high."

In Jonah, the sailors "rowed hard to put back to land, but in vain" (1:13), as in the psalm, "their seamanship was all in vain." The sailors "called on the LORD and said, O LORD, do not let us perish" (Jon. 1:14); in the psalm, "they cried to the LORD in their trouble." In Jonah, "the sea stopped raging" (1:15), and in the psalm, "the storm sank to a murmur, and the waves of the sea were stilled." In Jonah, the "crew were filled with the fear of the LORD and offered sacrifice and made vows to him" (1:16), as in the psalm, those saved from the storm are advised to "offer sacrifice of thanksgiving."

Early Christians regarded the career of Jonah as a type, a prefiguring, of the career of Jesus. As Matthew put it, Jesus' generation would be given the "sign of the prophet Jonah"; for as "Jonah was in the sea-monster's belly for three days and three nights, . . . in the same way the Son of Man will be three days and three nights in the bowels of the earth" (Matt. 12:39-40). Likewise, if the Lord stilled the sea in the case of Jonah, the same must happen in the case of Jesus. Mark was the first of the evangelists to write the story; he received it from Greek-speaking Christian tradition and did not seem to be aware of its source in the book of Jonah. In the story, we find Jesus' disciples ferrying him across the Sea of Galilee in an open fishing boat,

> A heavy squall came on and the waves broke over the boat until it was all but swamped. Now he was in the stern asleep on a cushion; they roused him and said, "Master, we are perishing! Do you not care?" He awoke, rebuked the wind, and said to the sea, "Hush! Be still!" The wind dropped and there was a dead calm. He said to them, "Why are you such cowards? Have you no faith even now?" They were awestruck and said to one another, "Who can this be? Even the wind and the sea obey him." (Mark 4:37-41)

Either Mark or his source was aware of this story's relationship to the psalms, for in the story Jesus' statement to the sea uses the vocabulary of Ps. 105 (106) LXX: as Jesus "rebuked" (*epetimēsen*) the Red Sea (105:9 LXX). Though we cannot be sure whether Mark regarded his story of the stilling of the storm as prefigured in the Old Testament, it is quite clear that Matthew did regard the story thus, for he rewrote Mark's account, deliberately changing its vocabulary so it would align with the language of the Septuagint "predictions."

Matthew got his first clue from the statement in Mark about Jesus' rebuking the sea. Clearly familiar with the Septuagint psalms, Matthew went back to the source of this remark and proceeded with its guidance.

Whereas Mark had written that the waves "broke over [*epeballen*] the boat until it was all but swamped [*gemizesthai*]," Matthew preferred to write that the boat was being "covered [*kalyptesthai*] by the waves" (Matt. 8:24). He did this because he knew that in the very psalm in which the Lord "rebuked" the Red Sea (the psalm lying behind part of Mark's vocabulary), the water "covered" *(ekalypsen)* the Egyptians. And just as the Lord's mighty acts were seen as "wonders" *(thaumasia),* so too the disciples "wondered" *(ethaumasan)* at Jesus' act (Ps. 105:7 LXX; Matt. 8:27).

And though Mark may not have known that his story of the stilling of the storm was based in part on the book of Jonah, Matthew certainly knew, for again he rewrote his version of Mark's narrative on the basis of Jonah, chapter 1, which he recognized as a predictive type of the story of Jesus. Matthew was unhappy with the disciples' rude remark to Jesus in Mark: "we are perishing! Do you not care?" so he changed the statement: "Save us, Lord, we are perishing" (Matt. 8:25). If we look at the Septuagint of Jonah, the version Matthew used, we find the reason Matthew felt justified in making such a change in Mark. Matthew saw that the source of part of the disciples' speech in Mark was the speech of the sailors in Jonah: as they say, "Forbid it, Lord. Let us not perish [*medamōs, Kyrie. Mē apoplōmetha*]" (Jonah 1:14 LXX); the disciples say to Jesus, "we perish [*apollumetha*]" (Mark 4:38). But Matthew also observed that the ship's captain says to Jonah, "call upon thy God, that God may save us, and we perish not [*hopōs diasōse ho Theos hemas, kai ou mē apolometha*]" (Jonah 1:6 LXX). Thus Matthew takes the key words from Jonah—"Lord," and "save us,"and "we perish"—and rewrites Mark's account accordingly. Matthew's version of the stilling of the storm is a fictional correction of Mark's fictional account, each based in its own way on the Old Testament.

With this in mind, we may grasp the nature of the rest of the miracle story as Mark first wrote it. Does it seem strange that Jesus could sleep in the stern of a small, open fishing-boat in the middle of a storm so violent that the waves were breaking over the vessel and filling it with water? The answer is that Jesus' "sleep" is not a description of an event but a literary necessity, a "fulfilment" of what was taken to be an accurate typological prediction: "Jonah had gone down into a corner of the ship and was lying sound asleep when the captain came upon him. 'What, sound asleep?' he said. 'Get up, and call on your god'" (Jon. 1:5-6). Does it seem strange that Mark delays in saying that the disciples were afraid until *after* the storm has been stilled, writing that they were frightened at the stilling, not at the storm? The answer again is that the story presents not an event but an antitype, a literary fiction built from a supposed prefigurement; for after the storm is stilled in Jonah, we learn that the men "feared [*ephbethēsan*] the Lord with great fear [*phobō megalō*]" (Jon. 1:16 LXX), just as in Mark, after the sea is calmed, the disciples "feared very greatly [*ephobēthēsan phobon megan*]" (Mark 4:41).

NOTES

1. Northrop Frye, *Harper Handbook to Literature*, 191.
2. Northrop Frye, *The Great Code*, 78.
3. Ernst Käsemann, *Essays on New Testament Themes*, 48.
4. Matt. 11:2-5.

R. Joseph Hoffmann*

Other Gospels, Heretical Christs

At the outset it is necessary to state what I mean by the title "Other Gospels, Heretical Christs." What I do not propose to deal with—at least not in detail—are the so-called apocryphal gospels and their various representations of Jesus. Not that these gospels are unworthy of attention: it would be great fun indeed to talk about the precocious little Jesus of the *Infancy Gospel of Thomas* who makes clay pigeons and causes them to fly, then slays a playmate who has vexed him with only a word; or the Jesus of the *Gospel of Peter,* who is seen by the guards posted outside his tomb on Easter morning bearing his cross, his head arching high above the clouds; or the Jesus of the *Gospel of Nicodemus* who batters down the gates of hell, binds Satan in irons, and leads Adam and the patriarchs out of captivity into heaven; or the gnostic Jesus of the *Gospel of Philip,* who is said to love Mary Magdalene more than the other disciples and offends his followers by kissing her hard and often on the mouth. Our attitude toward these tendentious literary creations may be shock or amusement; perhaps among university undergraduates it is more often than not something closer to amazement that so much material exists outside the fences of the New Testament canon, material that for one reason or another is disqualified from membership in the body of inspired books. But as I say, my subject here is not the fictional elaboration of the four gospels. It is rather the relation of the four gospels to each other, and only then their relation to extracanonical materials.

Simply stated, my argument is that every gospel is tendentious in relation to any other; that is to say, every gospel has its own reason for being written, and that reason is quite independent of its reason for being in the canon.

---

*R. Joseph Hoffmann is Associate Professor of Ancient and Biblical Studies at the University of Michigan, Ann Arbor.

By this standard, every New Testament gospel is other than the one before it: different in terms of the author's intention in writing it; different, often markedly so, in its view of the Christ; different in respect of the audience to which it was originally addressed; and different in terms of the purpose it was intended to serve in the Christian community. By this standard as well, every Christ is to a certain extent heretical when measured by the yardstick, theological or literary, of any other gospel. To talk about the Jesus of the gospels is rather like talking about the Christian church: everybody might agree that there is such a thing, but just as surely everybody disagrees about what it is or where it is: Is its center Rome; Lynchburg, Virginia; Salt Lake City; or the heart of every believer? Just so with the Jesus of the gospels: we may be quite certain that a historical personage with a specific identity and a particular message is buried beneath these terribly uncooperative literary and theological creations, but he has, as Schweitzer ably showed in his *Quest of the Historical Jesus,* persistently refused historical capture, and he has done so, ironically, because the gospels cover rather than illuminate his identity. Is he the preexistent logos who can say to his disciples, "I am in the father and the father is in me" (John 14:11); or the affrighted victim who just before the kill can cry "Abba—Father—take this cup from me?" Is he the heretical rabbi of Matthew's story, who announces that not one stroke of the law may be abolished before the final consummation (Matt. 5:18f.), or the Jesus of Mark's gospel who specifies which transgressions defile a Christian and declares all foods clean? Again, is the real Jesus the Jesus of Mark's account, who initially refuses to help a Greek woman whose daughter is possessed because the woman is not a Jew and is hence, to use the language ascribed to Jesus, a dog; or the Jesus of the Fourth Gospel who, in spite of the risk of defilement, begs a drink of a Samaritan woman (John 4.8; Mark 7:24)?

What we do know or can know, little as it is, we know not from the gospels but from the interstices between them: from reading between the theological and apologetic lines and listening as closely to what is not being said by an evangelist as to what actually is said. This may seem a cynical way to approach books that have been so highly regarded for so long: Aren't such scholarly habits really based on one's own personal wish to see divine revelation discredited, a misuse of reason, as Cardinal Newman described the rationalist biblical interpretations of his day?

It seems to me that there are two reasons for rejecting the notion that a reading of the gospels that emphasizes their otherness, their inherent differences, reflects only a wish to dismember the claims of Christianity.

First, Christianity bases its distinctive claims not on the law as a revelation of God's will, as does Judaism, or on a prophetic revelation, as does Islam, but on what theologians call a particular revelation. This means, simply put, that the truth claims of Christianity are tied to historical events, but more especially to a historical person in a way that is not typical of other religions. Its claim to truth is a claim that must be decided based on what is asserted of a historical figure who is, by orthodox Christians, believed to be God incarnate. Given such a claim, it is obvious that our best and only roughly contemporary documents dealing with this figure, the gospels and the letters of Paul, must bear careful scrutiny, scrutiny being the nether part of reverence.

Second, we must acknowledge that the canon, that is, the collection of twenty-seven books we know as the New Testament, is itself a historical development. Space is too limited to outline the rather complicated evolution of this body of literature, but in any discussion of the canon two things must be observed: first, that there is no widely recognized inventory or list of books that corresponds exactly to our canon until the year 367, when the champion of the doctrine of the trinity, Athanasius of Alexandria, names them in a famous Easter letter to the churches in his jurisdiction. Second, in the writings of the major church fathers before the fourth century there is a wide difference of opinion about what should and what should not be regarded as sacred—inspired—scripture. Irenaeus, for example, in the second century, does not acknowledge the authority of 2 and 3 John, James, or 2 Peter, while Clement of Alexandria recognizes some obscure works such as the *Preaching of Peter* and the *Apocalypse of Peter* as being inspired. It was not until 692 that the church decided on the acceptability of the book of Revelation, and even then there was considerable grumbling among the Greek bishops about its status. It is certainly the case that the four gospels we possess achieved popularity and prestige long before the closure of the canon; but by the same token, we cannot use the closed canon of the fourth century as a way around the theological and literary differences between sources that were compiled before a definitive canon had emerged. Bluntly put, the canon does not settle these differences; it freezes them into a permanent structure.

These two considerations—the particularity of Christian claims about Jesus Christ and the articulation of these claims in a body of literature regarded by the vast majority of Christians as inspired, "God breathed," and authoritative—are tied together in such a way that no separation of them is possible. Thus, history and historical study are relevant to Christianity in a way that cannot be set aside in favor of groundless theological premises concerning the way in which revelation operates in scripture: if Christian revelation is historical revelation, expressed in human language, then it is either meant to be understood or it is not. Since the idea of revelation presupposes the disclosure of some truth, it is simply nonsensical to talk about the problems of text and language and the like as though such problems were God's way of keeping truths hidden or his way of asserting the primacy of faith over reason. As the god of Christian theism is thought to be a god of peace and not of confusion, I should prefer to think that his peace extends to the orderly investigation of biblical texts.

In the next few pages, I want to illustrate what I have described as the otherness of the gospels—their wide-going differences from each other—and also to suggest why these differences are important for the understanding of the New Testament.

At a crucial moment in the Gospel of Mark, Jesus is depicted as giving his disciples a kind of pop quiz: "Who do the people say that I am?" The answer comes back that some are saying he is John the Baptist, others Elijah, others one of the prophets. Indeed, Mark reveals people are saying all kinds of things, and no one is getting it just right, at least not in Mark's view. So he urges Jesus to ask a second question, this time directly of the disciples: Who do you say that I am? To this Peter responds "You are the Christ." Taking Mark's cue, Matthew's Peter replies "You are the Christ, the son of the living God" (16:16), thus splicing together two originally discrete titles. Luke's Peter responds, "You are the Christ of God" (Luke 9:20). The Fourth Gospel, traditionally ascribed to John, finds all this secrecy and circumspection rather wearying and so provides a Jesus who announces rather than inquires about his divinity: "I do not rely on human testimony," he says (John 5:34), "My testimony is valid even though I do proclaim myself, because I know where I come from and where I am going" (John 8:14). John's Jesus announces a dazzling array of things about himself: he is the light of the world, the bread of life, the preexistent logos of God, the true vine, the good shepherd. Not only is he a good controversialist and a creator of powerful signs, but he also shows a knack for metaphor and paradox that the apocalyptic prophet of the earlier gospels seems to lack. All this would seem ordinary enough if it were not the case that the Jesus of the Fourth Gospel and the Jesus of the synoptics do not merely have different technical vocabularies. They also say different things about themselves in language so markedly dissimilar that scholars have long since concluded that the Fourth Gospel must be a theological characterization—if anything—of the things said by Jesus, a "spiritual gospel," as Clement of Alexandria called it. That is indeed a handy way around the problem. It is also a dog that will not hunt. We are beyond the point where it is possible to let John off the hook by reading his version of the sayings of Jesus as though it was his intention merely to epitomize the essence of what Jesus said or meant to say. More than any other writer, the author of the Fourth Gospel means for his record to be taken strictly and claims to have inside, shall we say cultic, knowledge of what Jesus said. How do we know this?

In chapter 21 we find a bewildered Peter asking after the welfare of the beloved disciple, who is following along behind Peter and the risen Christ. "When he caught sight of him Peter asked, 'Lord, what will happen to him,' and Jesus said, 'If it should be my will that he wait until I come, what is that to you.'" That saying of Jesus became current in the brotherhood and was taken to mean that the disciple would not die, but in fact Jesus did not say that he would not die; he only said, "If it should be my will that he wait until I come, what is that to you." Obviously the situation that occasions this kind of explanation, tortuous as it is, must be the death of the founder of a Christian community, someone whose prestige was guaranteed by his claim to have seen Jesus, to have been a close follower of Jesus, and someone who claimed to have been promised or was expected to be alive at the time of the second coming. His death has thrown the community into doubt, just as the deaths of some Christians at Thessalonica cause Paul to write that church a reassuring letter about the end of the world. Not content with saying that the death of the disciple is not contradictory of anything Jesus may have promised, the writer ends his gospel with the unlikely assertion that "Indeed, it is this same disciple who attests what has been written. It is in fact he who wrote it, and we know that his testimony is true." Preoccupied as he is with exactness of expression and the problem of authority and witness, problems he has tried to solve by making evidence and authority central concerns of his Christ (cf. John 7:15ff.; 8.54ff.; 10.37ff, etc.), we cannot conclude that John means merely to offer a characterization of Jesus' words. No, he means them to be taken as signed, sealed, and delivered by the disciple. And if this is so, then all the theological maneuvering and imaginative sidestepping in the world (and my colleagues and I have seen a bit) cannot alter the fact that the Jesus of the Fourth Gospel and the Jesus of the synoptics—Matt, Mark, and Luke—are very different Jesuses.

Now I suppose it is tempting to think something like the following: John, being the later gospel, must represent the later view, the more developed Christology. Therefore, the view of Jesus in the gospel that can be shown to be the earliest must bring us nearest to the historical Jesus—

closest to what he actually said and did. This intuition can be supported if we are also inclined to emphasize, as Schweitzer did at the beginning of this century, that the historical Jesus was radically apocalyptic in his own outlook; he expected the end of the world to occur within his own lifetime, or at latest in the lifetime of his hearers. "Truly, I say to you," says Matthew's Jesus, "you will not have gone through all the towns of Israel before the Son of Man comes." As it did not happen as predicted, these words must be authentically Jesus', for no one would have wished to preserve his errors unless the prediction was so early and so undeniably his view that it has been embedded in the gospels. Further, manipulations of the text, as in Mark 13:32 where Jesus is given to say that no one knows when the end will come, not even the son but the father alone, show attempts to soften the impact of the delay of the second coming and the final catastrophe. Thus was the historical Jesus a preacher of apocalyptic woes, goes the thinking, and any view of Jesus that minimizes the apocalyptic aspect of his teaching must be a step further away from the historical figure. On this premise, the gospel of John is furthest away of all, since its Jesus is preoccupied with himself and not the end of the world. But, as Professor Wells has so well reminded us, there are problems with using the apocalyptic context as a standard to which the historical Jesus might be expected to conform, and reasoning our way round to the conclusion that the historical Jesus was an apocalyptic teacher.

What I mean by this is that the context exists quite apart from any particular expression of it. The fact that the Jesus of the early writers expresses views about the end of the world is no more an argument for his historicity than is the existence of a tradition of deifying kings, philosophers, and especially capable military leaders proof of their divinity. It is one of the oddities and perhaps one of the most unfortunate legacies of German theological scholarship that the discovery of a Jesus who might have been wrong about the timing of the end of the world resulted in elevating wrongness—or empirical disconfirmation or dissimilarity between forecast and outcome, to use the more elegant language—to the level of a methodological principle to be used in sorting out what Jesus might have said from what he might not have said. To give only a trivial analogy, I do not normally count a weatherman's errors as his only true words simply because I count it likelier that he should be wrong about the weather than that he should predict it accurately. By the same token, I can argue that it is as likely that Jesus said things that corresponded to an eventual outcome as that he made mistakes that needed to be remedied, in some fashion, by his followers. There is simply no way of knowing about the former, that is, what he may have predicted himself, since we disbelieve in prophecy even more than we disbelieve weathermen. Lacking criteria for what the histori- cal Jesus might have said, we are stuck with the plain fact that the evangel- ists wanted their ^ommunities to think that Jesus said the things they said he said.

We are also stuck with the fact that however we may finally sort out the so-called synoptic problem, that is, the literary relationships of the gospels, and the connection between the synoptic gospels and John, we have in the New Testament a Jesus who says very different things in different and even contradictory ways. I do not wish to go into the mani- fold problems that attach to such a statement: I recognize of course that adherents of the doctrine of divine inspiration can invoke it at random to make any discrepancy a fault of human perception rather than a fault of the texts. But my own want of perception is not for me a satisfactory explanation of why in John 14:28 Jesus is given to say "The father is greater than I," while in John 10:30 he reports, "I and the father are one"; or why on a rather niggling level the disciples are charged by the Jesus of Matthew's gospel to go barefoot and not to take a staff with them, while in Mark 6:8 the apostles are instructed to wear sandals and to carry a staff. I have no way of explaining it, that is, unless I begin with the assumption, one that I regard as absurd, that the God who inspired the evangelists caused them to include these disparities as a test of people's faith, rather like the way the God of Israel tested Abraham's faith by asking him to set aside his better instincts for the sake of obedience to some higher design. I detect no such design in the gospels; I detect rather the voice and purpose of the evangelists in the voice of Jesus. I hear about communities who believed widely different things about who Jesus was and what he taught and how he died and where he was seen after his death by believing followers who, according to Luke, had hoped he was the Messiah of Israel. These different voices, none of which can be equated with the voice of Jesus, are all attempts—earnest ones, I think—to answer the question, "Who do men say that I am?" That verse is the decisive one because it suggests quite clearly that the historical Jesus is not being offered up by any New Testament writer as a subject for biography or intellectual assent. Whatever the cross-purposes of the evangelists, none of them has it as his goal to prove the existence of Jesus. The Jesus about whom they write is simply a subject for their interpretation, a creature of their faith. And what they say about him they say in order to evoke the faith of others: These things here written, says the author of the Fourth Gospel, have been recorded so that you might hold the faith that Jesus is the Christ, the Son of God, and that through this faith "you may possess life in his name." Nothing could be clearer than that what is included in a gospel is determined by its propagandistic value, its power to persuade and proclaim. Yet for the same reason, we are badly mistaken to make a jump from the discrepancies in the gospels, most of which residuate from these theological cross-purposes, to the notion that nothing was known about him, or that the gospels are the contrivance, as Bruno Bauer once reckoned, of a second-century writer who knew very well that no such character had ever lived.

Given Bauer's premises, his conclusion is not an unfamiliar one. Those who hold, to use the language of the liturgy, the holy Catholic faith that comes to us from the apostles are bound to think any fault in the structure of the faith comes from the malice of the originators of the tradition. Indeed, even Marcion thought so in the second century and acted on the assumption by reducing the New Testament to one gospel, much altered in substance, and a few of Paul's letters, perhaps the first attempt to restore some semblance of order to these wayward reports. Luke's gospel, as we can judge from his intention in chapter 1 of his work, was another; there can be no question that he has wearied of the reports circulating about him and undertakes to provide an account to end all accounts, one he says is based on the testimony of eyewitnesses. Indeed, it must be a travesty of Luke's intention that his work was finally included in a canon of four disparate gospels, one account among other accounts. And I think, judging from the last chapters of John, the same can be said for the Fourth Gospel; it was never meant for inclusion among the others, but was intended to become the gospel to end all gospels.

Our own sense of frustration at the diversity of reports and sayings and stories must also have been Luke's and John's and Marcion's: we are not the first to feel slightly cheated at the ways in which the question "Who do men say that I am" has been answered. But we do a foul injustice to the integrity of the gospels when we imagine that these four ever wished to move into the same neighborhood. Thus the facile evangelical dilemma—either the gospels are true or else Jesus was a liar or a madman—begins with the false assumption that the point of view represented in the gospels is univocal, and, perhaps worse, that it is univocally Jesus' view. I would quite agree that a man who commanded secrecy in one gospel and then went about openly proclaiming himself equal to God in another, and who taught in one place that the end of the world would be preceded by specific signs and in another that no signs would be given to "this wicked generation" might be quite mad. I would agree to this if I regarded any of these things as being attributable to Jesus himself. But I do not. As a historian, the discrepancies I see belong to a text, and not to the historical figure: they belong not to biography but to the Christian mission. By its nature, missionary literature looks as much to its audience for confirmation as it does to its subject for definition. It is the sort of literature that might tend to rationalize Jesus' deadline for the end of the world or show him the intellectual better in disputes with Pharisaic teachers. It is the sort of literature that might, depending on its audience, portray him saying positive things about the law in one case and negative things in another, or advising people to pay taxes, in response to the suggestion (as Luke frames the charge) that he subverts the nation by opposing the payment of taxes to Caesar (23:1). It is the sort of literature in which an original picture of the apostles as slow and even obstinate pupils of the master might need to be revised to make them the very eyewitnesses on whom the report depends, as indeed Luke reverses it in his account of the encounter between the apostles and the risen Christ. The revision of sources, it should be stressed, does not arise from an interest in providing a more historical view based on better information. Luke, it is true, constructs a historical framework for his sources and offers us the closest thing to a chronicle he can manage. He gives, for example, a genealogy that tells us that the birth of Jesus took place during the reign of Augustus and in the time Herod was king of Judaea, and even that John began ministering to people in the fifteenth year of the emperor Tiberius. But he also tells us that the angel Gabriel was sent from God with a message to Joseph in the sixth month of Elizabeth's pregnancy, and ends his ninth chapter with this historical marker: "As the time approached when he was to be taken up to heaven, Jesus set his face resolutely toward Jerusalem and sent messengers ahead" (9:51f.). This curious blend of the historical and suprahistorical reveals nothing so clearly as Luke's theological premise that the saving event of Jesus Christ can be located *in* history, and that in itself is a theological, not a historical, assertion.

To say that the New Testament writers are not especially interested in the historical Jesus is also to say that there is notable continuity between the gospels and the letters of Paul. Paul, it is well known, shows a positive disregard for the historical Jesus: What does knowing Jesus according to the flesh mean, he asks, when we know him now only as the risen Christ and Lord. Doubtless, Paul's disregard of historical tradition says less of what he may or may not know about the historical data (and from Galatians 4, it appears he knows something) than that he is forced by those in authority in Jerusalem to defend his right to preach the gospel on what the super-apostles, as he calls them, consider spurious grounds. I myself consider the Gospel of Mark to bear the imprint of Paul's polemic against his predecessors in the faith, and I would not be surprised to learn that the earliest gospel text emerged in Pauline circles. It is undeniable, however, that within the framework of the synoptic tradition, this is a Jesus who gradually becomes more historicized, and, not surprisingly considering Luke's view of Paul's mission as being subordinate to that of the Twelve, most historicized in Luke's account. This would entail, of course, that one of Luke's purposes in writing his gospel was to supply the framework by which the authority of the original eyewitnesses could be maintained against the claims of Paul and his followers to possess the true gospel of Jesus Christ. Nor am I convinced that Paul's references to this gospel, as in Galatians 1, can be shrugged aside as general references to his preaching, simply on the grounds that he never actually tells stories familiar to us from the canonical accounts. The evolution of the gospel tradition begins with Paul, and not with Mark's adaptation of the Pauline message.

This leads us to the conclusion that a purely biographical interest in Jesus is absent from the earliest phase in the history of the gospels, and only emerges as the raw and unruly kerygma begins to require the sort of historical grounding that an audience, increasingly curious about the when and where of the events proclaimed by Paul, asserts itself. Without doubt, however, this emphasis would amount to a kind of heresy from Paul's point of view, just as from Luke's Paul having been made an apostle on his own recognizance, without approval of the Twelve, is heretical.

The gospels are not biographies. If they were so intended they would be worthless. If they were, we would know nothing about Jesus' family because the fabricated genealogies of Matthew and Luke are self-evidently apologetic in purpose. We would know nothing of a birth in Bethlehem, as do neither Mark nor John; indeed, John denies such a provenance for Jesus (7:52). We would not know who killed him, whether his was an orderly crucifixion carried out by the Romans as Mark wants grudgingly to suggest, or whether he was a victim of Jewish mob justice as John tries incoherently to maintain. We would not know what happened at the site of the grave: whether one woman arrived at the tomb in Jerusalem, found it empty, and ran to tell Peter, who remained in Jerusalem after the crucifixion; or whether a score of women went to the tomb, found it empty, and ran back to tell Peter and the rest; or whether three women, finding the tomb empty, were instructed to tell a Peter who had already returned to Galilee about the resurrection, but, because they were afraid, said nothing to anyone. With respect to the resurrection we should expect uniformity in the story, but we get none. Instead, we get traditions particular to different communities—Matthew's, Mark's, Luke's, and John's—views that a later editor of Mark's gospel has tried to harmonize with the rather slipshod addition of some twelve verses. Taken together, however, it is pretty obvious that the stories about the resurrection enshrined in our gospels and elsewhere, as in Acts 10, where no appearances other than to the apostles are cited (Acts 10:40) and in Paul's first letter to the Corinthians (15:5), where an appearance to over five hundred at once is mentioned, are the fanciful contrivances of early Christian storytellers. And this recognition undergirds the point I have tried to make in this little essay. The gospel writers were not interested in harmonizing their views, but in saying particular things in a particular way to communities with particular interests. The need to protect certain views of Jesus is a dominant element in the composition of the gospels, nor does any gospel exist that does not betray its writer's wish to supersede the others in some fashion.

What does all of this mean for the study of the gospels—this fact of their uncooperativeness on the literary and theological level? In the first place it means, I think, that we cannot expect a gospel to yield information about Jesus as a biography yields information about its subject. They are, in the main, spiritual exercises written by men already committed to the view that Jesus was the Christ and Son of God, and motivated by the desire to get others to accept that belief. Yet Paul's complaint about the preaching of gospels and Christs other than the one he is preaching (Gal. 1:1f.) suggests that already in the forties there was no agreed view of how these theological views should be expressed. This does not mean that the gospels yield no factually significant information about Jesus; it does mean that what they yield is not primarily factual. What they yield primarily are the views of their writers and the various Christian communities whose views these writers represent.

But, it may be asked, is there any level at which the disagreements, the otherness of the gospels, disappears? After all, many of us are less concerned with knowing how many angels were in the tomb on Easter morning, or how many donkeys Jesus rode into Jerusalem, or how many demoniacs were living among the Gerasene tombs than with the historical truth of the resurrection or the possibility of miracles. To talk of discrepancies in the accounts of things we can no longer believe may seem foolish to any rationalist who has made the mistake of looking beneath the waters of the Sea of Galilee for the stones that supported Jesus on his walk across the water. Their assumption, of course, is that nothing mythical is true, and that the elimination of anything that smacks of the supernatural from the gospel accounts leaves one with a residue of historical fact. I am sorry to report that that is not the way it works, for the gospels are less factual in one sense than the rationalists have given them credit for being, and truer in another than their mythological content and structure would lead one to believe. What is important to emphasize is that they are the products of belief, and it is very difficult to approach them when the beliefs they embody have been, a priori, rejected. Certainly one cannot believe contradictions out of existence, or through belief provide the coherent biography of Jesus that the gospels fail to supply. At the very least, however, an appreciation of their character as products of belief helps us to avoid the mistake of faulting them where no fault lies. If I may use an Old Testament analogy: to use the gospels as biographical sources is like using Genesis as a science textbook. Clearly, the authors of Genesis imagined no such use for their work; their task was simply to declare God the author of the created order. It is we who are mistaken when we overlook the kerygmatic function of a religious book and require of it things for which it was never intended. And just as Genesis was not intended to teach science to high-school students, the gospels are not intended to prove the existence of Jesus. By the same token, the absence of this intention need not lead us to think that no historical person stands behind the narratives. I suspect that the Jesus of Sunday-school piety and church sermons is as vague and anemic as he is because preachers and priests persistently try to make him a man of the present, an object of history, and more often of our history rather than his own. He has been made into a man whose teachings can be studied, his life and goals imitated, his personality known through a careful synthesis of appealing texts. So and only so can he be the Jesus of the IRA and of the British establishment, the Jesus of the Afrikaaners and of Bishop Tutu, of the German Greens and the Salvadoran reds. It is almost pointless to say that these Jesuses and all who have gone before them have merely an ideological existence, pointless because the Jesus of the gospels has precisely *that* sort of existence and in that sense is no more historical—no more real—than the Jesus of the political and religious special interests. If I may, however, I would like to say a word in favor of the four gospels and their heretical Christs: Unlike the artificially consistent Jesus of the ideologies, the Jesus of the gospels exists in tension with himself. In proclaiming him the evangelists can almost be heard saying, "No—he was like this"; "No—he must have done this"; "No—he must have said this." I detect in this desire for getting it right not only the special interest of the evangelist, or the community; I detect uncertainty as well, and this uncertainty, by a chance of history, has been frozen into existence in the canon. What this means, for good or ill, is that the Jesus of the gospels is an iconoclastic standard against which the Jesuses of doctrine, trend, and fad are sure to crumble. As they are singular, he is persistently plural; as their vision is clear, his is ambiguous; as their Jesuses are modern, the Jesus of the gospels belongs to the past. "The historical Jesus," wrote Schweitzer, "will be to our time a stranger and an enigma." That, to be blunt about it, is what the gospels have made him.

Robert M. Grant*

The Christ at the Creation

THE COSMIC CHRIST

Before the Christian gospels were written, the apostle Paul, who knew Jesus as one who, crucified and risen, had revealed himself to him, made an astounding confession about the cosmic Jesus Christ in a "credal" passage in 1 Cor. 8:6. Though pagans might accept "many gods" or "many lords," Christians believed in

> one God, the Father,
>> *from* whom are all things, and
>> *for* whom we exist, and
> one Lord Jesus Christ,
>> *through* whom are all things,
> and
>> *through* whom we exist.

The universe was created through the crucified and exalted Messiah whom Paul proclaimed in his preaching.

Whether or not Paul wrote Colossians, it too contains an awesome Christological statement. Christ is

> the image of the invisible God,
> the first-born of all creation; for
>> *in* him all things were created, in heaven and on
> earth,
>> visible and invisible,—

*Robert M. Grant is Professor of Early Christian Literature at the University of Chicago.

> whether thrones or dominions or principalities
> or authorities—
> all things were created
> *through* him and
> *for* him. He is
> *before* all things, and
> *in* him all things hold together. (Col. 1:15-17, RSV)

Or, again,

> *In* the beginning was the Word,
> and the Word was *with* God.
> and the Word was God.
> He was *in* the beginning *with* God;
> all things were made *through* him,
> and *without* him was not anything made that was made.
>
> (John 1:1-3, RSV)

Within a few decades after the crucifixion, then, Christians were taught that the Christ had been God's agent in creation. The claim was startling but not unique. The supreme Father resembled the supreme Zeus of pagan worship, while the work of the Lord Christ was much the same as that of the various lesser gods, usually sons or daughters of Zeus, to whom cosmic functions were assigned, as we shall see. Converts to Christianity could recognize that Jesus, the Son of God, did what the cosmic gods did. But Christians were speaking of a human being whose crucifixion was "a stumbling-block to Jews and foolishness to gentiles." The notion was paradoxical, as Paul well knew. "For those who are called, both Jews and Greeks, Christ [is] the power of God and the wisdom of God" (1 Cor. 1:23f.). The later passages in Colossians and John do no more than re-affirm the basic statement in 1 Corinthians.

Pagans made similar statements about their gods, but Christians denied the reality of these gods and held that Christ was the only Demiurge (shaper or fashioner) to have existed.

POSSIBLE ORIGINS OF THE IDEA

An important modification of Jewish monotheism is already present in the book of Proverbs, where God's Wisdom is personified. God creates or generates her to be his agent in the creation of the world. This text was to be especially meaningful for Hellenistic Jews and Christians who thought about cosmic mediators. For Hellenistic Jews the evidence comes from Sirach, the Wisdom of Solomon, and Philo; for Christians, from the passages we have already cited, especially 1 Corinthians and Colossians. In 1917 Rendel Harris published a collection of texts to show that everything in John's prologue, except for the *Incarnatus est,* could be paralleled in the Wisdom literature.[1]

There is one obvious difference between John and the others. In Greek the word *sophia* is feminine, while *logos* is masculine. Presumably the change was welcomed by those who shared Philo's view that the divine wisdom really ought to be masculine. Philo was pleased to discover that Bethuel, which means "daughter of God," was a name applied to a male in Gen. 28:2. This enabled him to say that "while Wisdom's name is feminine, her nature is manly." Wisdom is called feminine just because she is second and inferior to the masculine Maker of the Universe. "Pre-eminence always pertains to the masculine, and the feminine always comes short of and is lesser than it."[2] We may hope that John did not fully share this view even though he did change the name from Wisdom to Word.

Some have tried to relate Wisdom to oriental religion, specifically to ideas about the Hellenized Egyptian goddess Isis. According to the hypothesis of W. L. Knox, a cosmic presentation of Isis is served as a model for the goddesslike figure of Wisdom in Proverbs and related books.[3] Similarly Hans Conzelmann endeavored in "Die Mutter der Weisheit" to relate Sirach 24:3 and following to the Egyptian goddess.[4] The creation of the world was supposedly ascribed first to Isis, then to Wisdom. The theories of both Knox and Conzelmann are hard to prove, however, for cosmic theologizing about Isis comes almost entirely from the Greek world. The personal opinions of Plutarch and the religious experiences of Apuleius were set forth in the second century of our era, when the dossier of Greek texts provided by Werner Peek also arose,[5] as did the cultic equivalences noted in Oxyrhynchus papyrus XI 1380. All these are much later than the Proverbs passage and reflect Greek philosophical meditation rather than "oriental" musing.

We do not question the reality of Isis as a cosmic goddess in Greek circles. Later we shall take up the evidence in relation to oriental gods in the Hellenistic-Roman world. But this evidence proves nothing about the supposed derivation of Wisdom from Isis.

In Hellenistic Judaism we find Wisdom at the creation in about 150 B.C. when a certain Aristobulus provided exegesis of Genesis and insisted that the one God made the universe. He allowed the supreme god to use a mediator, however, stating that when God said, "Let there be light," the text might refer to Wisdom, "for all light is from her," and he cited Solomon in Prov. 8:22 for her existence before heaven and earth. Aristobulus thus referred to Wisdom as God's instrument in creation.

Philo of Alexandria wrote several centuries later and strongly influenced Christian thinkers. In his treatise *On the Creation* he referred to mediators as implied by Gen. 1:26: "Let *us* make," and elsewhere he laid emphasis on the work of such subordinates as Logos and Sophia, Word and Wisdom, calling them (among other things) the Son and the Daughter of God.

COSMIC INTERPRETATION OF THE LESSER PAGAN GODS

The doctrine of the cosmic Christ was proclaimed in a setting where the "many lords" were often related to the supreme god Zeus. These lesser gods could be expected to intervene in human affairs for the benefit of humanity and individuals, but beyond such interventions there was the supreme example of beneficence, as Plato had already intimated, in the creation of the world. Therefore several of the lesser gods came to be viewed as cosmic in nature.

In general the ideas were developed and expressed by religious-minded rhetoricians who tried to say as much as they could in praise of various gods. We should not suppose that they were creating a kind of pagan orthodox theology, though this was the way in which some ideas widely held and, indeed, often insisted upon came to prominence among both pagans and Christians.

We now examine the cosmic functions ascribed to some of the gods subordinate to Zeus, not discussing every case but a few of the most prominent ones. We expect to find not the source of Christian theological statements but rather environments in which Christian statements might be acceptable because they are familiar.

Cosmic Apollo

A third-century manual of rhetoric ascribed to Menander of Laodicea devotes a special chapter to the praises of Apollo, ending with the numerous alternative names of the god and noting even that "Persians call thee Mithras, Egyptians Horus, Thebans Dionysus."[6] Apollo can even be called Sun or Mind or Demiurge of all, for he abolished chaos and brought about order. The current powers of the god seem less impressive.

They are his skill in archery, in prediction, in medicine, and in music. The music is important, however, for the author believes that the universe moves in tune with Apollo's music.[7]

The cosmic role of Apollo is often expressed in what is said of the sun. In the sixteenth tractate of the *Corpus Hermeticum* the Sun is described as the Demiurge, subordinate to the supreme God (chap. 18), even though the name Apollo does not occur.

Cosmic Athena

Apollo's sister Athena was greater. In Plato's *Cratylus* (407B) she is already identified as the mind *(nous)* of God *(theos)*, though we never know how seriously Plato wanted his etymologies taken. The Stoic Chrysippus gave an allegorical explanation of the birth of Athena from the head of Zeus. Athena was Zeus's thought *(phronesis)*, coming out of his head. A pupil wrote "On Athena" and set forth the same doctrine. He was criticized for it not only by Cicero but also by a Christian apologist.[8]

The Christian apologist Justin mentions pagans who hold that Athena, the daughter of Zeus, was not generated from sexual intercourse. When Zeus considered *(ennoetheis)* making the world through his reason *(logos)*, his first thought *(ennoia)* was Athena. Justin comments rather feebly that "we consider it ridiculous that the image of a thought should be female in form."[9]

The orations *To Zeus* and *To Athena* by the late second-century rhetorician Aelius Aristides provide excellent parallels to Christian theology and indicate the environment in which this theology was acceptable and meaningful. The rhetor states that

> Zeus made everything and all things are works of Zeus; rivers and earth and sea and heaven and whatever is within these and whatever is beyond them, gods and men and whatever has life and whatever appears to sight and whatever one can think of. First he made himself, not the Cretan [Zeus] brought up in sweet-smelling caverns, nor did Kronos plan to consume him or consume a stone in his stead, nor was Zeus ever in danger or ever will be; there is nothing older than Zeus, for sons are not older than fathers nor things produced than those who make them, but he is first and oldest and chief of all, himself produced from himself. One cannot say when he came to be, but he was from the beginning and will be forever, father of himself and greater than one coming to be from another. And as Athena derived her nature from his head and he needed no partner to produce her, thus even earlier he made himself from himself and needed no

other for coming to be; on the contrary, everything began its existence from him.[10]

The relation of Zeus to Athena is described more fully in the other oration.

> He had nothing of the same rank from which to make her, but himself withdrawing into himself generated the goddess from himself and bore her, so that she alone is securely the genuine offspring of the Father, coming to be from a race equal to him and acknowledged. What is yet greater than this is that from the most excellent part of himself, that is, from his head, he produced her . . . therefore it is not right for her ever to abandon the Father, but she is always present with him and lives with him as being of the same origin; she breathes toward him and is present alone with him alone, mindful of her genesis and returning a suitable repayment for the birth pangs.[11]

There are striking Christian parallels to this interpretation, notably in the doctrine of Logos and Sophia advanced by the second-century apologists.[12] F. W. Lenz claimed that the Athena of Aristides had the Christian "homoousia" as its model but, since the doctrine of "homoousia" did not as yet exist, this cannot be right. It is wrong to treat Aristides as an imitator of Christian theology,[13] and it would be wrong to suggest that Christians relied on Aristides. The two interpretations reflect similar mediations with similar bases.

Cosmic Hermes

By the fourth century of our era there was some speculation about Hermes not only as revealer but also as creator. According to *Kore Kosmou,* a fragment of the hermetic literature, Hermes in heaven assured the supreme God that he would create "the nature of men" and set Wisdom and Temperance and Persuasion and Truth in them. He was the intermediary through whom "the Father and Demiurge," the "Monarch," would work.[14]

A contemporary papyrus provides a rather similar picture, though Hermes, not Zeus, is here the Demiurge. The father Zeus created Hermes out of himself and "to him he gave many commands, to make a most beautiful cosmos." While Zeus "rejoiced to behold the works of his illustrious son," Hermes went forth and ordered the elements to separate and live in peace. Then "the son of the all-creator" provided orderly arrangement for the universe. Hermes went through the skies, "but not alone, for with him went Logos, his noble son." Instead of treating Hermes himself as Logos, the author creates a genealogy from Zeus to Logos; the latter is now called "the swift herald [*angelos*] of the father's pure intention [*noema*]."[15]

As a god subordinate to the supreme Father, Hermes could play the role of assistant in the creation of the universe.

Cosmic Asclepius

Asclepius was a son of Apollo, and like his father he was sometimes considered a cosmic god, even though he was supposedly killed by Zeus, jealous of his reputation as a healer. The author of a second-century papyrus text (P. Oxy. XI 1381) deals with the praises of Asclepius (identified with the Egyptian god Imouthes)[16] and is concerned primarily with the healings for which the god was famous. The author refers, however, to a "physical treatise" in another book of his. It contains "the convincing account of the creation of the world" and thus extends "the fame of your [Asclepius's] inventiveness." He urges readers to come together if by serving the god they have been cured of diseases, or propose to follow virtue zealously, or have been blessed by benefits or saved from the dangers of the sea. "For every place has been penetrated by the saving power [*dynamis soterios*] of the god." He therefore intends to proclaim his "manifestations, the greatness of his power, and his benefactions and gifts."[17] Praises for his healings are most important, but they can be supplemented by comments on his cosmic functions.

To sum up: the gods and goddesses most often credited with cosmic creativity are children of Zeus who assist their Father. He remains above as the ultimate Demiurge; they do his work. We shall expect the situation of oriental deities not to be very different, since in Greco-Roman times they were ordinarily identified with the Greek gods.

An Oriental Cosmic Deity: Isis

Though Isis was not the prototype of the personified Wisdom of the book of Proverbs, in Greco-Roman times she acquired cosmic functions. In the of Werner Peek's inscriptions containing her praises, the one from Cyme on the island of Euboia, she describes herself as "the eldest daughter of Kronos" (5), the one who "separated earth from heaven, showed the stars [their] courses, ordained the path of sun and moon" (12-14). At Cyrene she declared that she was "sole ruler of eternity" and that "all call me the highest goddess, greatest of all the gods in heaven" (4, 7-8). "Nothing happens apart from me" (15). The goddess is also addressed in a hymn to Anubis from Bithynia and is called "blessed goddess, mother, many-named, whom Uranus son of Night bore on the marbled waves of the sea but Erebus brought up as a light to all mortals; eldest of the blessed ones in Olympus, bearing the sceptre," etc.

These examples suffice to show that in *Greek* circles Isis could be regarded as daughter of either Kronos or Uranus, as the supreme goddess, as one who had taken a leading part in the creation of the universe and now ruled over heaven and earth and whatever happened in either. The last passage cited shows that she was sometimes identified with Aphrodite, and such equivalences become fully clear in Oxyrhynchus papyrus XI 1380. There, after 119 lines (only a part of the original) of identifications, the author supplies nearly 200 more on the powers and functions of the goddess. She is "ruler of the world" (121), "greatest of the gods, the first name . . . ruler of heavenly things and the immeasurable" (142-45); "you bring the sun from east to west, and all the gods rejoice" (157-59; cf. the inscriptions); "you made the power of women equal that of men" (214-16); "you are the ruler of all forever" (231); "you have power over winds and thunders and lightnings and snows . . . you made the great Osiris immortal" (237-43).

Similarly in the second century Apuleius speaks of her care for humanity and explains that she unweaves the web of fate and keeps back the harmful course of the stars.

> The gods above worship you; the gods below reverence you; you turn the earth and give light to the sun, you rule the world, you tread upon Tartarus. The stars respond to you, the seasons return, the gods rejoice, the elements give service. By your will the winds blow, the clouds give nourishment, seeds sprout, fruits grow. . . . My voice lacks the strength to express what I think of your majesty, nor would a thousand mouths or tongues continuing to speak forever.[18]

Soon following this is a word of Athena-Isis that Plutarch knew: "I am all that has been and is and will be." Similarly the Christians Melito and Theophilus say that Christ or the Logos is rightly called "everything."[19] Another Christian apologist, Athenagoras, is acquainted with such interpretations. He knows the "physical explanations" that interpret Isis as "the origin of eternity, from whom all originate and through whom all exist."[20]

SECOND-CENTURY PHILOSOPHY

Philosophers in this period—roughly the second century of our era—had some contribution to make to the idea of a Demiurge or Creative Power different from the supreme god. Among them Numenius, from Apamea in Syria, was the most important to us, for he was certainly known to Clement and Origen, probably also to some of the Christian apologists before them. He claimed that the great Plato differentiated a Demiurge from a First Mind. "As Plato knew that among men only the Demiurge is known, while the first Mind, called Being in itself, is entirely unknown among them, for this reason he spoke like one who might say this: 'O men, he whom you conjecture as Mind is not the First; another, older and more divine Mind is before him.'" But this was Numenius's doctrine not Plato's.[21]

For authors like these there were thus at least two gods, with the second as the instrument of the first. Again Numenius writes that "if it is not necessary for the First to create, one must consider the First God as the Father of the one who creates." He then works out the implications of this thought.[22] Of course when he held that there was a third god, what was made by the second, he was rather remote from the Christian thought of his time, even though there are odd echoes of future trinitarian debates.

Some Gnostic teachers also stood close to Middle Platonism. The consort of Simon Magus was supposed to have been the first Thought that came from him, presumably when he was planning the creation. Similar language had already been used of the relation between Zeus and Athena. Not surprisingly, the Simonians had statues of Zeus and Athena, whom they evidently identified with their own hero and heroine. Again, Marcion regarded the good "unknown Father" as superior to the just Demiurge. And the Gnostic Ptolemaeus sharply differentiated "the perfect God" from "the Demiurge and Maker of this world."[23]

More orthodox Christians, like Justin who spoke of the "second God," were also acquainted with this kind of philosophy. Relying on scripture however, they insisted that "there is no other God above the Maker of all," and they usually referred to the Father as the Demiurge. Very occasionally they would use the term in regard to aspects of the Son's works. Normally, then, Gnostics agreed with Platonists that the perfect god was above the Demiurge, while Christians treated the Demiurge as supreme and his helpers as subordinate to him.

We cannot maintain, however, that any doctrine like that of Numenius was prevalent among philosophers either at the time when Proverbs was written or when Christians first spoke of Christ as the Wisdom or Word of God.

CONCLUSION

We thus see that the developments of cosmic theology in the background of early Christian thought were not universal and were usually related not to oriental deities but to the Greek gods who stood on a level just below Zeus. The creative powers of Zeus were extended to some of them, though not to others. This kind of religious thought apparently did not directly influence Christian theology until later, but the congenial environment permitted both Christian and pagan theology to develop at the same time.

Since thought about the cosmic Christ was based on the Old Testament figure of Wisdom, he had no direct pagan antecedent. There was, however, a pagan or gentile milieu in which this kind of doctrine was meaningful.

NOTES

1. *The Origin of the Prologue to St. John's Gospel,* cited with approval by Rudolf Bultmann and used, oddly enough, to support his theory of a Gnostic origin for the prologue.

2. *De fuga* 51.

3. "The Divine Wisdom," JTS 38 (1937), 230-37.

4. *Zeit und Geschichte,* ed. E. Dinkler (Tuebingen, 1964), 225-34.

5. *Der Isishymnos von Andros und verwandte Texte* (Berlin, 1930).

6. L. Spengel, *Rhetores Graeci* III 446, 2.

7. Ibid. 438, 11; 441, 1; 442, 30.

8. SVF II 908-9; Cicero, *Nat. deor.* 1. 41; Minucius Felix, *Oct.* 19. 20.

9. Justin, *Apol.* 1. 64. 5. So too Athenagoras knows that "they say Athena is thought pervading all things" *(Leg.* 22. 8).

10. Aelius Aristides, *Or.* 43. 7-9, p. 340, 14-30 Keil.

11. *Or.* 37. 2-4, pp. 304-5.

12. Cf. my *After the New Testament* (Philadelphia, 1967), 66f.; for further speculations, 70-82.

13. "Der Athenahymnos des Aristides," *Rivista di Cultura Classica e Mediaevale* 5 (1963), 329-47, esp. 339-40.

14. *Kore Kosmou* 23, 29-30 Nock-Festugière.

15. D. L. Page, *Greek Literary Papyri,* I (London, 1942), no. 136.

16. Imouthes was the Greek name of Imhotep, famous physician and architect, who became a god of Egypt.

17. Cf. E. and L. Edelstein, *Asclepius: A Collection and Interpretation of the*

Testimonies (Baltimore, 1945), I, 1969-75 (no. 331).

18. *Metam.* 11. 25. The last words are typical of rhetoricians praising Sarapis or Asclepius or, for that matter, the creation story in Genesis; cf. Aristides, *Or.* 45. 16; 47. 1; Theophilus, *Ad Aut.* 2. 12.

19. Melito, *Hom.* 9, pp. 6-7 Hall; Theophilus, *Ad Aut.* 1.3.

20. *Leg.* 22. 8.

21. Frag. 17 Des Places; cf. Dillon, op cit., 366-74.

22. Frag. 12; cf. E. des Places, *Numénius: Fragments* (Paris, 1973), 10-14.

23. Justin, *Apol.* 1. 26. 3; Irenaeus, *Adv. haer.* 1. 23. 4; Epiphanius, *Haer.* 33. 7. 3-4.

Rowan A. Greer*

The Leaven and the Lamb
Christ and Gregory of Nyssa's
Vision of Human Destiny

It is a common, indeed virtually a universal experience to find the writings preserved from the early church obscure and inaccessible; the reader has the sense of entering an unfamiliar landscape. What explains this experience is in part the simple fact that the conventions of the world view of late antiquity are both different from and sometimes offensive to our own, tied as it is to the empirical and committed to giving primacy to the world of our own experience. But it is also true that much of the theology of the fourth and fifth centuries looks like futile quibbling about inconsequential details. Is the Son of God *one* in being with the Father *(homoousios)* or *like* in being to the Father *(homoiousios)?* Is the incarnate Lord to be recognized as one *out of* two natures or one *in* two natures? Indeed, the dogmas that are the product of the first four general councils of the church, held between 325 and 451, appear to be a kind of esoteric mathematics. The Trinity is one substance and three persons, so that three times one equals one. And Christ's person is two natures in one person, so that one plus one equals one. In order to understand what the fathers of the church were saying it is necessary not only to recognize the initial difficulties I am mentioning but also to penetrate them. It is as though we encountered an obscure poem: understanding comes only by the willing suspension of disbelief that allows us to enter the conventions of the poem in order to interpret it.

Theology in the fourth and fifth centuries, as I have implied, revolved around two controversies about the identity of Christ. The Christ of the Arians was neither divine nor human, but imagined as the first of God's creatures, a sort of gigantic archangel through whom God created the rest

---

*Rowan A. Greer is Professor of Early Christian Literature at Yale University.

of the universe and who appropriated a human body to become Jesus, the Savior. The church responded to this view by drafting what we call the Nicene Creed and by insisting that the "one Lord, Jesus Christ" was "God from God, Light from Light, true God from true God, begotten, not made, of one Being with the Father." The second controversy begins when Nestorius, the patriarch of Constantinople, refused to call the Virgin Mary "Theotokos" (God-bearer) and so appeared to divide Christ's humanity from his divinity. And it concluded with a dispute over the opinions of the monk Eutyches, who insisted there was but one nature of the incarnate Lord. At the council of Chalcedon in 451 the church issued a definition meant to specify how the Nicene Creed's statements about Christ should be understood. Against Arius Christ is one divine nature, one in being with God the Father. Against Apollinaris he is one human nature, one in being with us. These two natures are not divided into two Sons or two Lords, as Nestorius said. Nor are they to be confused with one another, as Eutyches supposed. The two dogmas of the Trinity and of Christ's person were not intended so much to be authoritative doctrines identifying Christ, as grammatical rules that must be observed in constructing such doctrines. And they were meant to insist upon three basic convictions. First, since Christ is the Savior and since only God can save, Christ must somehow be God. Second, since the only way God can save is by touching us and our condition directly and fully, Christ must somehow be identified with our humanity. Third, these two aspects of Christ's identity must be kept distinct but must not compromise his unity.

The convictions just outlined, together with their dogmatic expression, cannot be understood unless we realize that they were intended to preserve the meaning of scripture and to safeguard the proper expression of the Christian life in worship and in its moral aspect. The New Testament speaks of Christ as "one" with the Father (John 10:30), as "the image of the invisible God" in whom "all things were created" (Col. 1:15ff.), and as the one "who though he was in the form of God, did not count equality with God a thing to be grasped" (Phil. 2:5ff.). Yet it also distinguished the Son from the Father: ". . . the Father is greater than I" (John 14:28). And it speaks of Christ not only as God the Word, Lord and God (John 1:1, 20:28), but also as one who increases "in wisdom and in stature, and in favor with God and man" (Luke 2:54, cf. 2:40), who is limited in his knowledge and power (Mark 6:5, 15:34; Matt. 24:36), and who suffers and dies. The church's theological task, then, was to sort out and make sense of these apparently contradictory assessments of Christ. Moreover, the task was more than a theoretical one, since it was designed to define Christ as the object of Christian piety, worshipped in the liturgy and imitated in the Christian's life. Were he not God and distinct from the Father, he would not be a worthy and clear object of worship. Were he not human, he would not bring salvation to his worshippers and would not supply them with a paradigm of true humanity to assist them in their lives.

The work of Gregory of Nyssa, who lived from about 335 to about 394, illustrates the general points I have been making. He is preoccupied with the question of Christ's identity, and is one of the architects of the dogma of the Trinity that was drawn up at the council of Constantinople in 381. His refutation of Apollinaris's view of Christ, a view that denied Christ's full humanity by refusing to admit he possessed a human soul, not only bears witness to his involvement in Christological disputes but also demonstrates that he anticipates the Definition of Chalcedon, drawn up more than half a century after his death. Moreover, Nyssa's concern is to treat dogmatic conclusions as principles by which scripture can be properly interpreted. His genius is that he is able to place dogma in a positive doctrinal structure designed to have a direct bearing upon the Christian life. His later writings succeed in creating an ideology, as it were, for monasticism, a monasticism not understood as a special form of the Christian life but as a full and concrete expression that should, in principle, be embraced by every Christian. In what follows I shall argue that Nyssa's assessment of Christ, while it is in part fashioned by his response to Arius and to Apollinaris, makes sense only in terms of his own larger theological framework, and that this framework is meant to have a direct bearing upon the Christian life.

The fundamental puzzle found in Nyssa's account of Christ has to do not with his treatment of the divine Christ, but with apparentlycontradictory statements about Christ's humanity. As divine Christ is, for Nyssa, one in being with the Father, a distinct person of the Trinity. As human, however, Christ is sometimes identified with human nature thought of generally and corporately, and sometimes identified with the concrete and individual human being Jesus. On the one hand, Nyssa can speak of the incarnation as the eternal Word of God appropriating to himself the whole of our nature. The Son of God is the Good Shepherd, who saves the lost sheep of humanity by putting it on his shoulders. The lost sheep is not a specific human being, but humanity taken in its entirety.[1] On the other hand, Nyssa can speak of "*the* Man" the Word assumed or "*the* Man who bore God."[2] These expressions presuppose that the incarnation is the union of God the Word and a specific individual human being. This concrete individual is like leaven placed in a lump of dough; and just as we can distinguish the leaven from the lump, so we can distinguish the concrete humanity of Christ from human nature taken as a whole. The puzzle, then, is how we are to make sense of these two different assessments of Christ's humanity. Is it the lost sheep and human nature corporately understood? Or is it the leaven and human nature individually and concretely understood? Or is it somehow both of these? Let me explain these questions first in the context of Nyssa's technical account of Christ as we find it in his refutation of Apollinaris, and then turn to the broader structure of his theological vision.

Apollinaris, a friend of Athanasius and a champion of Nicene orthodoxy, is one of the most attractive of Christian heretics. In thinking through the orthodox position against Arius he sought for some way of arguing that the eternal Son of God was not affected in his nature by the incarnation. The prince, though entering into our pauper's condition, remained the prince. In Apollinaris's view this position could be maintained only by denying that the incarnate Lord possessed a human soul, since this spiritual principle would have competed with the spiritual principle of the divine Word. The human soul, said Apollinaris, is inevitably subject to condemnation; and its rebellion against the divine Word would render the Christological union unstable.[3] Consequently, the Word appropriated a human body without a rational soul and governed that body in such a way that the body and its motions never affected the Word, but were instead continually controlled by the Word. Nyssa attacks this account of the incarnate Lord in two ways. First, the saving work of Christ depends upon insisting that the eternal Word of God touched and united himself with humanity in all its aspects, soul as well as body. Nyssa appeals to the principle that what the Word did not assume, he did not redeem. Consequently, Apollinaris gives an inadequate account of salvation. Second, from another point of view Apollinaris, by arguing that Christ in the incarnation is a single being composed of divine Word and human body, posits so highly a unitive view of Christ that either the divine Word loses his divine status and is reduced to the created status of the body he governs, or, contrariwise, the truncated humanity of Christ is so divinized that it can no longer be regarded as truly human. Nyssa's argument, that is, attacks Apollinaris for confusing Christ's divinity and his humanity and for failing to observe any distinction between the created and the uncreated.

What succeeds as a double refutation of Apollinaris's account of Christ fails when Nyssa begins to draw out the positive implications of his polemic. Nyssa's first line of attack implies positively that we must insist upon the fullest possible union of divinity and a complete humanity, and he draws that implication boldly. While the humanity "exists in its own essence," it is so "mingled" with the divinity that like a drop of vinegar placed in the sea and assimilated to it, "it is transformed to the sea of immortality—as the Apostle says 'death is swallowed up by life'" (cf. 1 Cor. 15:54).[4] The "mingling" implies that we must think of the Christological union as the analogy of the union between a human soul and a human body, and it is difficult not to conclude that Nyssa's soteriological attack upon Apollinaris yields a theandric Christ whose humanity is so transfigured as to be translucent of his divinity. Nyssa's second line of attack, however, insists we must distinguish divinity and humanity in Christ. This view implies a very different vision of Christ. And once again Nyssa boldly draws out the implication. We cannot speak of a single essence. Instead, human suffering and human experiences refer to what is human about Christ, and the Word of God remained "unchanged and impassible even when he had fellowship [*koinōnia*] with human sufferings and experiences." The two natures are not *mingled* with one another, but are simply in *fellowship*.[5] It is almost as though Nyssa ends by painting two contrary portraits of Christ.

There is an obvious though, I shall argue, an incorrect way of explaining the problem by relating it both to the fundamental puzzle of Nyssa's account of Christ and to the Christological alternatives offered by the Alexandrian and the Antiochene fathers that eventually collided in the Nestorian controversy (428-51).[6] Nyssa's unitive view of Christ in which the divine Word is mingled with a complete human nature looks as though Christ's humanity is being defined in generic terms. It is humanity as a whole that the Word transfigures by uniting himself with us. And from this perspective Nyssa's Christology seems not to differ significantly from Athanasius's and Cyril's, and so looks Alexandrian. The mystery of the incarnation is located in the condescending love and power of God's Word, who appropriated our impoverished nature and transfigured it. On the other hand, when Nyssa distinguishes the humanity and the divinity and speaks of their fellowship with one another, he appears to treat Christ's humanity as concrete and individual. From this perspective what he says resembles the Antiochene Christology elaborated by Theodore of Mopsuestia, Nestorius, and Theodoret of Cyrrhus. The mystery of the incarnation revolves around the paradox that it is in the man Jesus, uniquely one in fellowship with God's Word, that we encounter God's saving love and power.

Nyssa, however, does not commit himself to either of these two contrary visions of Christ. He regards them as the products of two different ways of understanding the Christological union, and he not only recognizes the problems involved but also insists that they cannot be solved. "The union of flesh" implies the Alexandrian, unitive view; "the assumptive of man," the Antiochene, divisive view. Nyssa flatly states that "neither of these phrases which I am accustomed to use are meant as accurate definitions."[7] The same point of view lies behind the central argument of his "Address on Religious Instruction." There the question is posed in terms of how the Word can be united with humanity without being made passible. The question keeps emerging, and Nyssa suggests at least two ways of handling it. If "passion" means vice, then the sinlessness of Christ leaves the Word impassible. If "passion" means human weakness—hunger, thirst, suffering, death—then in the case of Christ these are better seen as divine activities than as human passions; and the Word remains impassible even in the incarnation. But neither explanation suffices. We can only conclude that "sick people do not prescribe to doctors their manner of treatment."[8] In other words, the objection is dismissed even though it cannot be explained away. Like the Chalcedonian definition Nyssa sees that we must speak of two complete natures, unconfused and undivided, but that we cannot be sure how to press beyond these negative requirements to a positive exposition of the Christological union. My conclusion is that the technical dimension of Nyssa's Christology fails to explain the basic puzzle of his double assessment of Christ's humanity as both individual and corporate. The problem of the unitive and the divisive accounts of Christ that emerge from Nyssa's polemic against Apollinaris cannot be successfully correlated with this puzzle.

Although we can arrive at no satisfactory account of Nyssa's Christology by comparing him to Alexandrians and Antiochenes, we can find a resolution if we look in a more obvious place, the broad structure of his own theology. His treatise "On the Making of Man" supplies us with a reasonably clear exposition of that structure, and his ideas focus upon the biblical theme that humanity was created as the image of God. According to Gen. 1:26 ("Let us make man in our image, after our likeness") God intended to create humanity as the image of the Trinity. But the next verse in Genesis states that what God actually did stands in some contrast with his intention, since he created humanity not just as his image but as "male and female." Nyssa further observes that in the age to come the distinction between male and female will be abolished.[9] By interpreting Scripture this way Nyssa concludes that we must distinguish between God's intention and the course of human history through which that intention must be realized. God's eternal purpose and its actualization in the age to come stand in contrast to the temporal order that comes before the completion of God's intention. Like Irenaeus two centuries earlier, Nyssa treats all of human history as a development analogous to the growth of an individual person from infancy to maturity. Creation is not so much an event that took place at the beginning as a process initiated then and completed by the age to come. Creation and redemption are really the same thing, and the two words refer to the same process, one from the point of view its inception, the other from the point of view of its completion.[10]

The image of God, then, is primarily a way of describing human destiny, since only in the age to come will God's purpose be realized. Nyssa's vision of human destiny under this rubric is a rich and complicated one. The image is a created resemblance of the Trinity and differs from God only because it belongs in the order of becoming rather than in that of pure being.[11] It possesses moral, intellectual, and spiritual characteristics that not only constitute it as God's image but also act as final causes for the Christian life as a growth toward human destiny.[12] And because the image is constantly becoming, this destiny is defined not as an entrance into the pure being and changelessness of God, but as a perpetual progress towards an infinite good.[13] Moreover, the image, properly speaking, does not refer to individuals, but to the plenitude of human nature.[14] That is, its meaning must be understood in corporate terms, and human nature is defined theomorphically. Just as the Trinity is a single, ineffable nature with a triple individuation, so humanity is destined to be a single, ineffable nature with individuation.[15] All human persons will be relations of one another the way Father, Son, and Spirit are relations of the one Godhead.

Nyssa's doctrine of the image begins at a purely spiritual and incorporeal level. Christian Platonist themes suffer a sea change by which the doctrine gains a corporate dimension. But the function of the image takes account of the body and of the physical creation. And at this level, too, the corporate character of the image gains pride of place. As God's image humanity ought to mirror God's freedom and sovereignty. What this means, to begin with, is that the mind, by reflecting God, gains the power to rule the body and to make it an image of the image.[16] The next step Nyssa takes is to broaden the idea of humanity's sovereignty. Since human nature is both physical because of the body and spiritual because of the mind, humanity is designed to bind together and to harmonize the two orders of creation, the physical (beasts, plants, and even sticks and stones) and the spiritual (the angels). It is humanity thought of corporately that fulfills this function, and human destiny involves the destiny of the entire creation. The age to come will be a transfigured physical order perfectly united to the spiritual. And Nyssa thinks of this not only as a harmonized creation but also as a divinized order, with humanity both binding creation together and uniting it to God.[17]

We can immediately see that Nyssa's vision of human destiny requires the incarnation and the perfect union of God and humanity in Christ that alone enables human nature to fulfill its role of harmonizing and divinizing the entire creation. Nyssa does not make the point explicitly in "On the Making of Man," but he implies it by his citation of Pauline texts referring to the new humanity in Christ.[18] And the point is made explicitly at a number of points in Nyssa's other writings. One example occurs in his allegorical interpretation of Song of Songs 5:9ff. The bride is challenged to explain "what is your beloved more than another beloved"; and she responds not by describing Christ in his divine, invisible, and incomprehensible aspect but by reference to the incarnation when he "clothed himself with human nature."[19] Just as Saint Paul argues that the visible creation makes the invisible God known (Rom. 1:19ff.), so the bride explains the beloved, the Word of God, by speaking of the new creation of the church. The incarnation creates the new humanity, which may be regarded as a new heaven and a new earth. We become the stars and the luminaries of this new universe as "the light of the world" (Matt. 5:14) and "lights in the world" (Phil. 2:15). In a poetic fashion Nyssa treats Christ's humanity as a cosmos and human beings as aspects fully ordered in it.[20] The metaphors of the body and the temple also provide a way of speaking of the new humanity of Christ in a general and corporate fashion, including the plenitude of humanity as parts integral to the whole. I should conclude that when Nyssa speaks of Christ's human nature in corporate terms, what he has in mind is a vision of human destiny in which the plenitude of all human beings has been completed so that we all become relations of one another in Christ's humanity, the way the persons of the Trinity are relations of the one divine nature. This corporate humanity, then, fulfills God's eternal purpose by harmonizing, divinizing, and so transfiguring the entire universe.

Once we understand Christ's corporate humanity in relation to human destiny, it becomes clear that his individual humanity must be related to the process by which God achieves that destiny and fulfills his creative intention. The very metaphor Nyssa repeatedly employs confirms this interpretation. To speak of Christ's humanity as leaven not only distinguishes it from the lump of dough, the rest of humanity, but also suggests that it is meant to leaven the whole lump. From this point of view Nyssa adopts a dynamic understanding of Christ's headship over the church:

> Christ is the head of the body, the church. And by "Christ" we do not now mean to be referring this name to the eternity of the Godhead. Rather we are speaking of the man who received God, who appeared on earth and conversed with human beings, the fruit of the Virgin birth, in whom the fulness of Godhead dwelt bodily (Col. 2:9), the first fruits of the common lump (Rom. 11:16), through whom the Lord clothed himself with our nature and made it pure, cleansing it of all the passions which had grown up with it.[21]

So long as the process is at work we may distinguish Christ's humanity over ours and treat it as a concrete individual. But once the process has been completed the distinction between his humanity and ours disappears, just as the leaven and the lump of dough can no longer be distinguished once the bread has been baked. The leavening process is, of course, designed to overcome the fall of Adam and its effects. But, more broadly, it is necessary to bring to completion God's eternal purpose and the initiation of that purpose at what we usually call creation. We might broaden (and perhaps trivialize) Nyssa's metaphor by thinking of God as a baker who assembles the ingredients of his bread at creation, introduces the yeast at the incarnation, and bakes the loaf at the end of the world.

The final point to make in my argument is that Nyssa's version of the Christian story functions not as an end in itself, but as a context for what he wants to say about the Christian life. His short treatise "On Perfection" handles the subject in a Christocentric fashion. Saint Paul's exclamation "It is no longer I who live, but Christ who lives in me" (Gal. 2:20) acts as a rubric for what Nyssa wants to say.[22] And there are two aspects of this identification of the believer with Christ. "What we can grasp of Christ, we imitate; and what our nature cannot grasp for imitation, we adore and worship."[23] What Nyssa seems to mean is that our participation in Christ is partly his work and partly our own. In the incarnation God the Word "through his love for humanity became the image of the invisible God, so that by the form he assumed and made his own he might be formed in you and might transform you once more through himself to the pattern of the archetypal beauty."[24] It is Christ's humanity that is described as the image of God, and that image draws the rest of humanity into conformity with itself. We become members of the body of which the human Christ is the head.[25] And just as in the individual the mind governs all the members and senses of the body, so macrocosmically Christ's new humanity governs all human individuals. They remain distinct but are so united with their head that they cease being divided from one another.[26] The perfection of this new humanity is the new creation of the resurrection.[27] "Therefore, just as the first fruits of the lump was made proper to the true Father and God through purity and impassibility, so shall we, too, the lump, be joined through similar paths to the Father of incorruptibility by imitating so far as we can the impassibility and changelessness of the mediator."[28]

The last part of what Nyssa says shifts attention from God's part in our redemption to our own. Although from one point of view we can do nothing but adore and worship the God who became incarnate and in this way established the corporate human image of God, destined for perfection in the transfigured world of the resurrection, from another point of view God's work is persuasive and demands our efforts to make the pattern our own by imitating Christ. Initially, this means the renunciation of vice and our progress in the moral life, the establishing of peace both with those around us and within ourselves.[29] But it involves the mind and the spirit as well as the will, and Nyssa insists that our progress must be moral, intellectual, and spiritual.[30] The themes that are integral to his discussion are a reworking of Origen's contemplative ideal into the notion that the true vision of God is perpetual progress in the good. Nyssa's treatise "On Perfection" concludes by exhorting the reader not to be sorry when he sees that we are by nature doomed constantly to change, but to rejoice that we can continually be changed from glory to glory without finding any limit to our growth towards an infinite perfection.[31]

Nyssa's dogmatic and doctrinal judgments about Christ find their proper function in his account of human destiny and in the role that vision plays in urging his readers to embark upon the Christian life. The corporate humanity of Christ becomes an image of the Trinity and redefines our individuality so that we become relations of one another in Christ, rather than isolated centers of consciousness. That new humanity transfigures the entire creation, providing a setting for our perpetual progress towards God. That progress is, moreover, an imitation of the incarnate Lord. Christ, for Nyssa, is the eternal Word of God united to humanity in order to bring us redemption. And Nyssa would surely have to be judged orthodox by Chalcedonian standards. But he refuses to try to solve the mystery of precisely how divinity and humanity are united in Christ. Instead, he seeks to think through Christ's identity in terms of his understanding of the Christian story and the Christian life. And that identity, or at least the aspect of that identity we can grasp, must be equated with the new humanity of the age to come.

NOTES

1. Cf. Address on Religious Instruction 15 (LCC III, 290); Antirrheticus adversus Apolinarium, ed W. Jaeger III,i, 152; Commentarius in Canticum canticorum, oratio II, ed. W. Jaeger VI, 61f.

2. Cf. Address on Religious Instruction 16, 27, 32 (LCC III, 293-94, 305, 310).

3. Hans Lietzmann, ed., *Apollinaris von Laodicia und Seine Schule,* Texte und Untersuchungen I (Tübingen: J. C. B. Mohr, 1904), 178-79, 204, 247. The weakness of the human soul is, for Apollinaris, the product of the old creation rather than of the fall.

4. Antirrheticus adversus Apolinarium, ed W. Jaeger III,i, 200f.

5. Ibid., 168.

6. See Kelly's opinion that Nyssa's Christology "owed much both to Origen and to the Antiochene school" (J. N. D. Kelly, *Early Christian Doctrines* [New York: Harper and Brothers, 1958], 298). Grillmeier argues that "one sentence" in Basil's homily on Psalm 45 "shows how Cappadocian Christology is approaching 'Antiochene' conceptions," and says of Nyssa that compared with Nazianzus his "language is much more diphysite in tone." He goes on to analyze Nyssa's Christology in terms of Stoic conventions, but concludes that "The picture of Christ in his preaching and in his Christ mysticism transcends his theory" (Aloys Grillmeier, *Christ in Christian Tradition,* ET [London: J. S. Bowden, A. R. Mowbray & Co., 1965], 279, 282, 290). Both Kelly and Grillmeier reflect attempts to explain Nyssa's Christology in terms of the debate between Alexandria and Antioch, but Grillmeier appears to recognize the limitations of this approach.

7. Antirrheticus adversus Apolinarium, ed. W. Jaeger III,i, 183f.

8. Ibid., 294.

9. On the Making of Man, XVI.5-8, XVII.2, XXII.3 (NPNF, 2nd series, vol. V, 404f., 407, 411).

10. I should defend this conclusion despite the fact that Nyssa sometimes speaks of redemption as a restoration of an original perfection in paradise. His assessment of the original state of humanity is difficult if not impossible to pin down.

11. On the Making of Man XVI.12 (NPNF V, 405).

12. Ibid., V (NPNF V, 391).

13. The most familiar discussion of the point may be found in Nyssa's allegorical treatment of the thick darkness on Mt. Sinai into which Moses enters. See Life of Moses, ed. W. Jaeger VII,i, 86-89, 110-22.

14. On the Making of Man XVI. 16-18 (NPNF V, 406).

15. Cf. On Not Three Gods, LCC III, 257f., where Nyssa insists that the term "human nature" does not properly refer to individuals.

16. On the Making of Man XII.9 (NPNF V, 398f.).

17. Ibid. XVI.9 (NPNF V, 405). Cf. Address on Religious Instruction 6, 16 (LCC III, pp. 278f., 294). See also David L. Balás, *Metousia Theou: Man's Participation in God's Perfections according to Saint Gregory of Nyssa,* Studia Anselmiana 55, I.B.C. (Rome: Libreria Harder, 1966), especially chap. 1.

18. On the Making of Man XVI.7 (Gal. 3:28), XXII.3 (1 Cor. 15:47), XXX.33 (Col. 3:9f.) (NPNF V, 405, 411, 427).

19. Commentarius in Canticum Canticorum, oratio XIII, ed. W. Jaeger VI, 384.

20. Ibid., 385.

21. Ibid., 390-91, commenting on Song of Songs 5:11.

22. De Perfectione, ed. W. Jaeger VIII,i. 175
23. Ibid., 178.
24. Ibid., 195.
25. Ibid., 198.
26. Ibid., 199.
27. Ibid., 202.
28. Ibid., 206.
29. Ibid., 184.
30. Ibid., 210.
31. Ibid., 214

John Dart*

Jesus and His Brothers

A journalist should come bearing news, and all the better if it is a great story. What I will summarize all too briefly I consider to be more important news than anything I've done in eighteen years of covering religion for the *Los Angeles Times.* The story has not appeared in the *Times* (at least not yet) because my own conclusions are involved. My research, now exceeding seven years, has been for a book.

The "news" (about 1900 years too late) is that the brothers of Jesus— James and Judas—can finally be cleared of their "bad press" in the New Testament Gospels and be recognized for conveying the earlier, more authentic Jesus in certain apocryphal gospels.

The canonical Gospels give the distinct impression that the brothers were unbelievers who stayed in Galilee during Jesus' ministry and only later, after the resurrection, came to believe in his divinity. New Testament criticism of the brothers was stronger than would seem necessary if that were true. Actually, a strong polemic is introduced in the Gospel of Mark against all personages close to Jesus, and other gospels only soften it somewhat or introduce new polemics. While Mark undermined the authority of Judas and James, the apostle Paul, a couple of decades earlier, was combating the basic Wisdom theology we now can associate with the brothers of Jesus (if not with the early movement entirely). Such evidence would have been impossible except for two key texts attributed to brothers Judas and James, rediscovered only forty years ago. The Nag Hammadi Library, which was discovered in upper Egypt in 1945, had more than fifty treatises in an earthen jar; these treatises were classified primarily as Christian gnostic writings. Gnosticism included schools of thought that tended to be eclectic and very other-worldly. They speculated about the divine origins of human spirits in counterpoint to their unhappy view of a debilitating world. But among the Nag Hammadi works (Coptic translations

*John Dart is religion writer for the *Los Angeles Times.*

181

of tractates written in Greek) were documents showing primitive stages of the Jesus tradition.

Very significant for the study of the sayings of Jesus were the *Gospel of Thomas* and the *Apocryphon (secret book) of James*. The document attributed to James—obviously James of Jerusalem who was known to be Jesus' brother—purports to be a discourse between the risen Jesus and two trusted disciples, Peter and James. The *Gospel of Thomas* is a collection of 114 Jesus-sayings said to be written down by Judas. The opening line of this text says, in a Greek fragment (Oxy. pap. 654) found around the turn of the last century, that what followed were the "secret sayings which the living Jesus spoke and which Judas who was called Thomas wrote down." The Coptic version of the *Gospel of Thomas* differs in calling him "Didymos Judas Thomas." The name "Thomas" means "twin" in Aramaic (as does "Didymos" in Greek); but the principal name is Judas, whom we know as another brother of Jesus. (Obviously I am convinced that there was an actual person Jesus if I also believe that he had real-life brothers.)

First, let us affirm that the brothers of Jesus were indeed brothers of Jesus. They are considered stepbrothers, cousins, or merely "relatives" by the great Eastern churches and Roman Catholicism. Protestant scholarship today takes the use of the word "brother" as meaning a male sibling.

The apostle Paul, writing in the fifties, referred to more than one brother when he asked why he and his co-worker Barnabas should not receive the benefits accorded to others in the ministry. (The struggle for respect that Paul had with the Jerusalem church, by the way, should be a reminder of who carried the most authority in the first decades of the Jesus movement.) Paul wrote: "Do we not have the right to our food and drink? Do we not have the right to be accompanied by a sister as a wife, as the other apostles and the brothers of the Lord and Cephas?" (1 Cor. 9:4-5).

Thus, most important were Cephas (Paul's most common name for Peter), the brothers of the Lord, and other apostles. At another point Paul gave the name of one brother: "I saw none of the other apostles except James the Lord's brother" (Gal. 1:19). Judas, or Jude, was probably the only other active brother of Jesus, as indicated by other New Testament writings. Two "letters" toward the back of the Bible are credited to the well-known James and to Jude—both short documents written well after their lifetimes. Neither writing says that they are brothers of Jesus and neither really writes about Jesus. But the letter of Jude does identify the writer as the "brother of James" (Jude 1:1). If anything, the admonition-filled works seem to be token gestures to the places of James and Judas in the early church.

The Gospel of Mark says that Jesus had four brothers. They are named in a hometown scene, where townspeople asked incredulously about Jesus, "Is this not the carpenter, the son of Mary and brother of James and Joses and Judas and Simon, and are not his sisters here with us?" (6:3). The Gospel of Matthew follows Mark, with some differences, but still naming four brothers (13:55). The Gospel of Luke does not mention any names of brothers, but it does say that Jesus was Mary's firstborn son (2:7), implying that more sons followed. And in Acts, written by the author of Luke, the opening chapter depicts the unnamed brothers in prayerful accord with the closest followers of Jesus (1:14).

Among references outside the New Testament, the Jewish historian, Josephus, in the late first century, referred to "James the brother of the so-called Christ" in the reporting of James's execution by stoning. The year of James's death is thought to be 62 C.E. Both Josephus and the New Testament make it clear that James was a central church figure in Jerusalem. As for Judas, Hegessipus, the Christian historian, writing late in the second century, told about the grandchild of Jude, a man said to have been a brother of Christ according to the flesh. However, the brothers' importance to the story of Jesus was quickly eclipsed. Churches developed a growing adoration for the mother of Jesus despite her less-than-exalted image in the Gospels of Mark and John. Nascent orthodoxy expanded on the nativity stories in the Gospels of Matthew and Luke. Elaborations included a second-century text that added story "details" about the Virgin Mary and Joseph, who was singled out as her husband when the maiden was only sixteen years old. Joseph is reported to have replied anxiously, "I (already) have sons and am old, but she is a girl" in the *Protogospel of James* (9:2). By having Joseph say that he already had sons, this text turns the "brothers" of Jesus into stepbrothers by a previous marriage.

The argument over family relationships continued, however, as late as the fourth century. One church father who was to influence the Roman Catholic church indelibly and who wrote "The Perpetual Virginity of the Blessed Mary" was Jerome. Through a complicated argument about which women were watching the crucifixion in the different gospels, Jerome determined that the "brothers" were really cousins.

A joint Lutheran-Catholic study on *Mary in the New Testament* (Fortress, Paulist, 1978) found many areas of agreement. But they waffled on the question of whether the brothers were also sons of Mary. They conceded that "there is no convincing argument from the New Testament against the literal meaning of the words 'brother' and 'sister' when they are used of Jesus' relatives." They concluded only that, "The solution favored by scholars will in part depend on the authority they allot to later church insights"—namely, whether Catholic dogma is considered authoritative in this case.

It must be said, however, that being a blood brother of Jesus was not supposed to carry any weight among the disciples whom Jesus gathered into a new spiritual family. A well-attested saying of Jesus—found in Mark 3:31-35, Matt. 12:46-50, Luke 8:19-21, and *Thomas* 99—says so pointedly: When told that his brothers and mother were outside, Jesus responds to his disciples, "Those here who do the will of my Father are my brothers and my mother" (*Thomas* 99). Other sayings likely to be authentic make it clear that one must leave one's natural family and become a child—reborn into a new family in which the Father in heaven may be addressed intimately as "Abba" or Daddy. A nearly identical saying in Luke 14:26 and *Thomas* 55, cf. 101, says that a disciple must indeed "hate" his mother and father.

There is good reason to suspect, on circumstantial evidence alone, that James and Judas were disciples of Jesus, despite the rather consistent willingness of even liberal biblical scholars to accept the gospel accounts that they were not. For an early church creed recited by Paul (1 Cor. 15:3-7) says that the risen Christ "appeared" to a number of witnesses, but the only individual witnesses (besides himself, verse 8) were Peter and James. Indeed, Paul, somewhat sarcastically, said in his letter to the Galatians (2:9) that James, Cephas, and John—in that order—were reputed to be "pillars" (of the church). And when Peter got out of line by sharing a meal with gentiles (Gal. 2:12), Paul said that "men from James" confronted Peter with that violation of Jewish law; Paul said that he berated Peter as well. In other words, Paul's references to the privileged authority of the brothers of the Lord (1 Cor. 9:4-5), and especially to James, would indicate altogether that the brothers were well regarded, in contrast to what certain gospels would have us believe.

The tone of the Gospels of Mark and John should have made biblical scholars more suspicious about the portrayal of the disciples. Many prominent specialists still think of the thickheaded and weak-willed disciples in Mark as simply a valid historical portrayal. Many specialists say that no gospel author in the early church would write disparaging things unless he had to admit it was true. Nonsense. Mark purposely depicted the disciples and all those close to Jesus progressively worse as his narrative unfolds.

"Mark is assiduously involved in a vendetta against the disciples. He is intent on totally discrediting them," wrote Theodore J. Weeden (*Mark— Traditions in Conflict* [Fortress, 1971]).

The first gospel author, whose work guided most of Matthew's and Luke's content and influenced the Gospel of John, begins in his third chapter by saying that Jesus' "own," his mother and brothers, set out to seize Jesus because they thought his activities, including healings, proved that "he is beside himself" (3:21). Later, in the hometown scene, Mark identifies Jesus' full family but mentions no father and indeed has the townspeople call Jesus, "son of Mary"; this could mean that, in that day, the father was unknown. Mark's scene leads up to a traditional Jesus saying (*Thomas* 31 and parallels) about no man being a prophet in his home country. Mark has Jesus say more: "A prophet is not without honor, except in his own country, and among his own kin, and in his own house" (6:4). Sayings of Jesus often deemed authentic would justify Mark's disparagement of Jesus' natural family, but Mark goes well beyond this point in his polemic.

The brothers never appear again in Mark's narrative, although James's name is used to identify mother Mary at the cross. Mark cannot resist a dig—Jesus' brother is called here (15:40) "James the Less," and not the kindly rendering of "James the Younger" in many Bible versions.

In the Gospel of John, the disciples are a bit dull, but they do believe (2:11, 22). The never-named "brothers" of Jesus do not fare so well. They chide Jesus to show his stuff in Judea during the time of a festival when it might be safe. The brothers urged him, "For no man works in secret if he seeks to be known openly. If you do these things, show yourself to the world" (7:4). The gospel author then adds in an aside to the readers (7:5): "For even his brothers did not believe in him." For some scholars who would not otherwise rely on John for historical data, this oddly has become a decisive statement. The joint Catholic-Lutheran study, for instance, wrote: "In the light of 7.5 it is clear that the brothers were not disciples during the ministry."

The brothers do not reappear in the Gospel of John. Nevertheless, a final indignity comes during the crucifixion (19:26-28). Jesus directs his mother to be the mother of the "beloved disciple." This unnamed, model disciple takes her home to live with him.

That is how "the brothers" were treated. But most of Jesus' followers sustain rough handling as well (especially in Mark). Peter's answer to Jesus, "You are the Christ," turns out to be unsatisfactory in Mark: Jesus rebukes Peter, "Get behind me, Satan" (8:27-33). Peter later vows that he will never lose faith (14:16-22); but, indeed Peter does deny Jesus three times after Jesus' arrest (14:16-22).

When Peter is joined by James and John, the disciples called the "sons of Zebedee" and the "sons of thunder" by Mark, the image of the big three suffers just as badly. The three do not know what to say to Jesus during his mountain-top transfiguration (9:2-8) because they are frightened.

James and John, later, shock the other disciples (and presumably the readers) when they tell Jesus that first they want him to "do for us whatever we ask of you," and then they ask him to let them sit on either side of him in heaven (10:35ff). The other ten disciples were rightly "indignant" (10:41). This episode in Mark is best understood as part of an ever-building attack.

When Jesus is in danger of being arrested, the inner three (Peter, James, and John) are to keep watch, but they fall asleep repeatedly. The disciple who actually betrays Jesus to the authorities is called Judas Iscariot, but all the disciples in Mark are betrayers: at his arrest all of them flee from the scene. Mark uses outsiders to show that some people recognized Jesus' destiny—the woman who pours a symbolic ointment on Jesus (stirring a misplaced furor by the disciples in 14:3-8), the centurion at the cross who utters, "Truly this man was the Son of God" (15:39), and Joseph of Arimathea who volunteers to take care of Jesus' burial (15:43-46).

The final blow to the disciples' authority and even to Jesus' mother's, Mary Magdalene's, and Salome's authority was struck at the very close of the gospel. Two of the best manuscripts show that Mark ends at 16:8 and that "longer endings" were added later. At this point, a young man at the empty tomb tells the three women that Jesus is risen and the disciples are to meet Jesus in Galilee. However, the women are frightened and tell no one. The original gospel ends here. This means Mark declared that any claims that the disciples and the women had seen the risen Jesus and received secret teachings had to be false.

The changes wrought by Mark in the early Jesus movement cannot be underestimated. A number of dialogues of Jesus with his disciples found at Nag Hammadi and elsewhere have these exchanges take place after the resurrection—the *Gospel of Mary* and the *Dialogue of the Savior,* for instance. These texts show definite gnostic influences and, in their final form, may derive from the second century. But Matthew, Luke-Acts, John, and the expanded Mark all favored some postresurrection conversations between Jesus and the disciples; this indicates that we have grounds to say that Mark's story is in part a reaction to earlier postresurrection dialogues.

One text that Mark's gospel may have needed to combat is the *Secret Book of James* from Nag Hammadi. James M. Robinson of Claremont Graduate School has called attention to turning points in Mark and *Secret James*. In the Nag Hammadi document, the risen Jesus says to James and Peter, "I first spoke with you in parables, and you did not understand. Now, in turn, I speak with you openly, and you do not perceive" (7:1-7). When Mark's Jesus made the first of his three predictions of his suffering and death, the author added: "And he said this plainly" (8:51). Even though Robinson said the *Secret Book of James* probably represented the type of postresurrection presentation of Jesus that Mark fought against, I think that continued study of the *Secret Book of James* will show that its core is an essentially non-gnostic writing that can be dated in the first century and prior to Mark.

We also need to talk about the coincidence of names in Paul's letters and Mark's gospel. Paul says that the three "pillars" of the church in Jerusalem were James, Cephas (or Peter), and John. About twenty years later, Mark says that the three most important disciples of Jesus were Simon Peter (Paul did not use the name "Simon") and James and John— except that James and John were brothers of each other and sons of Zebedee. Rice University's Werner Kelber has suggested that somehow the coincidence of names is probably no coincidence. Kelber sees the choice of these three disciples and their disgrace in the gospel as an attack on the Jerusalem church (*Mark's Story of Jesus,* Fortress). More was at work than seems to have met scholarly eyes. In a technique that may be called "historicizing," Mark has provided an enormous amount of detail about disciples, their nicknames and relationships, and a plethora of detail about places where Jesus went in his itinerant ministry and performance of miracles.

Most important for our purposes, Mark writes James and Judas out of the picture. To anyone who claimed to follow the teachings of Jesus according to James, the Lord's brother, a reader of Mark's gospel would say, "I don't see him among the Twelve, but only James the son of Zebedee (or James, son of Alphaeus)." Matthew and Luke tamper very little with Mark's list of the Twelve but the Gospel of John, significantly, does not name the entire twelve, never mentioning James and John as disciples. (The "sons of Zebedee" are mentioned in the twenty-first chapter, but that is widely classified as a postscript chapter added to the gospel by a later hand.) I think that the reason why the Fourth Gospel stays away from James and John is that the Johannine community knew that its namesake authority was not the "son of Zebedee" and not the brother of James.

Rather than conflict with Mark, John does not put the two men into the narrative at all.

Brother Judas was dealt the same blow as brother James. The only Judas in the Gospel of Mark is Judas Iscariot, the traitor. The name "Judas" was an authoritative one, as indicated by the letter of Jude in the New Testament and the inclusion of Judas (just "Judas") as one of three questioners of Jesus in the *Dialogue of the Savior*. Reconstruction of the original, non-gnostic *Gospel of Thomas* will help us to understand what happened in the last third of the first century to give us two "Judases." When the Gospel of Mark received sufficient circulation, those who cherished the collection of sayings that were said to have been written down by Judas had to be thunderstruck. The only Judas who was privy to Jesus' teachings in Mark was Judas Iscariot. The believers loyal to Judas the brother needed a solution. One of the few disciples in Mark who bore no further identity and played no part in the gospel was Thomas, the nickname meaning "twin." A way was found to return Judas to the twelve! A title was added to the end of the sayings collection, "The Gospel According to Thomas"; saying number 13 that established "Thomas" as a recipient of secret teachings from Jesus was inserted along with some other sayings into the collection, and the beginning line of the collection was amended so that Judas became "Judas who was called Thomas." The double name Judas Thomas was used from the second century on in eastern Syria, where Thomas eventually was regarded as the founding apostle.

If this theory of how Judas got the nickname "Thomas" is correct, then we also have an explanation for why the "doubting Thomas" story concluded the Gospel of John. Mark had nothing bad to say about Thomas, but John said that Thomas would not take the word of the other disciples that Jesus had risen from the dead. After Jesus invites Thomas to examine his wounds, Thomas exclaims, "My Lord and my God!" (20:28). Thus, Thomas is made to call Jesus "God," as the gospel author suggested was the case in his opening lines (1:1). Jesus says to Thomas, "Have you believed because you have seen me? Blessed are those who have not seen and yet believe" (20:29). Thomas became a scapegoat in the Gospel of John because the author had to fight the sayings tradition now circulating under the name of Thomas. John, more subtle than Mark, presents Thomas as a skeptic, but he appropriated the disciple for his own theological understanding by saying, in effect, that now it can be told that Thomas finally came to believe the way we believe.

The Gospel of John, besides fighting a low Christology connected with the name Thomas, also is aware that there was a Judas among the followers. He takes a slap at that name by having "Judas (not the Iscariot)" ask impertinently, "Lord, how is it that you will manifest yourself to us, and not to the world?" (14:22). This is practically the same chiding question asked of Jesus by "the brothers" earlier in the gospel (7:4). Jesus does not really answer Judas-not-the-Iscariot but just keeps on talking in a previous vein.

If you doubt that John could be reacting to what I call "the brothers' tradition," listen to another example. The Gospel of John attempts to "correct" those who believe they can ascend to the heavens to gaze at God. John has Jesus say twice, early in the gospel, that "no one has seen God" except the Son (1:18) and again, "No one has ascended into heaven but he who descended from heaven, the Son of man" (3:13). The way to God, according to John, is through belief in Jesus.

This is not so for the *Secret Book of James* and the *Gospel of Thomas.* They contend that the believer will be able to ascend heavenward and see the Father. At the close of the *Secret Book of James,* Peter and James kneel in prayer and send their hearts, minds, and souls up to the first, second, and third heavens. This three-level heaven, in contrast to a seven-level heaven common in Jewish apocalyptic circles in the first century, is identical to the three heavens to which Paul says he ascended fourteen years before he wrote to the Corinthians (2 Cor. 12:2-4). The *Gospel of Thomas* has several sayings integral to the text that promise that the disciple will be able to see the Father in heaven (11a, 15, 27, 111a). Jesus says in *Thomas* 15, "When you see one who was not born of woman, prostrate yourselves on your faces and worship him. That one is your Father."

We can go back as far as the mid-first century to Paul's authentic letters to see him battle against the very same Wisdom theology catchwords we find in *Thomas* and the *Secret Book of James.* Paul wrote sarcastically in 1 Cor. 4:38, "Already you are filled! Already you have become rich! Without us you have become kings! And would that you did reign, so that we might share the rule with you!"

The word "filled" used in connection with being saved occurs a number of times in the *Secret Book of James.* But the term is also used in a beatitude found in Matthew, Luke, and *Thomas.* Saying 69 in *Thomas* reads, "Blessed are the hungry, for the belly of him who desires will be filled."

To become rich is the promise found in Jewish Wisdom literature and in *Thomas* 110 for the seeker of wisdom. As for "reigning," Jesus also talked constantly, albeit cryptically, about 'the kingdom." *Thomas* 2 promises, at the start, that those who seek and find will be astonished, and once that happens they will reign and finally be at rest (Oxy. pap. 654).

Thomas relates to the Pauline period in another way. The earliest sayings in the *Gospel of Thomas* speak of making the two into one (referring to the two sexes); that is, the genders of male and female are no longer distinguished when the believer is baptized. This is a return to the androgynous state known by the heavenly Adam. Yalé's Wayne Meeks published an article eleven years ago that made a good case for this kind of baptismal rite existing even before Paul's time. It is this rite, Meeks said, that was behind Paul's reference to the baptismal transformation in which believers became neither male nor female (Gal. 3:26-28).

James is certainly a teacher of plain and mysterious wisdom in the New Testament gospels, but that aspect is overshadowed by the biblical descriptions of Jesus as Messiah and the eventually returning Son of man. The *Gospel of Thomas,* for as long as it is analyzed just as critically as the New Testament Gospels for later editorial additions, has the promise of taking us close to the historical Jesus. However, the New Testament writers clearly had a more ambitious spiritual agenda than the early movement. Perhaps they felt justified in combating contemporary elitists who claimed Peter, James, and Judas as their mentors.

But texts such as the *Gospel of Thomas* and the *Secret Book of James* do not seem to display hypocritical, pompous, or elitist attitudes. One of Jesus' few ethical admonitions in *Thomas* is, "Do not tell lies and do not do what you hate, for all things are plain in the sight of heaven" (6b). The reactionary attacks by gentile-oriented New Testament writers toward a nonapocalyptic Wisdom theology and the early Jesus movement authorities combine to raise questions about where the truth lies. By using biblical critical methods on such promising documents as the *Gospel of Thomas* and the *Secret Book of James,* we have a chance to rehabilitate the witness of Judas and James, personages who knew Jesus better than any other followers.

IV

Philosophical and Theological Implications

Van A. Harvey*

New Testament Scholarship and Christian Belief

I

Anyone teaching the origins of Christianity to college undergraduates or divinity students cannot help but be struck by the enormous gap between what the average layperson believes to be historically true about Jesus of Nazareth and what the great majority of New Testament scholars have concluded after a century and a half of research and debate. Despite decades of research, the average person tends to think of the life of Jesus in much the same terms as Christians did three centuries ago: the humble manger birth in Bethlehem; the flight into Egypt to avoid the wicked King Herod; the baptism by John the Baptist, who recognized Jesus to be the long-promised Messiah; a three-year ministry in which Jesus' claims to divinity are met by the hostility of the Jews, who conspire to have him tried and crucified; and the burial in a garden tomb after which he rises from the dead.

So far as the biblical historian is concerned, however, there is scarcely a popularly held traditional belief about Jesus that is not regarded with considerable skepticism. It is not surprising, therefore, that any professor who today relies upon contemporary New Testament scholarship concerning the origins of Christianity meets with considerable student hostility and resistance. Whereas students of medieval or American history normally regard the teacher as an expert to be trusted, students of the origins of Christianity suspect that the teacher is a skeptic undermining their religious faith.

This gulf between the historian and the traditional Christian believer raises a number of important social, philosophical, and, as I hope to show,

*Van A. Harvey is Professor of Religion at Stanford University.

ethical issues. The social issue, although complex, may be put briefly in this way. Why is it that, in a culture so dominated by experts in every field, the opinion of New Testament historians has had so little influence on the public? The philosophical issue is also complicated, but it basically has to do with the important question concerning the role of presuppositions in professional historical inquiry. The conservative Christian student believes with some justification that the conclusions of biblical scholars are simply a function of their secular beliefs. Liberal New Testament scholars, it is said, create skeptical interpretations of the New Testament, while orthodox scholars create believing interpretations. Thus, it is not a case of objective scholarship versus faith; rather, it is simply a case of one faith colliding with another.

These social and philosophical issues, in my opinion, have ethical implications, because we are not dealing here with a mere difference of opinion about matters of fact; we are dealing with two normative policies concerning how one ought to go about reasoning about matters of historical fact. We have a conflict between two ideals concerning how historical beliefs should be acquired and maintained. These two ideals quite naturally find expression in two different tables of virtues and vices. We are dealing, in short, with a conflict between two "ethics of belief."

Anyone familiar with philosophical discussion of these matters will immediately recognize how complex and subtle these issues are, and I certainly cannot do them justice in the space allotted to me. Consequently, I am going to concentrate on only one of them—the conflict between the two ethics of belief. Moreover, in order to stimulate discussion, I will attempt to be provocative and argue from the standpoint of someone who believes that there is an implicit ethic in historical inquiry that conflicts with that of traditional Christian belief.

II

I first became aware of the moral dimension of this problem many years ago when, as a young theologian concerned with the integrity of Christian faith in a secular world, I turned to certain nineteenth-century intellectuals who had wrestled profoundly with the same issue. These intellectuals both attracted and frightened me. They attracted me because they took Christian faith so seriously, believing as they did that its loss could be catastrophic for Western culture. Moreover, they were themselves wistful for faith— drawn by its symbolic power and its metaphysical comfort in a world rapidly being demystified by the sciences. But these intellectuals frightened me because they regarded their own wistfulness not as a virtue but as a temptation to their intellectual integrity. Unlike their Christian contemporaries, they believed that faith, not doubt, leads one into temptation; that it is not faith that requires severity of conscience but skepticism and rational inquiry.

The viewpoint of these intellectuals is not best expressed by stating that they rejected Christian historical claims because they believed these claims to be false; rather, their position is best expressed by saying that they thought it was morally reprehensible to hold certain types of claims to be true "on faith." I say "certain types of claims" because they believed it was only wrong to hold "on faith" those propositions the truth of which could be adjudicated by some scholarly discipline. Not all Christian claims of course are the object of some sort of scholarly discipline in which there are widely accepted standards for judging their truth or falsity. There is no such discipline, for example, that has as its sphere of inquiry Christian claims about the triune nature of God. But some Christian claims—for example, those concerning the activities and teachings of Jesus—are historical claims and, as such, are also the object of highly specialized types of intellectual inquiry. Our nineteenth-century intellectual, I am suggesting, believed that it was morally reprehensible to insist that these claims were true on faith while at the same time arguing that they were also the legitimate objects of historical inquiry.

It is a measure of how distant we are psychically from the nineteenth century that most of us have a difficult time even understanding how this issue could be couched in moral terms. We can understand why someone might believe that certain statements about Jesus are false, but we cannot understand why someone should reject those claims on the ground that it is morally irresponsible to hold them "on faith." First of all, we do not understand how assenting to historical claims has anything at all to do with moral integrity. We can understand why someone might find certain claims difficult to believe, but to argue that one has a duty not to believe any such claim seems odd. Second, most of us are basically relativistic about matters of belief in general and historical beliefs in particular. We live in a culture in which people differ radically from one another as to what they can and do believe. Some believe that Mozart was poisoned, that Shakespeare was not the author of the plays that bore his name, that Kennedy was assassinated on orders from the CIA. Indeed, even historians differ among themselves about Joan of Arc, Luther, and the causes of World War II. "What has any of this to do with morality?" we ask.

In order to understand why we do not understand our nineteenth-century forebears in this respect, it is important to see that Victorian intellectuals believed that they had a special obligation for the health of culture or, as they would have expressed it, "civilization." The "clerisy," to use Coleridge's term for those educationalists, writers, lawyers, scientists, and civil servants who preside over the institutions that determine the nature of civilization, have a special responsibility for everything that molds the consciousness of a people. Consider language, for example. The clerisy believed that nothing determines the quality of civic discourse more than the way language is employed, because the discriminating use of language is crucial for the molding of those habits of reasoning and judgment upon which society depends. The future of a culture depends upon the level and precision of public debate, and the health of a culture can be measured by the lucidity of those debates through which the citizenry comes to judgment concerning its destiny.

The discriminating use of language and the patterns of reasoning it makes possible are not, it was argued, natural endowments. They are acquired in the same way that habits of character are acquired, namely, by self-discipline and training. Consequently, the clerisy exercises its responsibility for culture directly in its responsibility for those institutions in which the educated classes receive their training, which is to say, the schools. The aim of the schools is not merely to impart information; it is, rather, to inculcate those character traits or, to use Aristotelian language, those virtues that underlie and make possible the discriminating use of the mind. A child must learn through self-discipline the virtues of withholding premature judgment, of considering the evidence before assenting to a claim, of respecting alternative opinions, and of expressing one's opinions in a modulated and lucid fashion that conveys one's awareness of the degree of certainty to which one is entitled. The child must also learn to despise certain vices, above all, the vices of intellectual sloth and credulity, because these undermine all those qualities that are the foundation of an educated public. As one important interpreter of Victorian life, G. M. Young, once expressed it, the Victorian intellectual believed that children should be taught that they had no more right to an opinion for which they could give no reason than a pint of beer for which they could not pay.

It is a great irony that many educated people probably half-believe that it is arrogant and elitist to think that intellectuals have any special responsibility for the health of culture: an irony because at the very time that the ideal of public education has triumphed in our society, the ethic that propelled and nourished it has collapsed. But as a young Protestant theologian, I regarded this Victorian ethic of belief not as a manifestation of arrogance, but as a last vestige of the Protestant doctrine of vocation. Luther and Calvin had taught that one served God and neighbor not by becoming a priest but by fulfilling the duties of a secular vocation. One is called by God to be a judge or a carpenter or a businessman. And, if one is called to be a judge, then one obeys God by becoming an expert in the law; if a carpenter by becoming an excellent craftsman in wood; if a businessman, by becoming a first-rate entrepreneur. So, too, one fulfilled one's duties as an intellectual by acquiring those virtues of the self-disciplined mind.

Now it is characteristic of the intellectual vocations that they presuppose a rather general set of habits or virtues, on the one hand, and a rather specific set, on the other. Scientists, judges, engineers, journalists, humanists—all of them have the obligation to be honest and to make use of modes of reasoning that permit the assessment and criticism of arguments and the conclusions to arguments. All of the intellectual enterprises, one might say, require a general disposition to acquire evidence before coming to judgment and to submit one's conclusions to the criticism of one's peers. But intellectuals increasingly work in specialized communities of inquiry, each of which has their own rules and procedures. The historian's use of evidence and reasoning, for example, is different from that of the biologist, the neurologist, and the physician. In other words, the obligations of the intellectual are role specific, and it is because these procedures are role specific that we can speak of the unique expertise of the medieval historian in contrast to that of the urban sociologist, of the cultural anthropologist in contrast to the neurologist, of the historian of Greek philosophy in contrast to the logician.

Given this role-specific nature of intellectual inquiry, we are now in a better position to return to the issue with which I began. The gulf separating the conservative Christian believer and the New Testament scholar can be seen as the conflict between two antithetical ethics of belief. Viewed from the moral standpoint of the scholar, the issue may be put in two ways, both of which are morally offensive to the conservative Christian believer. The first of these is that New Testament scholarship is now so specialized and requires so much preparation and learning that the layperson has simply been disqualified from having any right to a judgment regarding the truth or falsity of certain historical claims. Insofar as the conservative Christian believer is a layperson who has no knowledge of the New Testament scholarship, he or she is simply not entitled to certain historical beliefs at all. Just as the average layperson is scarcely in a position to have an informed judgment about the seventh letter of Plato, the relationship of Montezuma to Cortez, or the authorship of the Donation of Constantine, so the average layperson has no right to an opinion about the authorship of the Fourth Gospel or the trustworthiness of the synoptics.

This conclusion, which initially sounds so outrageous and arrogant, is really nothing more than the extension of the attitudes of the scholarly community to its own fledgling members. Just as a classicist will listen with respect only to the opinions of another classicist on questions concerning the authenticity of the portrait of Socrates in the late Platonic dialogues and not, for example, to the opinions of an American historian, so, also, the New Testament scholar discounts the opinions of laypersons regarding the New Testament because they lack not only those tools essential to scholarship—Greek, Aramaic, Hebrew, form and tradition criticism, knowledge of ancient Near Eastern religions—but also those less easily defined but important qualities of judgment that characterize those who acquire distinction in their scholarly disciplines. In short, the result of the professionalization of knowledge has been to render amateurish most of the traditionally held beliefs of the average layperson and the conservative Christian.

I do not believe that the historic significance of this professionalization of knowledge of the Bible should be underestimated. Indeed, it constitutes an enormous wrench in the consciousness of Western humanity. Hitherto, the Bible, and especially the New Testament, has provided the fundamental text that has shaped the morality and ethics of Western culture. Since the Reformation, it has been assumed in Protestant countries that any literate person could pick up the Bible, understand it, and assent to its various claims. Evangelical Christianity, which rests on this basic assumption, presupposes that just such reading and understanding is the basis of conversion. It should not be surprising, therefore, that the emergence of a specialized scholarly discipline that implicitly rejects this claim should give rise to hostility and resentment. New Testament scholarship threatens to alienate the Western consciousness from one of its most cherished assumptions.

But I have said that the moral issue between scholar and believer can be expressed in two ways: The first, which I have already indicated, is that the scholar does not think that the layperson is entitled to an opinion about the historical Jesus. The second is even more serious. It is that the scholar believes that the ingression of traditional Christian belief into the inquiry concerning the truth of the historical claims of the New Testament tends to corrode the habits and virtues of historical judgment itself. This argument, of course, needs to be spelled out carefully, and I have attempted to do so elsewhere. But basically the issue is this: Whereas thᴜ average person feels no subjective need to have an opinion about the seventh letter of Plato, the traditional Christian, by contrast, identifies faith with certain claims about the historical Jesus. The Bible is believed to be divinely inspired, and this, in turn, guarantees the legitimacy of all the assertions within it. To be skeptical about these claims, therefore, is to be skeptical about faith itself. It could be argued, as certain liberal Christian theologians have, that this need not be the case, that the Christian could view the religious value of the Jesus story to consist not in its historical veracity, its truth as fact, but in its religious content. One might argue, as the theologian Paul Tillich has done, that the religious truth of the New Testament consists in the understanding of life mediated through the picture of Jesus, whether that picture is historically true or not. But the Christian who believes historical propositions "on faith" cannot accept this view. He or she takes an "infinite interest," to use Kierkegaard's language, in the "approximation process" of historical research. But the result, as Kierkegaard pointed out, is for the believer to become "comical," that is, to be infinitely interested in that which at its most accurate still always remains an approximation. Kierkegaard also saw, but was less interested in, the fact that this view leads to fanaticism, which is to say, the corruption of historical judgment itself, because the believer cannot be as disinterested as the scholar must. It was just this fanaticism that repelled our nineteenth-century intellectual. He believed that historical inquiry requires "subjective lightness," a methodological skepticism concerning sources and the testimony of alleged witnesses. When the Christian interjects faith or "subjective heaviness" into the historical approximation process, it inevitably undermines what R. G. Collingwood argued was the fundamental attribute of the critical historian, skepticism regarding testimony about the past.

But it is not only the autonomy of the historian that traditional faith undermines. Christian faith, when it is identified with specific historical beliefs, corrodes the delicate processes of historical reasoning itself. The reason for this, as F. H. Bradley once pointed out, is that all of our assertions about the past contain an element of judgment. Even the simplest judgment about the past is far from simple but presupposes a network of beliefs. In fact, we bring to every assertion what Bradley calleᴄ "the formed world of our existing beliefs." Thus what we call a historical fact is really an inference, and an inference is justified only against the background of our critically interpreted present experience. It is against the background of this critically interpreted experience that the historian can make all of his or her carefully modulated claims—that such and such is possible, improbable, or certain. The problem with traditional Christian belief is that, in contrast to all other texts, it sets aside our present critically interpreted experience when it comes to interpreting the New Testament. It assumes that in this case alone what our critically interpreted experience tells us is "impossible" is not only possible but probable and certain. "Heavy" assent is given to propositions that, in the light of present experience, deserve only light assent if not skepticism; claims with a very low degree of probability are converted into propositions that solicit heavy assent. Consequently, there is no way for the critical historian to enter into the lists of argument, because the background of our common beliefs that makes adjudication possible is set aside. The scholar's basic moral ideal of balanced judgment based on evidence and argument is undermined.

The moralization of the reasoning process, like that of the political, has its own dangers of fanaticism. Of that I am aware. Every normative ideal can be the vehicle of self-righteousness and arrogance. But it is even more dangerous to the community to assume that how one acquires one's beliefs is simply a matter of individual taste. And for that remnant few for whom the nineteenth-century ideal still reigns, certain words of Nietzsche still possess a measure of moral nobility. The "wrestle for truth," Nietzsche wrote, "requires greatness of soul: the service of truth is the hardest service. What does it mean, after all, to have integrity in matters of the spirit? That one is severe against one's heart, that one despise 'beautiful sentiment,' that one makes of every Yes and No a matter of conscience."

Antony Flew*

Historical Credentials and Particular Revelation

I

Once upon a time, when there was more concern than there is now both with the truth claims of Christianity and with finding some rational warrant for accepting these claims, much was heard of the scandal of particularity. It consisted in the fact that Christianity, alone among the great world religions, centers on what is supposed to have happened during a particular period, in a particular country, and upon this particular planet Earth. Christianity is in this to be distinguished even from Islam. For, although the providing of a revelation of Allah by the prophet was equally particular, its content was not: indeed to the Muslim, any suggestion of ar identification of Mohammed with Allah has to be supremely blasphemous. It is this scandal of particularity that must make the possibility of rational agents elsewhere in the universe embarrassing for Christians in a way in which for adherents of other religions it is not.

Another consequence of the same peculiarity is that any Christians so unfashionable as to want to produce evidences showing the reasonableness of their faith have had to try to come to terms with what, in a landmark paper, F. H. Bradley called "The Presuppositions of Critical History."[1] Christians have certainly not been alone in hoping to validate the claims of their candidate's revelation by maintaining that these claims have been, and perhaps still are, endorsed by the occurrence of miracles. Nor does this seem an unreasonable apologetic project. For if the laws of nature express practical necessities and practical impossibilities, as they surely do, then these could be overridden only by some supernatural power. So how

---

*Antony Flew is Emeritus Professor of Philosophy at the University of Reading, England.

better could such a power indicate its approval than by executing miraculous overridings of laws of nature? The peculiarity of Christianity lies in the fact that at least one miracle, and that a miracle of miracles, is not simply evidence for the authenticity of but the essential element in its supposed revelation. For, as Saint Paul so rightly insisted, "If Christ be not risen then is our preaching vain, your faith is also vain."[2]

II

What I propose to present is an argument to demonstrate this, and to show why that apparently not "unreasonable project" cannot after all be implemented. This argument is, of course, fundamentally the same as that first published in Section 10 of Hume's first *Enquiry*. But mine is a tuned-up version.[3] (Some tuning up is most urgently required. For, by denying earlier in that *Enquiry* that we either do or even can have experience of practical necessity and practical impossibility, Hume disqualified himself from distinguishing the merely marvelous from the genuinely miraculous.)

The heart of the matter is that the criteria by which we must assess historical testimony, and the general presumptions that alone make it possible for us to construe the detritus of the past as historical evidence must inevitably rule out any possibility of establishing, upon purely historical grounds, that some genuinely miraculous event has indeed occurred. Hume himself concentrated on testimonial evidence because his own conception of the historian, later illustrated in his own famous *History of England,* was of a judge assessing, with judicious impartiality, the testimony set before him. But, in the immediate present context, this limitation is not important.

The basic propositions are: first, that the present relics of the past cannot be interpreted as historical evidence at all, unless we presume that the same fundamental regularities obtained then still obtain today; second, that, in trying as best he may to determine what actually happened, the historian must employ as criteria all his present knowledge, or presumed knowledge, of what is probable or improbable, possible or impossible; and, third, that, since the word "miracle" has to be defined in terms of practical necessity and practical impossibility, the application of these criteria inevitably precludes proof of a miracle.

Hume illustrated the first proposition in his *Treatise,* urging that it is only upon such presumptions of regularity that we can justify the conclusion that ink marks on old pieces of paper constitute testimonial evidence. Earlier in the first *Enquiry* he urged the inescapable importance of the criteria demanded by the second. Without criteria there can be no discrimination, and hence no history worthy of the name. The application of both the second and the third contention can be seen most sharply in the footnote in which Hume quotes with approval the reasoning of the famous physician De Sylva in the case of Mlle. Thibaut: "It was impossible that she could have been so ill as was 'proved' by witnesses, because it was impossible that she could, in so short a time, have recovered so perfectly as he found her."

We need at this point to ask and to answer a question that Hume himself was in no position to press, because earlier he had denied the legitimacy of notions of practical (as opposed to logical) necessity and impossibility. That question is as follows: what, if anything, justified De Sylva in rejecting the proposition proved (or, he would presumably have written, "proved") by the testimony of witnesses? What, if anything, justified him in stubbornly continuing to maintain that the event allegedly witnessed did not in fact occur, because it could not have?

It is a matter of what evidence there is or can be, a matter of verification and of verifiability. The two crucial and conflicting propositions are of very different and quite disproportionate orders of logical strength, of confirmation and confirmability. For the propositions asserted by the putative witnesses were singular, and in the past tense: once upon a time, on one particular occasion, this or that actually happened. The days are, therefore, long past when that claim could be directly confirmed or disconfirmed. But the propositions that rule out the alleged miraculous occurrences as naturally and practically impossible must be general: it is either necessary or impossible for any so-and-so to be such-and-such. Nomological propositions, as these are called, can therefore in principle, if not necessarily and always in practice, be tested and retested anywhere and at any time.

And furthermore—as Damon Runyon characters loved to say—only when and insofar as one and all are agreed that some desirable occurrence would have been naturally impossible, and could have occurred, if at all, only through supernatural intervention, can any dispute about historical evidence possibly proving the occurrence of the miraculous be profitably undertaken.

III

Reasoning of the form so commendably exemplified by the physician De Sylva, like reasoning in all other valid forms, will sometimes lead to false conclusions. Hume himself, by dismissing reports of phenomena that the progress of abnormal psychology has since shown to be entirely possible, became exposed to Hamlet's too often quoted rebuke to overweening philosophy. What is practically or, if you like, contingently impossible is what is logically incompatible with true laws of nature. So if you mistake some proposition to express such a law when in fact it does not, then you are bound to be wrong also about the consequent practical impossibilities. But that a mode of argument must sometimes lead to false conclusions is no sufficient reason to reject it as unsound. The critical historian has no option but to argue in this sort of way.

To make clearer what is involved, consider an example derived from the work of the acknowledged father of critical history. This example has the advantage of being far removed from any ideologically sensitive area. Herodotus knew that, except where it is joined to Asia by an isthmus, Africa is surrounded by sea. But he did not know either that earth is— roughly—spherical and suspended in space, or all the consequences of these facts. So, in chapter 42 of book 4 of his account of ancient Greece's Great Patriotic War, he writes: "Necos, the Egyptian king . . . desisting from the canal which he had begun between the Nile and the Arabian gulf, sent to sea a number of ships manned by Phoenicians with orders to make for the straits of Gibraltar, and return to Egypt through them, and by the Mediterranean." This, in due course they succeeded in doing. "On their return they declared—I for my part do not believe them, but perhaps others may—that in sailing round Africa they had the sun on their right hand."

The incredulity of Herodotus upon this particular point was, as we know, mistaken. Indeed the very feature of the whole tradition that provoked his suspicion constitutes for us the best reason for believing that a Phoenician expedition did indeed circumnavigate Africa. But that Herodotus here went wrong upon a point of fact does not indicate that his method was unsound. On the contrary: his verdict on this point is only discovered to have been mistaken when later historians, employing the same fundamental principles of assessment, reconsider it in the light of subsequent advances in astronomy and geography. It was entirely proper and reasonable for Herodotus to measure the likelihood of this Phoenician tale against the possibilities suggested by the best astronomical theory and geographical information available to him in the fifth century B.C., as well as against what he knew of the veracity of travelers in general, and of Phoenicians in particular. It was one thing to believe that they had set off and returned as reported, since he presumably had other evidence for this, better than the word of Phoenician sailors; and if they had done these things they must have circumnavigated Africa, since it would have been impossible for them to overland their ships. It would have been quite another to believe a traveler's tale not made probable by any promising theory and unsupported by other evidence.

Similar considerations and principles apply whether, as here, attention centers on an alleged impossibility, or whether, as more usually, it is a matter of what, granted always some presupposed framework of known possibilities and impossibilities, is only probable or improbable.

IV

Faced by this Humean argument apologists are likely to be tempted to respond in various ways, all of which will get them nowhere. Notoriously "the good David" was so imprudent as to dismiss stories of two wonders wrought by the emperor Vespasian, two stories that, we now have excellent reason to believe, were surely true. We may, therefore, be seduced to suggest that, with further advances in our knowledge, several of the miracle stories in the Bible may be similarly sustained.

Indeed they may be; and perhaps some already have been. But this is not a bit of help to the apologist if the progressive verification is achieved— as in fact it always is, and has to be—only at the price of showing that, although what was said to have happened did indeed happen, its happening was not after all miraculous. Suppose that all the miracle stories in the New Testament were true, but that none of the events occurring were genuinely miraculous. Then we are left with no evidence[4] for believing the fundamental, essential, defining Christian dogma, that Jesus, bar Joseph, was God incarnate.

Nor is there any profit here in maintaining that the typically biblical notion is that of a sign, not necessarily involving any overriding of an established natural order. For, insofar as there is now nothing intrinsically remarkable and discernibly out of this world about the occurrences themselves, if any, these putatively revealing signs will have to be identified and interpreted as such by reference to precisely that system the claims of which require authentication.

Suppose, ᵗo⁻ the sake of argument, that we had been able to erect a solid and rich natural theology. And suppose too that this gave us good reason both for expecting that the God thus discovered had vouchsafed some supplementary revelation, and for believing that this revelation is bound to be identifiable as real by remarks of a certain type. Then for these marks to suffice it would not be necessary for their occurrence to constitute any kind of overriding of the ordinary order of nature. The situation here imagined, however, is very far from being that in which any of us actually find ourselves in that in our actual situation, with no solid and sufficiently rich natural theology, signs cannot substitute for true, traditional, completely supernatural miracles.

Again, someone is sure to want to remind us of Hume's own contention that we have and can have no experience of, and hence no conception of, physical as opposed to logical necessities and impossibilities. Others will be eager to assert that modern science has had to jettison the notions both of causality and of laws of nature. As that old Cambridge cynic Prof. C. D. Broad so loved to insist, "Some philosophers would say anything— except their prayers!"

There is, however, no call for us to try to refute such teachings here. It is enough to point out that our present opponents cannot by any means afford to accept them. If Christian apologists are to produce evidencing reasons for believing that they have hold of an authentic revelation, then they have to presuppose the existence of a strong natural order; an order the maintenance of which is ineluctably necessary, and that is practically impossible to violate. If truly there is no such order, then there can be no question of any overriding of it, and hence no question of referring to any alleged overridings in order to validate anything. (Much more is at stake as well: for instance, the very possibility of critical history. But that is a story for another place, another time.)

If, therefore, validation is to be achieved along these lines—and the Christian is scarcely overwhelmed by the problems of choosing between alternative apologetic avenues—then we have got to have a strong natural order. We have also got to have, and we have got to be able to recognize by natural (as opposed to revealed) means, overridings of that natural (as opposed to transcendent) order.

The crunch comes over the problem of identification. The temptation is to assume that we have some natural (as opposed to revealed) means of telling that something, notwithstanding that it did actually happen, nevertheless could not have happened naturally (in the other sense). We have not. Our only way of determining the capacities and the incapacities of nature is to study what does in fact occur. Suppose, for instance, that all previous observation and experiment had suggested that some performance was beyond human power; and suppose then we find, to our amazement, that after all some people can do it. Still this by itself is a reason not for postulating a series of infusions of supernatural grace, but for shaking up the psychological assumptions that these discoveries have discredited.

V

The upshot is that Hume was right in his main contention, that "a miracle can never be proved so as to be the foundation of a system of religion."[5] It is essential to realize that this important conclusion depends upon two things: first, an understanding of the methodological presuppositions of critical history; and second, a recognition of the impossibility of supplementing these by appealing to natural theology. Neither alone could be decisive. The two in combination are. To ignore either, or not to appreciate how they complement one another, is to fail altogether to take the measure of the force and the generality of the Humean offensive.[6] Given a rich and positive natural theology, the historian could perhaps find there natural means to identify overriding acts of God. He could thus distinguish what is naturally possible from what, on privileged occasions, in fact occurs. What is naturally impossible is nevertheless possible to God. If it were not for the fundamental requirements of critical history it might be legitimate to claim, as is so often done, that the historical evidence by itself shows that the crucial miracles did actually happen. If so, the claims of revelation might, at least to some extent, be authenticated thereby.

These fundamentals of critical history are, in their present application, still constantly ignored. One once and perhaps still popular book, *The Bible in the Age of Science,* first assures us that "in the twentieth century there is a developing recognition that the question whether the New Testament miracles happened is one that can be settled only by historical enquiry"; and then later offers—apparently as an "historical answer . . . given on the basis of historical evidence"—"that it is an historical fact that Jesus was known by his apostles to have risen from the dead."[7]

It was, I think, altogether characteristic of this particular author to write, not straightforwardly that "Jesus rose from the dead," but more deviously, that "Jesus was known by his apostles to have risen from the dead." This actually preferred formulation raises possibilities of slippery equivocation. There would be nothing in itself miraculous in the fact that people believed that a miracle had occurred. But to describe their belief as knowledge is, of course, to commit yourself to the further claims that what they believed was true, and that they were in a position to know this. It is these further claims that are needed to give point to the author's thesis.

He presents this stuff very confidently, having no patience for any philosophical criticism: "The one indubitable truth which we learn from a study of the history of philosophy is that of the impermanence of philosophical points of view." Yet it would not be quite right to say that methodological objections are totally ignored. For there is in one footnote a contemptuous phrase dismissing T. A. Roberts *History and Christian Apologetic* as "a clear statement of . . . the nineteenth century understanding of the historical method." This is glossed in the text: "The twentieth century has witnessed the disintegration of the old positivistic assumptions of Liberal historiography, especially the assumption that it is the task of the historian to construct an 'objective' account of 'what happened' in the past."[8] My sometime colleague Dr. Roberts was no doubt well content to be thus despised for his theologically unfashionable concern with historical truth.

A more worthy opponent is Cardinal Newman, who made an unusually serious attempt to come to terms with Humean criticism; yet even he seems to have failed to appreciate its full force and, in particular, how the two components work together. He is prepared to allow the general soundness of Hume's principles for the assessment of testimonial evidence. What he challenges is their application to "these particular miracles, ascribed to the particular Peter, James, and John." We have to ask whether they really are "unlikely supposing that there is a Power, external to the world, who can bring them about; supposing they are the only means by which He can reveal himself to those who need a revelation; supposing that He is likely to reveal himself; that He has a great end in doing so."[9]

This tempting argument overlooks something crucial I have not myself mentioned so far in my text. It is that Section 10 of Hume's first *Enquiry* is complementary to Section 11, and that in that later section Hume presented a most powerful argument for saying not only that we do not have any natural knowledge of the existence of such a power, but also, and here perhaps even more relevantly, that we could have no warrant for conjectures as to what upon this supposition might reasonably be expected. The response to all Newman's rhetorical questions should therefore be that any such conclusions about either likelihoods or unlikelihoods upon "the religious hypothesis" are surely without foundation: "it must evidently appear contrary to all rule of analogy to reason from the projects and intentions of men to those of a Being so different and so much superior."[10]

NOTES

1. F. H. Bradley, *Collected Essays* (Oxford: Clarendon, 1935).

2. 1 Corinthians 15:14. In England today, and no doubt elsewhere also, it is impossible to underline Saint Paul's point too heavily. For we have numerous clerics who, while ever eager to present their conventionally left-wing politics as part if not the whole of the teachings of Christianity, are in fact themselves not Christians at all.

3. For much more on this argument in Hume, and on how it both needs to and can be strengthened, see: first, my *Hume's Philosophy of Belief* (London: Routledge and Kegan Paul, 1961), chap. 8; and, second, my Introduction to *Hume: "Of Miracles,"* forthcoming from Open Court of La Salle, Illinois.

4. The contrast is between evidencing and motivating reasons. See, for instance, my discussion of the Wager Argument of Pascal in *An Introduction to Western Philosophy* (Indianapolis and New York: Bobbs-Merrill, 1971), 6:7.

5. *Enquiries concerning Human Understanding and concerning the Principles of Morals,* ed. L. A. Selby-Bigge, 3d ed. (Oxford: Clarendon, 1975), 127.

6. Section 11 of the first *Enquiry* is complementary to Section 10. See, for instance, *Hume's Philosophy of Belief,* chap. 8-9.

7. A. Richardson, *The Bible in an Age of Science* (London: SCM Press, 1961), 206, 132.

8. Ibid., 12, 125, 126. For more on Richardson's wretched but not unrepresentative book see my *God and Philosophy,* recently reissued as *God: A Critical Enquiry* (La Salle, Ill.: Open Court, 1984).

9. "Essay on the Miracles Recorded in Ecclesiastical History," in *The Ecclesiastical History of M. L'Abbé Fleury* (Oxford: J. H. Parker, 1842), 2 (viii):2.

10. Hume, *Enquiries,* 146.

John Hick*

A Remonstrance in Concluding

Most readers of *Free Inquiry* I presume would describe themselves as secular humanists. This article is written from a somewhat different point of view, that of a Christian. I started out a long time ago as a very conservative Christian—indeed, a fundamentalist Christian, though I have grown out of that. But I think it worthwhile to say that the fundamentalist wing within Christianity does serve an important purpose. Fundamentalism, or extreme conservative evangelicalism, can be an important phase through which to pass, though not a good one in which to get stuck. The conservative evangelicals do have the zeal to sometimes jolt young people out of an unthinking, self-centered materialism, and this can be very good. What is not good, of course, is for people to remain in that mold and become not simply enthusiastic young evangelicals but retarded adult ones.

From the liberal Christian standpoint, which I now occupy, I would like to ask two questions in connection with the subject of Jesus in history and myth. The two questions are: What do the liberal Christian and the secular humanist have in common? And where do we part company? We have in common, first, an opposition to the so-called creationists who are trying to turn the clock back in the teaching of science in the schools, and also an opposition to the people who are trying to impose Christian worship in the schools. So far as I am concerned, this opposition is in the interests not only of secularists but also of Jews, Muslims, Hindus, Buddhists, Sikhs, et al. This is a pluralistic country, and for that reason, quite apart from any other, there ought not to be required Christian worship in the nation's schools.

I spoke of the creationists. Notice how tricky language is. It seems to me a shame that the word "creationist" has become a label not only for

---

*John Hick is Professor of Systematic Theology at the Claremont Graduate School.

people who believe that the universe is God's creation but also for those who insist that biological evolution has not occurred. I too am a creationist in the sense that I believe that the universe is God's creation, but I believe that God's creative work is progressive and continuous and that biological evolution is a part of it. And so I am sorry that the word *creation* has become linked with the obscurantist rejection of evolution. The kind of creationism that I and other liberal Christians espouse is neither scientific nor antiscientific. The purview of science only goes back some fifteen billion years to the big bang. And, if the big bang should turn out to have been an absolute beginning, then science has nothing to say beyond it, though of course religion does.

Now let us turn to the Jesus of history. Was there a first-century person called Jesus or Joshua ben Joseph who was the founder of the Christian religion? This question of course has the rider that, if there was, he did not *intend* to found the Christian religion, since he believed that the end of the present age and the present order of history was going to come very soon. He could not possibly have had any idea of founding a religion that was to exist for twenty centuries, or indeed for one century. But the idea that there never was such a person goes back, I suppose, some one hundred and fifty years and has not been persuasive to more than a very small minority of those who have studied the matter carefully. Its status among historians is no higher than, and I would think in fact lower than, the theory among Elizabethan historians that Francis Bacon wrote the plays of Shakespeare. And, if I might offer a piece of friendly advice—and it is meant as genuinely friendly advice—to the secular humanist movement, it would be: Don't identify too closely with this kind of eccentric view. For the theory that Jesus never existed is not really a very probable one; and, further, the issue is, to say the least, not today at the cutting edge of research concerning Christian origins.

And I would extend the same advice to seeing the Dead Sea Scrolls as a stick with which to beat Christianity. The Dead Sea Scrolls are enormously important, but primarily, it would seem, in enlarging our understanding of the varieties of first-century Judaism. The idea that they have transformed the understanding of Christianity so as somehow to discredit it is not easy to sustain. . . .

So I really think that we are stuck, whether we like it or not, with the figure of the historical Jesus. Of course we do not see him directly, but through thick layers of first-, second-, and third-generation Christian faith. Some very interesting papers have appeared that have pointed out the various theological and sociological interests that entered into the growth and transmission of the New Testament tradition. It is clear, I think, that what we have is not just straight reporting but remembering in faith, with all the differences that faith makes to the remembering. But nevertheless it has been possible to give an approximate date to most of the documents, to set them in a probable chronological order, and to observe certain trajectories in the growth of the tradition. And when you have a documented forward trajectory you can to some extent reverse it and extrapolate back to the starting point. You have to do this very cautiously. You can do it only to a limited extent. But the growth of the tradition does seem to point back to a historical person who was Jesus.

We can say that Jesus lived in the first third of the first century and that he was a Jew—indeed, his Jewishness is becoming more and more fully recognized. He was evidently a charismatic preacher and healer. And it would seem, from the cluster of stories and parables and sayings that are associated with his name, that he must have had an extraordinarily intense and compelling sense of the reality and presence of God; also that he expected God's kingdom to come very soon on earth, wiping away the whole present order of society. And, furthermore, in the parables and sayings that are attributed to him, there is a very strong emphasis upon self-giving love, agapē. Furthermore, it seems clear that some of his disciples had visions of him after his death. And when his followers, going out in the enthusiasm of the transformed life that had come upon them, tried to make his existence meaningful to others they clutched at images that were there—floating, so to speak, in the air of their culture. There was the image of the son of man of Danielic prophecy, who was to come again in clouds of glory, and there was the image of the Messiah. However, it does not seem very probable that Jesus applied either of these images, or any other titles, to himself; rather, other people came to apply them to him.

Negatively—and this is very important—it seems pretty clear that Jesus did not present himself as being God incarnate. He did not present himself as the second person of a divine trinity leading a human life. If in his lifetime he was called "son of God," as is entirely possible, it would be in the metaphorical sense that was familiar in the ancient world. In this sense, kings, emperors, pharaohs, wise men, and charismatic religious leaders were very freely called sons of God, meaning that they were close to God, in the spirit of God, that they were servants and instruments of God. The ancient Hebrew kings were regularly enthroned as son of God in this metaphorical sense.

Now this original, biblical "son of God" language is entirely innocent, so to speak, entirely acceptable and understandable in the context of the ancient Nea' East. We use the metaphor today in an extended form when we say, for example, that all human beings are children of God. This is a metaphorical way of saying that all human beings are valued by God. But the fateful development that created what was to become orthodox Christian belief for many centuries occurred when this poetry hardened into prose and the metaphorical son of God, with a small s, was transmuted into the metaphysical God the Son, with a capital S. The philosophers then developed the explanatory theory that Jesus had two complete natures, one human and the other divine, and that in his divine nature he was of the same substance as God the Father, while in his human nature he was of the same substance as humanity.

Now I hold, as do many liberal Christians today, that a Christian does not have to accept those philosophical and theological theories of the third and fourth centuries. I think that we can base our Christianity upon Jesus' teachings concerning the reality and love and claim of God, and upon the love ethic that has developed out of it. This provides a framework for life regardless of how much or how little detail we know for sure about Jesus' life.

Christianity has, like every other religion, developed its own mythology. This mythology is at its height in the beautiful imagery that centers around the festivals of Christmas and Easter. And I would suggest that mythology is not necessarily a bad thing; it is not to be scorned. Indeed, there is today a rediscovery of the value of myth in human life. A considerable literature is growing up about its positive uses. Myths are not literally true, but they may nevertheless be mythologically true; that is to say, they may evoke in the hearer practical dispositions that are appropriate to the ultimate subject matter of the myth. They may be a good way of communicating the claim of the transcendent upon us.

Having said that Christianity provides a good framework for the religious life, I do not go on to say that it provides a *better* framework than is provided by Rabbinic Judaism, or Islam, or Hinduism, or Buddhism, and so on. Rather, for many of us it is the framework into which we were born, which has therefore formed us in its own image, and which accordingly suits us better than a framework that is alien to us. Accordingly, I do not seek to convert people of the other great world religions to Christianity, though I would be very happy if I could convert secular humanists to any one of the great world religions—whichever one happened to be most suitable to the particular individual—because they all provide windows onto the transcendent. They all lead to what religion is ultimately all about, namely, the transformation of human existence from self-centeredness to reality-centeredness.

Having referred to the other great world religions, let me mention a parallel between the historical Jesus, known as the Messiah or the Christ, and the historical Gautama, known as the Buddha. It occurs to me that it would be quite possible for someone to come along and question the existence of the historical Buddha. It would be possible to suggest that maybe there was no such person; certainly one cannot strictly prove that there was. But, just as the trajectories of the physical universe, when you follow them backward, lead to the postulated big bang, so the trajectories of Buddhist development lead back to the spiritual big bang of a man who had attained enlightenment, and so also the trajectories of Christian development point back to the spiritual big bang of a man who was overwhelmingly conscious of the dynamic presence of God. And I think that it is religiously important that we know something, even if something rather general and minimal, about the lives of Gautama and Jesus. It adds something important to the Buddhist message of the transcendence of ego to know that this man Gautama, who attained that total transcendence of ego that is nirvana, did not then retreat from the world to enjoy this bliss but spent the next forty years of his life strenuously traveling around India teaching other people, helping them to attain that which is beyond the ego state. Thus, if we knew nothing about the man who gave the teaching, we would be impoverished. And, likewise, it seems to me that it adds something important to the Christian message of the reality and love of God, and of the claim of love upon all human life, to know that the person who so powerfully taught this lived, as did Gautama, in relative poverty, that he gave his time and energies to others, and that he was willing to accept the rather grisly death that came to him.

Reverting now to the role of one giving friendly advice, in which I suggested that secular humanism should not become the last refuge of eccentric theories about Jesus, I also want to suggest that secular humanists should not spend too much time fighting yesterday's battles. It was, for example, back in the eighteenth century that the argument from miracles to the truth of Christianity was flourishing. Today it can no doubt be found among some of our evangelical brethren, but it does not play a large part in the ongoing encounter of Christianity with the modern world. The contemporary issues in the philosophy of religion are very different from those of the eighteenth century. They include such topics as the epistemology and sociology of knowledge, and the place of interpretation, and thus of faith, in all world-views and also in historical knowledge; the study of interesting developments in contemporary scientific cosmology;

the problem of the apparently conflicting truth claims of the different world religions; the epistemological question of foundationalism; fascinating new forms of the ontological argument; the application of Bayesian probability theory to theism; the encounter between Christianity and Marxism. These are some of the live issues today; and there are so many live issues that there seems to me no need to continue to spend a lot of time on dead ones.

Let me end by asking: If one takes this kind of liberal Christian stance, is one still a Christian? Well, if you see Christianity as a body of propositions that have to be the same in the twentieth century as they were in the fourth century, then probably not. But of course Christianity has never been as unchanging and monolithic as both conservative believers and conservative unbelievers like to think. It has always been an actively developing tradition. And it has always been internally pluralistic. Even in the earliest period there was a plurality of Christologies. There are different trajectories moving out of the New Testament, and today, with the collapse, or partial collapse, of ecclesiastical authority, these differences are flourishing again.

But I think it is noticeable that some secular humanists would rather like Christians to stick with the ancient, outdated forms of Christianity that arose in long-past phases of Western culture. They want us to hold as absurd beliefs as possible, presumably because then it is much easier to fight against these beliefs. But I suggest that they would do better not to join the fundamentalists in trying to deny to Christians the right to go on thinking, developing their tradition in the light of modern knowledge and in relation to the contemporary world. So my final piece of friendly advice to secular humanists is to avoid the tempting role of the fundamentalist disbeliever who aligns with the fundamentalist believer in trying to stop the process of Christian development.

And I end, literally now, with a footnote about the bishop of Durham, David Jenkins. You may perhaps know, and it is this that makes news about the bishop particularly significant, that he ranks fourth among the Anglican bishops in England, after the archbishops of Canterbury and York and the bishop of London. Of course it is a delightful joke that he said that he did not believe in Christianity and then proceeded to attack Margaret Thatcher for being un-Christian. But I imagine that your common sense has already told you that that can't be literally true. What he denied was the physical virgin birth. He said that it has symbolic significance but is not a literal physiological fact. He also denied the bodily resurrection of Jesus, saying that Jesus lived beyond death, but not in a physical sense. Now it takes a fundamentalist, whether a Christian one or an anti-Christian one, to conclude that in saying this the bishop was disavowing Christianity. Personally, I think that he was right in what he said about the virgin birth and the resurrection, and also in what he said about Mrs. Thatcher!